Active Learning in Higher Education – Student Engagement and Deeper Learning Outcomes

Active Learning in Higher Education – Student Engagement and Deeper Learning Outcomes

Kayoko Enomoto, Richard Warner and Claus Nygaard (Eds.)
Foreword by Professor David Hyatt

THE INNOVATIONS IN HIGHER EDUCATION SERIES

First published in 2022 by Libri Publishing

Copyright © Libri Publishing

Authors retain copyright of individual chapters.

The right of Kayoko Enomoto, Richard Warner and Claus Nygaard to be identified as the editors of this work has been asserted in accordance with the Copyright, Designs and Patents Act, 1988.

ISBN 978-1-911450-47-4

All rights reserved. No part of this publication may be reproduced, stored in any retrieval system or transmitted in any form or by any means, electronic, mechanical, photocopying, recording or otherwise, without the prior written permission of the copyright holder for which application should be addressed in the first instance to the publishers. No liability shall be attached to the author, the copyright holder or the publishers for loss or damage of any nature suffered as a result of reliance on the reproduction of any of the contents of this publication or any errors or omissions in its contents.

A CIP catalogue record for this book is available from The British Library

Cover design by Helen Taylor

Design by Carnegie Book Production

Libri Publishing
Brunel House
Volunteer Way
Faringdon
Oxfordshire
SN7 7YR

Tel: +44 (0)845 873 3837

www.libripublishing.co.uk

Contents

Foreword
David Hyatt — vii

Chapter 1: Passive Learning and Active Learning in Higher Education: their Underpinning Learning Theories and Consequences for Teaching and Assessment
Kayoko Enomoto, Richard Warner and Claus Nygaard — 1

Chapter 2: How Voice Students Become Professionals through Active Learning Experiences
Anke Hoeppner and Anna Reid — 35

Chapter 3: Reflection towards Excellence: Empowering Learners to Become Reflective Practitioners
Hanna Olson — 63

Chapter 4: Using Co-designed Technology-enhanced Learning to Develop Postgraduate STEMM Students' Research Communication Competencies
Elena Forasacco and Jorge Freire — 83

Chapter 5: Partnering with Student Leaders: Active Learning through Integration of Peer Assisted Study Sessions into an Undergraduate Language Course
Kayoko Enomoto and Richard Warner — 107

Chapter 6: Impact of Learning Space Design on Students' Experiences in an Active Learning Classroom
Selin Üst and Orçun Kepez — 135

Chapter 7: Enhancing Students' Interpersonal and Leadership Skills through an Experience-based Service-learning Project: A Case of Active Learning
Lorina Culic and Anişoara Pavelea — 153

Chapter 8: Fostering Active Learning Online Using Interactive Video Lectures
Luis da Vinha   181

Chapter 9: Using Active Learning to Help Retention Rates for Women in Engineering through a Virtual Undergraduate Mentorship Program
Kristina Rigden   203

Chapter 10: Constructing the Employable Graduate through Active Learning Projects
Sarah Swann   229

Chapter 11: Pre-Service Second Language Teachers' Co-design of Virtual Exchanges as a Form of Active Learning in Higher Education
Giovanna Carloni   263

Chapter 12: Tracking the Mental Well-being of Pre-service Teachers in Post-secondary Health Methods Courses
Judy Jaunzems-Fernuk   289

Chapter 13: Teaching from the Native American Circle: A Future Campus-wide Sustainability Project as a Catalyst for Active Learning
Diana Schooling   319

Foreword

These are turbulent times for those teaching in higher education. The challenges and disruption of a worldwide pandemic have pushed teaching academics into an unexpected pivot to on-line teaching, often in contexts where their institutions are ill-prepared for such a transformation, in terms of logistics, support and staff development. Academics, both new and established, face institutional demands that push them to increasingly high workloads, in part caused by their desire to support their students. They face challenges in real terms to income and pensions, the growing casualisation of an expanding workforce, the unhelpful essentialisation of learners, and policy demands for increasing levels of bureaucratic demands, masquerading under discourses of 'accountability' and 'excellence'.

Within this seemingly shadowy landscape there are, however, beacons of light. Teaching academics enter the profession, not for prestige and riches, but with a burning passion to inform and inspire their students. Despite the constraints they face on a daily basis, I feel proud and humbled to work with such colleagues, and to meet fellow pedagogic travellers around the world, who strive to develop approaches to learning and teaching that foster a deeper engagement of their learners in the construction of, and reflection on, new understandings of their fields of study. These educators eschew an understanding of innovation and creativity as mere institutional marketing USPs and capture the true essence of these notions in describing the pedagogical affordances that emerge from an active learning orientation, and so encourage within their students a desire for, a love of, and a capability for deep, critical and reflexive learning.

The contributors to this book are such educators. In various forms, I have been writing on innovative approaches to higher education pedagogies for 27 years. In that time, rarely have I come across assemblage of chapters underpinned by a collective commitment to demonstrate the value and impact of approaches to teaching that challenge the ubiquity of transmission models. Such teacher-centred pedagogies, with their goals of the memorization and reproduction of decontextualised knowledge, have profound consequences for teaching, curriculum and assessment. At its heart this book embodies a decentering of pedagogic practice, problematizing the traditional relationship between teacher and student in terms of its power differential, often enacted in an asymmetric, hierarchical expert/novice dyad. Such relationships can trap educative relationships in a 'transmission' or 'training' mode, with students passively receiving 'instruction' from 'experts'. In contrast, this book offers a series of vignettes of active learning practices and the impact these have had on deep learning. The authors demonstrate how we can rethink, disrupt and disorient dominant conceptions of transmissive pedagogy, to build a more collaborative, collegial, decentred and active approach to student learning.

The process of compiling this book was important, with its cooperative and collaborative ethos mirroring the principles that the authors have embodied in each of their chapters. Authors have worked together supporting the development of each other's chapters, and adopting a common structure. This approach brings with it the benefits of intertextual and interdiscursive cross-referencing between chapters to ensure that the book is one which has a strong thematic coherence and integration, rather than representing a disparate bricolage of disconnected fragments. In the compilation of this collection, the authors and editors have adopted a process approach that frames their contributions around three key pillars: student engagement, active learning and deeper learning outcomes.

The book comprises thirteen chapters written by expert international authors from 9 countries across Europe, North America and Australasia. These chapters engage with important contemporary themes in active learning in higher education, such as: the importance and implications of learning theories on teaching paradigms; student voice and preparation for professional contexts; developing reflective practice and becoming reflective practitioners; the promotion of learning partnerships and the co-design of learning rich environments; the development of research communicative competencies; the benefits of peer mentoring and student partnership; the design of flexible and appropriate learning spaces; the enhancement of interpersonal and leadership skills, and active citizenship; interactivity in online learning spaces as a challenge to passivity in learning contexts; the challenging of instrumental discourses of employability through experimentation with career identities; the co-design of virtual exchanges and mentoring; the centrality in principled higher education of mental wellbeing; and the value of embracing and learning from indigenous and sustainable educative practices.

This is a book which will be of profound value to educators in higher education. It describes diverse active learning experiences and provides invaluable reflexive advice for those seeking inspiration in the deep and committed engagement of their students, the development of authentic and active learning communities and the fostering of deep learning in, and with, the learners they guide. It is a work that will be welcomed by those new to academia opening their eyes to new possibilities, but also by more experienced practitioners seeking to enhance the engagement and motivation of their students and to construct powerful and productive communities of learning. More importantly, the impact of this book will be felt by the students of those inspired by these chapters. It is those students themselves who will be the beneficiaries of the creative and innovative pedagogic practices espoused within these pages.

Professor David Hyatt

x

Chapter 1

Passive Learning and Active Learning in Higher Education: their Underpinning Learning Theories and Consequences for Teaching and Assessment

Kayoko Enomoto, Richard Warner and Claus Nygaard

Introduction

With the opening chapter of this book, *Active Learning in Higher Education*, we aim to inspire a motivated discussion of your university's dominant teaching paradigm and possibly a shift towards active learning methods. We argue for such a shift because we recognise, from our combined 75 years of experience with active learning in higher education and examples of active learning practised at universities worldwide, that active learning improves student engagement and student learning outcomes.

The idea of active learning itself dates back to the Greek philosopher Socrates (approximately 350 BC), who said: *"I know you won't believe me, but the highest form of human excellence is to question oneself and others"*. His active learning version, The Socratic Method, relied on the interaction between students themselves guided by the teacher questioning. Socrates introduced a problem which the students discussed in detail. As their teacher, Socrates would direct the conversation towards the key point if it was diverging. Socrates would then reveal his answer to the students, referring to their dialogue. Socrates, thus, did not lecture but practised his Socratic Method of questioning to help students discover and learn.

The Socratic Method of questioning remains strongly echoed in the learning and teaching literature in the twenty-first century. Halldórsdóttir (2014), for example, showed how case-based teaching helped students develop analytical thinking and reflective judgment, which improved their transferable skills. Picard and Guerin (2015) infused a research-based pedagogy with first-year undergraduate students, which improved the learning outcomes and employability of the students. Similiarly, Hørsted and Nygaard (2017) revealed how problem-based learning combined with internships increased student learning outcomes and employability. Ip (2017) illustrated how a collaborative project-based learning approach between student cohorts from two universities helped each other develop hands-on research skills and learn academic literacy more effectively. Moreover, this collaborative experience enhanced their social and communication skills as they worked in multidisciplinary and multicultural teams. In addition, Elbarrad and Saccucci (2018) evidenced how simulation-based learning discourages students from merely memorising the concepts without understanding but instead effectively enables students to meaningfully and deeply learn the concepts. Many examples showing possible positive impacts of active learning on students' deeper learning outcomes exist within the teaching and learning literature, which bears witness to the longevity of Socrates' influence. Yet, the Socratic Method of active learning, raising questions to students and inviting them to discuss the matters in question actively, is very different from its counterpoint: teacher-driven, theory-centred, didactic teaching – which we call 'passive learning'.

Passive Learning

In didactic teaching, the agency lies with the teacher responsible for providing the students with the requisite theoretical knowledge. To be didactic is to spell out things explicitly - to present the 'correct information', possibly in a dogmatic way. This is typically expressed in a traditional lecture theatre with a podium-bound teacher responsible for delivering predefined content to students. The likely characteristic dynamics of such a scenario sees the teacher actively engaged in giving information to students who take on the role of passive listeners. To simplify, the principal aim in didactic, theory-driven and teacher-centred higher education is to teach students to memorise the knowledge so well that they can apply it in relevant situations.

The term 'learning' in the Merriam-Webster dictionary (2021) is defined as: *"the activity or process of gaining knowledge or skill by studying, practicing, being taught...*". Similarly, The Cambridge Dictionary (2021) defines learning as: *"the activity of obtaining knowledge"*. Those are clear reflections of the idea that knowledge is gained by (for example) being taught by a teacher. Within the academic field of teaching and learning, similar definitions of learning also abound. Brown et al. (2014:11) see learning as: *"Acquiring knowledge and skills and having them readily available from memory so you can make sense of future problems and opportunities"*. Clark and Mayer (2016:12) argue that: *"Learning involves strengthening correct responses and weakening incorrect responses. Learning involves adding new information to your memory. Learning involves making sense of the presented material by attending to relevant information, mentally reorganising it, and connecting it with what you already know"*. Knowles et al. (2020:34) take a process-focused perspective, defining learning as: *"the process of gaining knowledge and expertise"*. Bingham and Conner (2010:19) build upon the notion of process to include a transformative element to learning: *"...the transformative process of taking in information that - when internalised and mixed with what we have experienced - changes what we know and builds on what we do. It's based on input, process, and reflection"*.

Consulting such standard definitions of learning, it is entirely foreseeable that teachers could reasonably think of their role as responsible for didactically providing students with information and knowledge through lecturing or similar distributive techniques. Table 1 (below) shows the main characteristics of didactic teaching as we see them.

Dimensions	Passive learning characteristics
Aim	To teach students
Goal	That students learn (=acquire knowledge)
Focus	Theory and knowledge
Curriculum	Syllabus/Teaching guide
Method	Transmitting knowledge to students (mainly by lecturing)
Orientation	Input
Agency	The balance of agency weights towards the teacher
Roles	The teacher is the authority, and the student is the recipient
Learning	Decontextual
Assessment	Summative

Table 1: The main characteristics of passive learning.

Advocates of didactic teaching see the goal of teaching as students' acquiring knowledge. Since learning is considered to be decontextual, all students who receive the same input learn the same, and that input method is usually through lecturing. The syllabus contains what needs to be delivered (transmitted) to students. Hence, the teacher's orientation is on the input - what the teacher needs to deliver to students. The agency is with the teacher who knows what input students need, and students become recipients of such input. Students' learning is usually assessed using summative methods such as end-of-term exams, a final project or a portfolio.

It may appear regressive to open a book on *Active Learning* with a section about *Passive Learning*. However, many of the ongoing teaching practices we have observed at universities can be categorised as didactic, theory-centred and teacher-driven. By that, we mean that the teaching method is based on a pre-planned lesson plan loaded with theory chosen by the teacher, who then carries out the teaching.

We wish to inspire a change in teaching and learning from didactic teaching to active learning with this book. Here in Chapter 1, we introduce and discuss the concept of active learning. In Chapters 2-13, authors from Australia, Canada, Italy, New Zealand, Romania, Turkey, the U.K. and the U.S.A. show prime examples of how active learning is implemented at their universities.

How our chapter focuses on active learning

Our chapter has three sections. In Section 1, we present three paradigms of learning. We do so because it is impossible to talk about active learning without defining learning. In Section 2, we present characteristics of active learning and give examples of active learning methods and their positioning before we introduce our Cyclical Model of Active Learning with its three elements: Student Engagement, Active Learning Method, and Deeper Learning Outcome. In Section 3, we take a closer look at the chapters in this book and their positioning in relation to the characteristics of active learning.

Reading this chapter, you will:
1. familiarise yourself with three learning theories that may inspire you to think about your understanding of learning and its consequences for your teaching; and

2. be presented with characteristics of active learning, which may help you plan your teaching to enhance students' agency.

Section 1: Three conceptualisations of learning

There appears to be no universally accepted definition of learning. At first sight, this may seem like a disadvantage to anyone working within the field of teaching and learning. However, it is possible to see commonalities between different definitions of learning. The ones we mentioned above (Merriam-Webster dictionary, 2021; Cambridge Dictionary, 2021; Brown et al., 2014; Clark & Mayer, 2016; Knowles et al., 2020; Bingham & Conner, 2010), for example, all have something in common. They emphasise an individual (subject) who has to learn something (object), and they view learning as a result of a stimulus (teaching) given to the individual.

Other definitions of learning do not emphasise this immediate relationship between the subject (individual) and the object (knowledge) and the stimulus (teaching). Shuell (1986:412), for example, defined learning as: *"An enduring change in behavior, or in the capacity to behave in a given fashion, which results from practice or other forms of experience"*. Driscoll (1994:8-9) saw learning as: *"A persisting change in human performance or performance potential as a result of the learner's interaction with the environment"*. They emphasise the individual's (subject) capacity to behave or interact. Here it is obvious that learning is not understood as giving stimulus to a subject, but rather an inter-relational process between the subject and the environment with which the subject interacts.

Yet other definitions of learning, put more focus on the social elements that mediate learning. Pahl-Wostl et al. (2008:NP) defined learning as a social endeavor: *"developing new relational capacities, both between social agents, in the form of learning how to collaborate and understand others' roles and capacities differently."* Another definition putting much weight on the social aspect was given by Cobb (2021:NP): *"People learn through interacting with each other; this learning – like all learning – changes them as individuals, but it also has the potential to change the broader groups within which they participate. I find the last part particularly powerful."* Here the focus moved from the stimulus (teaching) of objects (knowledge) given to individuals (subjects) to relations, collaborations, interactions, and participations in which the individual (subject) may take part while learning.

Reading these various definitions of learning, they appear to be positioned within different paradigms. They all talk about learning, but they perceive it in different ways. In our view, they subscribe to different learning theories. In the following part of our chapter, we briefly present three broad influential learning theories and relate them to *Active Learning*. We do so to wake a discussion of the possible consequences different learning theories may have for active learning, teaching and assessment.

Behavioural Learning theory

We start with Behavioural Learning theory. It can be traced back to Thorndike (1898), who published his theory of Law of Effect, which focused on the relationship between stimulus and response. He argued that no matter what the stimulus was, behaviour that led to pleasant consequences (positive response) would be reinforced, while behaviour leading to unpleasant consequences (negative response) was likely to stop - 'burnt child dreads the fire', so to speak. Thorndike (1898) argued that the behaviour could be managed by planning the consequences. Watson (1913) coined the term *behaviourism* in his article: 'Psychology as the behaviourist views it'. Later he wrote that the purpose of behavioural psychology was: "*To predict, given the stimulus, what reaction will take place; or, given the reaction, state what the situation or stimulus is that has caused the reaction*" (Watson, 1930:11). Within the behaviourist learning paradigm, the relationship between stimulus, response and consequences is the key to understanding behaviour. Therefore, it is argued that people learn how to respond - given a particular stimulus - in relation to the positive or negative consequences. The definitions of learning we presented in the Introduction can all be said to rest within the Behaviourist paradigm. They define learning as a positive consequence of a learning activity (response) to an input of knowledge (stimulus). A repetition of one of the six definitions of learning (given in the Introduction) clarifies this: "*Learning involves strengthening correct responses and weakening incorrect responses. Learning involves adding new information to your memory. Learning involves making sense of the presented material by attending to relevant information, mentally reorganizing it, and connecting it with what you already know"* (Clark & Mayer, 2016:12).

Consequences for teaching

Behaviourism fits neatly with didactic teaching, which is theory-based and teacher-driven. The teacher, when lecturing, provides the students with theory (stimulus), which primes student behaviour (response) that presumably leads to positive consequences (high grades). Since the stimulus-response mechanism is considered a law of effect (Thorndike, 1898), it is believed to a certain degree that all students can learn the same (response) when listening to the teacher (stimulus). Teachers practising didactic teaching may not think of the underlying stimulus-response mechanisms beneath it because most of what goes on in education is based on the teacher lecturing or explaining. Teachers may be encountered who, if a student fails the exam after having attended a series of lectures, say something akin to: *"I don't understand how the student could fail the exam because I have explained this several times in class"*. That is one example of a teacher who believes that the stimulus (the explanation in class) leads to a specific response (student learning).

Consequences for assessment

Within the Behaviourist paradigm, assessment is planned to measure if the stimulus had led to the desired response. Scriven (1967:72) coined the term *summative assessment* to account for this type of assessment. Examples of summative assessment are midterm exams, end-of-term exams, end-of-chapter tests, standardised tests to assess the students' knowledge at the end of a unit, course or program. In summative assessment, the focus is on the outcome, which is mostly measured using an absolute grading scale.

From primary schools to universities, education institutions use grading scales as a primary mechanism to reinforce the desired response to education (students learning). Students are honoured with marks. High marks = pleasant consequences (pleasant for the exemplary students who get high marks, unpleasant for those getting low marks and possibly failing the course). This attention to stimulus-response-consequences tends to make students very narrow-minded and focus merely on the outcome (grade). A teacher may experience a student who focuses on the outcome (passing or failing) if the student asks this question (or something similar) in the middle of a lecture: *"Excuse me, will this be part of the exam?"* This indicates a student culture that has been accustomed to summative assessment within the paradigm of Behavioural Learning theory.

Cognitive Learning theory

The second paradigm of learning we present is the Cognitive Learning theory, whose most prominent exponent was Piaget (1936), who developed the stage theory of child cognitive development. He argued that child development occurs through the use of schemata. As the child gets new experiences, these are related to existing schemata and adjusted to the world through either assimilation or accommodation.

According to Piaget, assimilation occurs when existing schemata are used to understand new experiences. Such fitting of new experiences into existing schemata is highly characteristic of human behaviour, contends Piaget (1936), because we seek order rather than disorder. So, in Cognitive Learning theory, we try to use what we already know to understand new experiences. When we can use assimilation, we are in a favoured state of equilibrium. More specifically, in education, we encourage assimilation when we ask the student to repeat a specific method and when we design exercises or assignments where students have to fit empirical data or new observations into known theories.

On the other hand, accommodation occurs when schemata have to be modified to fit with new experiences. This happens, Piaget (1936) states, after a phase of disequilibrium, where the new situation cannot be fitted into existing schemata. This is where new learning occurs, owing to the learner developing new schemata that help the student understand the new experience. Piaget (1958) later argued that accommodation requires an 'active learner' because the learner must cognitively discover accommodation – it cannot be programmed or taught.

Piaget (1936) saw cognitive development happening due to biological maturation (the child develops through stages) and interaction with the environment. Thus, learning is seen as an individual matter, which is also the case in behaviourism. From Piaget's perspective, the mind/brain (subject) and the environment (object) are dynamically interrelated.

Cognitive Learning theory places the individual student (the subject) in a learning environment (among objects). Cognitivists argue that our brain/mind is responsible for processing, organising, and interpreting information and therefore is responsible for learning which results from our mental activity.

Consequences for teaching
Where Behaviourism is an objectivist theory, Cognitivism is a constructivist theory, meaning that not all students will learn the same, although taking part in the same learning situation. Some students will be assimilating while others will be accommodating. It is a matter of the existing schemata of students when they engage in the learning situation, and it is a matter of their preferences for equilibrium or disequilibrium. In education, we encourage accommodation when we use pedagogical practices that challenge students to work with active discovery. We encourage accommodation when we ask students to investigate, analyse, and synthesise to emerge with new knowledge. Problem-based learning, Inquiry-based learning, and Case-based learning are active learning methods that could help students reach a new equilibrium through accommodation. Within Cognitivism, the teacher's role changes from direct tuition to the facilitation of learning and also to help students plan and govern their learning process.

For Cognitivists, the role of the teacher is to design a learning environment (object) whereby the student (subject) gains the best conditions for learning. Once the learning environment is established, the student is individually responsible for learning. Curriculum design focuses on creating the best possible learning environment, such as designing specific ways to distribute information to students (such as through lectures, books, or technology-enhanced techniques) or activating students in various learning activities (such as group work, projects, or internships). Because Cognitive Learning theory argues that humans process the information they receive rather than responding to a stimulus, changes in behaviour are only an indicator of what goes on in the learner's mind. Therefore, active discovery, problem-solving, engaged learning and the like are fruitful techniques in education, as they become a mirror of students' actions, reflections, and thus learning. Such active learning methods live side by side with cases of teacher-driven distribution of information to individual students, who are themselves considered to be responsible for engaging in cognitive learning processes. Cognitive Learning theorists would argue that students learn based on their cognitive abilities (the mind/brain of the subject) and as a consequence of the learning environment in which they are placed (the object). And such theorists believe that students would learn the same if they had the same cognitive abilities. They would probably design the curriculum with a mix of lectures and exercises. However, they would be aware that one type of learning environment would appeal to students with particular cognitive abilities.

By way of contrast, another learning environment would appeal to students with other cognitive abilities. Some students would prefer a teacher-driven learning environment, whereas others would prefer a student-driven one. Some students would prefer to work online, while others would prefer to work face-to-face and so forth. Students engage in pre-designed learning situations, expected to enhance their learning (or the learning of the good students- those students with the right cognitive abilities).

Consequences for assessment

Since learning is a cognitive process, and because what is learned is stored in the students' brain/mind, it becomes possible to assess students' learning using an absolute grading scale. Tests, quizzes and similar exams can assess students' absolute knowledge. Students respond in pre-programmed ways by solving a pre-designed assignment; they are assessed using a uniform assessment method suitable for the exercise in question and graded using a uniform grading system. Bloom et al. (1956) determined three taxonomies that enabled teachers to distinguish between different levels of student learning, the so-called classifications of learning objectives. One taxonomy for the cognitive domain, a second for the affective domain, and a third for the psychomotor domain. The taxonomy covering the cognitive domain crucially differentiated between 1) remembering, 2) comprehending, 3) applying, 4) analysing, 5) synthesising, and 6) evaluating.

A taxonomy like Bloom et al.'s (1956) helps educators and students to formulate learning goals and assess learning. One of the consequences of Cognitivism is that assessment is mostly linked to the student's cognitive capacity. Following an exam, teachers may conveniently talk about their students as excellent, good, or bad based on their results. In this perspective, the assessment method perfectly assesses students' cognitive abilities. We often see that no matter what type of learning activity students have participated in, they are assessed with an end-of-term test, an oral exam or a similar form of summative assessment. Learning itself is considered purely cognitive and can therefore be measured by cognitive tests, such as examinations and IQ tests.

Social Learning theory

The third paradigm of learning we present is Social Learning theory, which studies how social relationships (social embeddedness) and communication (discourse) both contribute to peoples' understanding of situations (contexts/learning environments). This is slightly different from Cognitivism, where the argument is that the student (the subject) is placed in a learning environment (the object). In Social Learning theory, the student is not placed in an objective learning environment. Instead, the student constructs the learning environment. This means that the subject-object dichotomy from Cognitivism is dissolved and becomes an integrated recursive dualism, where the subject constructs the object while at the same time being recursively affected by the object under construction.

Therefore, in Social Learning theory, there is no such thing as a designed learning environment. Rather the learning process is situated in an ever-changing context. McDermott (1993:290) wrote about context: *"...context is not so much something into which someone is put, but an order of behavior of which one is a part"*. Seeing the learning context as an order of behaviour, as opposed to an object, shifts the focus from the classroom's design or layout or the online platform's design to the ongoing relational processes between students and their peers, teachers and other stakeholders in students' learning processes. For Social Learning theorists, learning is perceived as a socially embedded process, influenced by the individuals' position, in what Granovetter (1985:487) called 'ongoing systems of social relations' whereby: *"Actors do not behave or decide as atoms outside a social context, nor do they adhere slavishly to a script written for them by the particular intersection of social categories that they happen to occupy. Their attempts at purposive action are instead embedded in concrete, ongoing systems of social relations"*.

Chapter 1

Social Learning theory is closely linked to the theory of Communities of Practice presented by Lave and Wenger (1991). Their theory points out the relationship between practice, identity, and learning, seeing the behaviour as a product of the practices of the community in which we are legitimate members. This means that student learning goes hand in hand with their socially constructed identity as human beings. The idea that learning occurs as we reflect upon our practice against the practice of others is not entirely new. Vygotsky (1978) argued that the child's learning occurs through social interaction with a skilful teacher. And he coined the term *More Knowledgeable Other* to explain the role of the teacher who guides the child through collaborative dialogue. With collaborative dialogue, he stresses the importance of seeing learning as an interrelated process, in which both child and teacher must engage. Following his theory, the teacher changes from an instructor to a role model.

Consequences for teaching
Arguing within the realm of Social Learning theory, the role of the teacher is to help facilitate a situation whereby students are encouraged to take part in the various ongoing systems of social relations that make up the education. Curriculum design then becomes a matter of designing a learning environment where students can meet and identify themselves with *More Knowledgeable Others* (may it be fellow students, teachers, or others) and thereby engage in their identity projects (trying to become whom they aspire to be). Social Learning theorists believe that students learn something different from their studies, even if they are exposed to the same input (such as a teacher lecturing, watching a film, reading a book, chatting on an e-learning portal, engaging in group work and taking an internship). Therefore, teaching will use various pedagogical methods and technologies, many of them being student-driven activities, where students' thoughts, ideas, and feelings about the learning environment, that they take part in constructing are an important element. Social Learning theory, more than the Behavioural and Cognitive Learning theories, therefore calls upon active learning.

Consequences for assessment

Because learning is a social process, there is little value in simply assessing students on their response to stimuli (how they solve pre-designed assignments). Students participate in iterative learning situations, where they interpolate between what they do know and what they do not know, and their learning is affected by their embeddedness in ongoing social relationships with *More Knowledgeable Others*. How students direct themselves in this social process is what affects their learning. They each respond in unique and different ways. Therefore, within Social Learning theory, students are assessed using mixed assessment methods to assess how students engage in ongoing social relations. They also have to assess the methods students use to direct themselves. Assessment is concerned with how students engage in ongoing social relations, the methods they use to direct themselves, and their reflections of how they become who they dream of becoming. Assessment should also relate to how what they learn in the context of the university may be transferred to other contexts. The assessment of such learning may well be graded using a uniform grading system. This can include formative assessment methods linked to case-based and problem-based methods that focus on students' progress and the transferable skills of students tie in well with Social Learning theory. Indeed, students' transferable skills do tie in well with Social Learning theory, as the assessment also has to examine students' reflections of how they become their desired selves and the transferability of what they learn in university to alternative contexts. All of this may well be graded using a uniform grading system. This can include formative assessment methods (Scriven, 1967) linked to case-based and problem-based methods that focus on students' progress.

A summary of the three learning theories

To sum up, the key aspects of the three learning theories are presented in Table 2.

	Behavioural Learning theory	**Cognitive Learning theory**	**Social Learning Theory**
The key argument about learning	Learning is a consequence of stimulus-response	Learning is a consequence of cognitive abilities and a process of adaptation to the environment	Learning is a consequence of fitting ones identity project to the order of behaviour in which one is embedded
The key mechanism of learning	Learning occurs due to operant conditioning	Learning occurs due to discovery (doing and actively exploring)	Learning occurs due to the social construction of meaning in a given situation
Consequences for educational design	Input oriented and teacher-driven education, where students are given tasks and challenges and assessed and evaluated on their performance	Process-oriented and teacher inspired, where students are challenged with active methods that require reconstruction of known schemes	Process-oriented and mainly student-driven, where students are responsible for their learning process
Key thinkers	Thorndike (1898, 1905); Watson (1913, 1930); Skinner (1936)	Piaget (1936, 1958); Bloom et al. (1956); Bruner (1960, 1961, 1962, 1996); Freeman (1999)	Bandura and Walters (1963); Vygotsky (1978); Lave & Wenger (1991)

Table 2: Key aspects of three different paradigms of learning (Nygaard, 2019).

With these three learning theories fresh in mind, let us look further into active learning and see how it relates to the learning paradigms.

Section 2: Active learning

Active Learning, as a concept, deals with teaching and learning methods that give students agency and thus multiplies their engagement in their learning activities. Tyler (1949:24) framed active learning in the context of education when he stated: *"Learning takes place through the active behavior of the student: it is what he does that he learns, not what the teacher does"*. Decades later, Revans (1980) presented two important equations related to active learning:

$$L \geq C$$

and

$$L = P + Q$$

The first equation shows that learning (L) is key to managing change (C). Revans (1980) argued that the learning rate has to be equal to or greater than the rate of change. If not, individuals (or organisations, the management of which Revans (1980) was also theorising about) would not survive. Relating $L \geq C$ to university education, it becomes evident that the learning that takes place within the university has to be equal or greater than the rate of change in the society in which graduates have to work. Otherwise, graduates will not survive in the job market.

The second equation shows that learning (L) is made up of both programmed knowledge (P) and questioning insight (Q). In this way, Revans (1980) argued that learning is more than programmed knowledge and that questioning insight, in particular, is an essential factor for enhancing learning. Learning could never exceed the programmed knowledge presented to students if it were not for the addition of the questioning insight. So, to sum up, active learning is meaningful because it brings forward the concept of questioning insight (Q), a vital component of learning (L) that has to be equal or more significant than the change (C) facing the learner.

There are many different active learning methods that, in their unique ways, introduce the component of questioning insight (Q) that Revans (1980) presented in his equation. Some of them are (and the list is not exhaustive):

- Case-based learning (Harvard Law School, 1870);
- Inquiry-based learning (Dewey, 1916, 1935, 1938);
- Discovery Learning (Bruner, 1960, 1961, 1962); and

- Experiential Learning (Kolb, 1984).

In the following subsections, we briefly examine their characteristics and relate them to Revans' (1980) equation: L = P + Q.

Case-based Learning (Harvard Law School)

Under the leadership and inspiration of Dean Langdell, the case method was pioneered as early as 1870 at the Harvard Law School (Carter & Unklesbay, 1989). Case-based learning was used to train the students in generalising from law cases to principles of law (Merseth, 1991). Today, case-based learning is implemented in multiple disciplines at universities worldwide. In case-based learning, the student's learning process is scaffolded through a purposeful structure, where the teacher consciously uses guiding questions (Q) to challenge students to consider new aspects, which they had not thought of themselves when reading the case or the course material (P). Much of case-based learning occurs through conversations between students and teachers and between students. This is in line with the Socratic Method of active learning, mentioned earlier in this chapter, where the teacher raises questions to students and invites them to actively discuss (Q) the matter (P). In case-based learning, the context of relevance is often brought to students in the form of written cases, and in that way, students are also addressing the ongoing change (C) that goes on, for example, in industry or society. In that way, we can relate case-based learning to Revans' (1980) above-mentioned equation.

Inquiry-based Learning (Dewey)

Dewey (1916) presented a need for an experimentalist education based on a three-stage process of 1) inquiry, 2) knowledge formation, 3) restoring balance. This was important, Dewey (1935:164) wrote because students who were educated to *"find the right answer..."* had *"...no clue to the situation in which they are to live"*. Dewey (1938:IX) labelled it *"progressive education"*, which was *"a product of discontent with traditional education"*, and its core was to include socially engaging learning experiences which matched the level of children. For Dewey (1916, 1935, 1938), social interactions were the most effective way to enhance learning in schools, and he argued that schools should represent real-life situations. In that way, children would learn from participating in learning activities in different social settings (Dewey, 1938). Students would learn less when being abruptly introduced to academic content (P), and they would learn more if they 1) engaged in inquiry (investigating a problem) (Q) and 2) came to their understanding and formed their own knowledge (L = P + Q), and 3) restored balance at their new level of knowledge. In that way, we can use the equation of Revans (1980) to reflect on Dewey's (1916, 1935, 1938) inquiry-based learning.

Discovery Learning (Bruner)

Bruner (1960) presented cognitive constructivism that had a profound effect on the way of thinking. For Bruner (1960, 1961), the most important learning method was Discovery Learning. For him, the primary purpose of education was not to get students to learn an exact discipline by heart (P), but rather to educate students in methods by which they can acquire attitudes, skills and knowledge that can enable them to understand the world of which they are a part. Some of the methods inherent in Discovery Learning were knowledge as symbolic representations, a scaffolding of learning and discovery (Q). Learning by doing is one of the main ideas stemming from Bruner's (1960) work. Later in his career, Bruner (1996) emphasised culture because the learner is culturally embedded, and so is learning. His cultural view on education opposed the Behaviourist's computational view (Bruner, 1996), which perceived learning as a process of being taught the right programmed knowledge (P) and then sorting, storing, and retrieving the right information. For Bruner (1962), the goal of education then became discipline understanding rather than performance, meaning that knowing (P) was insufficient for learning (L). Through the ability to discover (Q) and structure knowledge, the student can expand and deepen knowledge and move beyond what is simply given (L = P + Q). In that way, we can use the equation of Revans (1980) to reflect on Bruner's (1960, 1961, 1962, 1996) Discovery-based Learning.

Experiential Learning (Kolb)

Kolb (1984) developed the Experiential Learning theory as a holistic and dialectic theory. Being holistic means that learning takes place at all levels, from individual to team and organisational learning to societal learning. Being dialectic means that learning is driven by a dialectic between two dimensions: 1) action/reflection and 2) experience/abstraction. When students learn, Kolb (1984) argues that they work to integrate the two dimensions. While learning on one dimension (action/reflection), students try to grasp their experience. While learning on the other dimension (experience/abstraction), students try to transform their experience into new knowledge. Kolb (1984) describes this dialectic learning as a recursive spiral, where students investigate (Q) contextual matters. This spiralling process of grasping and transforming knowledge is in stark contrast to a linear transmission of existing knowledge to students (P) (what we called 'Passive Learning' in the Introduction of this chapter). For Kolb (1984), it is important that students are both receivers of knowledge (P) and creators of knowledge through experiential activities (Q). This is how Kolb's Experiential Learning theory (1984) can be related to Revans' (1980) equation.

Summarising Active Learning in contrast to Passive Learning

Following this brief introduction to four well-known active learning methods/theories, in Table 3, we summarise the characteristics of active learning as we see them and add to them the characteristics of passive learning as presented in Table 1. In Table 3, active and passive learning characteristics are compared in terms of how they differ on the dimensions: aim, goal, focus, curriculum, method, orientation, agency, roles, learning and assessment.

Advocates of active learning see the goal of teaching as students acquiring learning skills, which means that students become familiar with knowledge production. Here, learning is contextualised, meaning that all students who receive the same input will not learn the same because they are embedded in different contexts. Students have different backgrounds, support structures, and ambitions; each learning situation is different due to such variables as content, time, pace, and level. Therefore, the preferred learning method is one where the student is actively engaged in the learning process, hence the term active learning.

	Active learning characteristics	Passive learning characteristics
Aim	To engage students in learning activities	To teach students
Goal	That students learn to learn (=becomes familiar with the process of knowledge production)	That students learn (=acquire knowledge)
Focus	The practice of learning (which involves getting to know theories and knowledge)	Theory and knowledge
Curriculum	Learning-centred action plan	Syllabus/Teaching guide
Method	Active learning methods	Transmitting knowledge to students (mainly by lecturing)
Orientation	Output	Input
Agency	The balance of agency weights towards the student	The balance of agency weights towards the teacher
Roles	The student is the learner; the teacher is the authority on facilitating learning activities	The teacher is the authority, and the student is the recipient
Learning	Contextual learning/situational learning	Decontextualized
Assessment	Formative/developmental	Summative

Table 3: The main characteristics of active learning in contrast to passive learning.

In active learning, the curriculum is not centred around a syllabus or list of literature. Instead, the curriculum is seen as a learning-centred action plan, which concentrates on the learning activities students have to take part in. Here the orientation of the teacher is on the output, meaning what students are learning. The role of the teacher is as the authority facilitating learning activities in which students take part. The teacher most probably spends the time before teaching preparing learning activities to enable the students to get feedback on their learning. The balance of agency is weighted towards the student, as it is the student who learns.

Often teachers will discuss which methods are best to use for accelerating learning under contextual circumstances. Students' learning is usually assessed using formative methods, including immediate feedback, peer-review, logbooks, self-assessment, and quizzes related to learning activities. Assuming that all students learn differently, at a different pace, and to a different level, the assessment of student learning has to be formative and developmental, engaging the student much more in both learning design and evaluation design.

A Cyclical Model of Active Learning: Student Engagement - Active Learning Method - Deeper Learning Outcome

The above discussion of *Passive Learning* vs. *Active Learning* and the presentation of the three learning theories (*Behavioural Learning, Cognitive Learning* and *Social Learning*) is included to encourage teaching staff to reflect upon their perceptions of learning and its consequences on their teaching and assessment methods. Our aim has not been to present a new theory or necessarily integrate the concepts and theories further. We will argue that Active Learning and the variety of methods nested within the concept lean toward Cognitivist and Social Learning theories, as it favours the cognitive development of students embedded in social situations, social relations, and social contexts, and society. The chapters in the book, where authors from universities in Australia, Canada, Italy, New Zealand, Romania, Turkey, the U.K. and the U.S.A. all show how the cognitive development of students is affected by social embeddedness and how they engage students through uses of active learning to develop deeper learning.

To stress this important relationship between Student Engagement, Active Learning Method, and Deeper Learning Outcomes, we have created a Cyclical Model of Active Learning (Figure 1), which also serves as the central model for the book. Each chapter in the book, therefore, positions itself using this model.

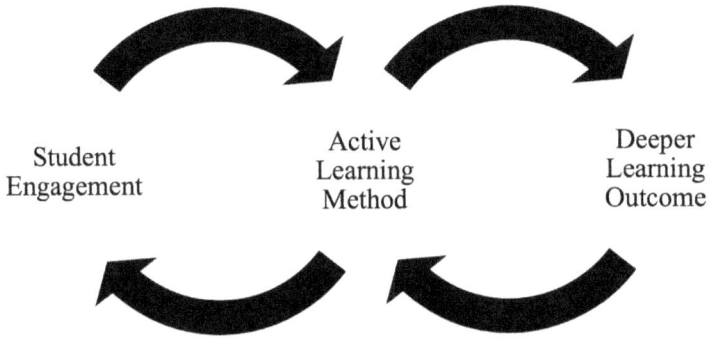

Figure 1: Cyclical Model of Active Learning.

Active Learning Method

Above, we have already presented *Active Learning* and some of its different methods, such as Case-based Learning (Harvard Law School, 1870), Inquiry-based Learning (Dewey, 1916, 1935, 1938), Discovery Learning (Bruner, 1961), and Experiential Learning (Kolb, 1984). In the chapters within this book, the following variations of active learning can be located:

- authentic project-based learning (Chapter 2);
- case-based learning (Chapter 3);
- flipped and peer learning (Chapter 4);
- students as partners framework (Chapter 5);
- learning space design (Chapter 6);
- experience-based learning (Chapter 7);
- technology-enhanced learning (Chapter 8);
- research-based learning (Chapter 9);
- project-based learning (Chapters 10 and 13);
- virtual exchange co-design (Chapter 11); and
- inquiry-based learning (Chapter 12).

In our cyclical model (Figure 1), *Active Learning Method* is in the middle. It is the focal point of the book and its chapters. The model is cyclical, meaning that the active learning method affects student engagement. Then, student engagement affects the active learning method, which in turn affects students' deeper learning outcomes. These deeper learning outcomes then affect both the active learning method and students' further engagement in the cycle. Hitherto, we have accounted for active learning. Yet, in the remaining part of this section, we shall briefly look at the two other important parts of the model: Student Engagement and Deeper Learning outcomes.

Student Engagement

Gibbs (2014) called student engagement the new educational buzzword, which has a negative ring to it. The reason for this talk of a buzzword is the dominant focus on student engagement, which arose in higher education a decade ago and has increased throughout the decade. To move from buzzword to mindset and identified practice requires an explicit strategy for engaging students. Nygaard et al. (2013) suggested three dimensions of student engagement, which may be useful when forming and implementing an explicit student engagement strategy:

1. identity;
2. motivation; and
3. community.

Identity

The way of teaching and scaffolding student learning greatly impacts how students perceive themselves, and students tend to identify themselves through the active learning method in which they are engaged. The cyclical processes between active learning methods and student engagement can create students' identity. Being engaged through active learning methods will make students look upon themselves in a certain way. In Chapter 2 of this book, Hoeppner and Reid (2022) examine how students develop professional identities through active learning. Extending the concept of identity yet further, in Chapter 11, Carloni (2022) discusses how active learning helps pre-service language teachers develop a sense of identity while learning to reflect on their future practice.

Motivation

Just as student engagement is the fuel that drives action learning methods, a personal or collective motivation to participate is the fuel that drives student engagement. Saeed and Zyngier (2012) linked Ryan and Deci's (2000) Self-Determination-Theory (extrinsic and intrinsic) motivation with Schlechty's (2001) engagement framework (authentic; ritual; passive compliance; retreatism; and rebellion). They found that extrinsically motivated students engaged ritually and with retreatism, whereas students who felt both intrinsically and extrinsically motivated showed both authentic, ritual, retreats and rebellious engagement. Ryan and Deci (2009) showed that motivation and well-being (see also Jaunzems-Fernuk Chapter 12 in this book) were closely related to learning outcomes.

Community

Tinto (2003) argued that creating learning communities would enhance student engagement and student success. Gerber (1996) showed how extra-curricular activities positively affected students learning outcomes. This sense of community aligns with Social Learning theories, such as that of Lave and Wenger (1991), mentioned above. Communities of practice lead to further engagement as students become legitimate members of the community and identify more with their study group, class, education, or university. In Chapter 9 of this book, Rigden (2022) shows how a sense of belonging among engineer students who identify themselves as female leads to improved retention. In Chapter 13, Schooling (2022) presents the design of a campus-wide sustainability project that aims to create a learning community.

In this book, all authors present ways of engaging students. Reading the chapters, you will see a wide range of engagement methods:

- a song competition (Chapter 2);
- practice logbooks (Chapter 3);
- technology-enhanced activities and real-life practices (Chapter 4);
- 360° feed-forward model (Chapter 5);

- student-centred learning activities (Chapter 6);
- a service-learning project (Chapter 7);
- interactive video lectures (Chapter 8);
- a virtual mentorship program (Chapter 9);
- the posing of real-world problems (Chapter 10);
- engagement in course co-design and reflection (Chapter 11);
- openly track and share well-being (Chapter 12); and
- a campus-wide sustainability project (Chapter 13).

Deeper Learning Outcome

Both student engagement and active learning have been shown to improve students learning outcomes (Kuh et al. 2008). Moreover, there is empirical evidence that students' learning outcomes are affected by their approaches to learning and their motivation to learn, as we saw in the work of Saeed and Zyngier (2012) above. Looking into learning outcomes, Marton and Säljö (1976) developed the concepts of deep and surface learning. They defined four types of responses to learning: passive and active deep learning and passive and active surface learning. From the beginning of the learning process, students with a deep learning approach would engage to understand the meaning and engage actively in academic discussions. On the other hand, students with a surface learning approach would work to reproduce the knowledge presented to them and apply a strategy of memorising what they thought important.

Enomoto (2012a, 2012b) showed how student attitudes affected their choice of either memorisation-based surface learning or deeper learning characterised by analysing, evaluating and creating knowledge. Surface learning utilises reproductive strategies, such as rote learning, with little by way of an attempt to assimilate information (Lizzio et al., 2002). In contrast, deep learning utilises such strategies as reading extensively and linking parts to a whole, applying and comparing ideas for greater understanding (Lizzio et al., 2002). Thus, deeper learning approaches are inherent requisites for any active learning method.

Furthermore, active learning *"requires engagement in activities (writing, discussion, and presentation) and externalizing cognitive processes in the activities"* (Mizokami, 2018:79). Therefore, an imperative step for active learning is student engagement with deeper learning approaches. Such engagement must involve meaningful interactions between teacher and student and amongst students themselves, necessitating a deeper approach to learning. Thus, deep active learning is defined as: *"learning that engages students with the world as an object of learning while interacting with others and helps the students connect what they are learning with their previous knowledge and experiences as well as their future lives"* (Matsushita, 2018:v).

As you read this book, you will see how the authors have enhanced various deeper learning outcomes by engaging students using active learning methods. The specific deeper learning outcomes are:

- development of graduate attributes (Chapter 2);
- reflective practitioners (Chapter 3);
- research communication competencies (Chapter 4);
- enhanced course engagement (Chapter 5);
- enhanced learning experiences (Chapter 6);
- interpersonal and leadership skills (Chapter 7);
- engaged learning (Chapter 8);
- a sense of belonging for the purpose of retention (Chapter 9);
- graduate employability (Chapter 10);
- digital pedagogy and professional skills (Chapter 11);
- enhanced well-being (Chapter 12); and
- retention and employability (Chapter 13).

In the first two sections of our chapter, we have introduced the concepts of *Passive Learning* and *Active Learning* and three learning theories: *Behavioural Learning, Cognitive Learning* and *Social Learning*. We have shown some of their implications for teaching and assessment. We have also presented the central model of our book, touching upon how its elements, Student Engagement, Active Learning Methods, and Deeper Learning Outcomes are cyclically interrelated. We hope that our presentation and arguments have inspired a motivated discussion of your university's dominant teaching paradigm and possibly a shift towards active learning methods.

In the final Section 3, we briefly introduce the other 12 chapters in this book.

Section 3: A brief introduction to the chapters in this book

Chapter 2, written by Anke Hoeppner and Anna Reid from Australia, is titled: *How Voice Students Become Professionals through Active Learning Experiences*. Their chapter describes how they have used a song competition to engage students in authentic project-based learning to facilitate the development of graduate attributes and deeper learning outcomes in the context of professional preparation. This was done to prepare vocal students specialising in Western Art music for their future lives as professional singers. The chapter shows the effectiveness of incorporating the song competition into a core German diction curriculum for developing graduate attributes.

Chapter 3, authored by Hanna Olson from New Zealand, is titled: *Reflection towards Excellence - Empowering Learners to Become Reflective Practitioners*. The author demonstrates how they have used practice logbooks to engage students in case-based learning to successfully educate them as reflective practitioners within a Bachelor of Oral Health (BOH) program. Following Kolb's experiential learning cycle, reflective practice is used by students to gain a profound clinical work skillset and improve their knowledge and understanding to ultimately provide a high standard of patient care, fuelling their active, purposeful learning.

Chapter 4, written by Elena Forasacco and Jorge Freire from the UK, is titled: *Using Co-designed Technology-enhanced Learning to Develop Postgraduate STEMM Student's Research Communication Competencies*. They share how they engaged postgraduate research and postgraduate coursework students in technology-enhanced activities and real-life examples using flipped and peer learning to successfully develop their research communication competencies. This chapter analyses and shares strategies that facilitate the synergic collaboration between a learning designer and a teacher, students and other stakeholders, with inputs from supervisors to co-design digital learning-rich courses.

Chapter 5, written by Kayoko Enomoto and Richard Warner from Australia, is titled: *Partnering with Student Leaders: Active Learning through Integration of Peer Assisted Study Sessions into an Undergraduate Language Course*. They present how they used the Students as Partners framework to design their 360° Feed-forward Active Learning Model that enhances students' course engagement, leading to deeper learning outcomes. They show how the 360° Feed-forward Active Learning Model was implemented in partnership with a learning community of students participating in Peer Assisted Study Sessions (PASS) attached to an undergraduate Japanese language course.

Chapter 6, authored by Selin Üst and Orçun Kepez from Turkey, is titled: *Impact of Learning Space Design on Students' Experiences in an Active Learning Classroom*. They present how they have used learning space design to engage students in various student-centred learning activities, leading to enhanced learning experiences and deeper learning outcomes. Content analyses of open-ended written feedback from 79 students revealed privacy and ergonomics to be the sub-themes for their individual experiences, whilst flexibility and appropriateness for various activities were also found to be sub-themes for their collaborative experiences.

Chapter 7, written by Lorina Culic and Anișoara Pavelea from Romania, is titled: *Enhancing Students' Interpersonal and Leadership Skills through an Experience-based Service-learning Project: A Case of Active Learning*. The authors show how they have used experience-based learning to engage students in a service-learning project to enhance their skills as reflective practitioners by exploring how a service-learning project incorporated into a university course can be seen as an active learning tool. They demonstrate the effectiveness of their service-learning methodology for developing students' skills and attitudes towards active citizenship, social responsibility and personal accountability in changing communities.

Chapter 8, authored by Luis da Vinha from Australia, is titled: *Fostering Active Learning Online Using Interactive Video Lectures*. The chapter outlines how to integrate technology-enhanced active learning strategies that promote engaged learning when developing and producing online video content, providing an example of the multiple methods of interaction that can be used to engage students successfully. The author demonstrates how they have used Interactive Video Lectures to transform passive educational materials into technology-enhanced active learning resources in the context of undergraduate and postgraduate courses in an International Relations and Political Science program.

Chapter 9, written by Kristina Rigden from the US, is titled: *Using Active Learning to Help Retention Rates for Women in Engineering through a Virtual Undergraduate Mentorship Program*. The author shows how they have used a virtual mentorship program to engage undergraduate engineering students, who identify as female, in research-based learning to develop their sense of belonging and improve their retention effectively. This program utilised research-based learning to focus on belonging and social relationships through 1:1 mentoring with mentees and peer mentors and group mentoring with industry and teacher mentors. The chapter describes how mentees and peer mentors who participated in the program developed a sense of belonging within the engineering community.

Chapter 10, authored by Sarah Swann from the UK, is titled: *Constructing the Employable Graduate through Active Learning Projects*. The author shows how they engaged students to pose real-world problems using project-based learning to productively enhance their graduate employability on the BA (Hons) Childhood Studies degree. Through the author's lenses, the reader will be able to reflect on broader questions about how university degrees might help students explore and 'try on' different career identities.

Chapter 11, written by Giovanna Carloni from Italy, is titled: *Pre-Service Second Language Teachers' Co-design of Virtual Exchanges as a Form of Active Learning in Higher Education*. This chapter presents how they used a virtual exchange co-designing procedure to engage pre-service language teachers in course co-design and reflection-on-action. To develop their digital pedagogy and professional skills through active learning, the chapter describes a conceptual framework suitable for facilitating pre-service language teachers' virtual exchange co-design in a Master's program.

Chapter 12, authored by Judy Jaunzems-Fernuk from Canada, is titled: *Tracking the Mental Well-being of Pre-service Teachers in Post-secondary Health Methods Courses*. The author details how the well-being of students was enhanced and supported through the tracking and sharing of mood and stress levels at the start of every class in an undergraduate health methods course. Guided by a process of active learning known as Aware-Care-Cope (ACC), students attended to their well-being through daily in-class check-ins and course assignments, resulting in a final project that summarised a reflexive practice of inquiry focusing on well-being.

Chapter 13, written by Diana Schooling from the US, is titled: *Teaching from the Native American Circle: A Future Campus-wide Sustainability Project as a Catalyst for Active Learning*. In this chapter, the author describes how to engage students in a future campus-wide sustainability project using project-based learning to improve their retention and enhance their employability. This chapter outlines how the sustainability project has been designed, directly informed by 'Teaching from the Native American Circle' (Schooling, 2021) to be implemented at a Tribal College serving the educational needs of Tribal communities in Washington, Oregon and Idaho.

---oOo---

This book showcases inspirational accounts of learning theory-informed active learning in a variety of higher education contexts worldwide. We hope that reading these chapters will inspire you to continue developing your own active learning methods - for the improvement of student engagement and deeper learning outcomes.

About the Authors

Kayoko Enomoto is a Senior Lecturer, Head of Asian Studies and Director, Student Experience in the Faculty of Arts at the University of Adelaide, Australia. She can be contacted at this email: kayoko.enomoto@adelaide.edu.au

Richard Warner is an Adjunct Lecturer in the School of Education in the Faculty of Arts at the University of Adelaide, Australia. He can be contacted at this email: richard.warner@adelaide.edu.au

Claus Nygaard is Professor and Executive Director of The Institute for Learning in Higher Education. He can be contacted at this email: info@lihe.info

Bibliography

Bandura, A., & Walters, R.H. (1963). *Social learning and personality development*. New York: Holt Rinehart and Winston.

Bingham, T., & Conner, M. (2010). *The new social learning: A guide to transforming organizations through social media*. Berrett-Koehler Publishers.

Bloom, B. S., Engelhart, M. D., Furst, E. J., Hill, W. H., & Krathwohl, D. R. (1956). *Taxonomy of educational objectives: The classification of educational goals. Handbook I: Cognitive domain*. New York: David McKay Company.

Brown, P. C., Roediger, H. L., & McDaniel, M. A. (2014). *Make it stick: The science of successful learning*. Cambridge, MA: Harvard University Press.

Bruner, J. S. (1960). *The process of education*. Cambridge, MA: Harvard University Press.

Bruner, J. S. (1961). The act of discovery. *Harvard Educational Review*, 31, 21-32.

Bruner, J. S. (1962). *On knowing: Essays for the left hand*. Cambridge, MA: Belknap Press.

Bruner, J. S. (1996). *The culture of education*. Cambridge, MA: Harvard University Press.

Carloni, G. (2022). Pre-service second language teachers' co-design of virtual exchanges as a form of active learning in higher education. In K. Enomoto, R. Warner, & C. Nygaard, C. (Eds.), *Active learning in higher education* (pp. 263-288). Oxfordshire, U.K.: Libri Publishing Ltd.

Carter, K., & Unklesbay, R. (1989). Cases in teaching and law. *Journal of Curriculum Studies*, 21(6), 527-536.

Clark, R., & Mayer, R. (2016). *e-Learning and the science of instruction* (4th ed.). Wiley.

Cobb, J. (2021). *How to Define Social Learning*. Online: no page numbers. Retrieved from https://www.leadinglearning.com/define-social-learning/

Dewey, J. (1916). *Democracy and education*. New York, N.Y.: The Free Press.

Dewey, J. (1935). *The need for orientation*. The later works 11 (pp.162-166). Illinois: Southern Illinois University Press.

Dewey, J. (1938). *Experience and education*. New York: Macmillan.

Driscoll, M. P. (1994). *Psychology of learning for instruction*. Needham Heights, M.A.: Allyn & Bacon.

Elbarrad, S., & Saccuci, F. (2018). Using a simulation game to teach students principles of cost accounting. In K. Enomoto, R. Warner & C. Nygaard (Eds.), *Innovative teaching and learning practices in higher education* (pp. 101-114). Oxfordshire, U.K.: Libri Publishing Ltd.

Enomoto, K. (2012a). A Study Skills Action Plan: integrating self-regulated learning in a diverse higher education context. In X. Song & K. Cadman (Eds.), *Bridging transcultural divides: Asian languages and cultures in global higher education* (pp. 101-129). Adelaide, Australia: Adelaide University Press.

Enomoto, K. (2012b). Promoting deeper learning through a scaffolded language curriculum: double tasking language-specific and research-skills development. In J. Hajek, C. Nettelbeck & A. Woods (Eds.), *The next step* (pp. 347-360). Melbourne: The University of Melbourne. https://www.lcnau.org/publications/2011-proceedings/

Freeman, W. J. (1999). *How brains make up their minds*. Phoenix, A.Z.: Orion Books.

Gerber, S. (1996). Extracurricular activities and academic achievement. *Journal of Research and Development in Education, 30*(1), 42-50.

Gibbs, G. (2014). Student engagement, the latest buzzword. *Times Higher Education, 1*. Retrieved from https://www.timeshighereducation.com/news/student-engagement-the-latestbuzzword/2012947.article

Granovetter, M. (1985). Economic action and social structure: The problem of embeddedness. *American Journal of Sociology 91*, 481– 510.

Halldórsdóttir, S. (2014). The cycle of case-based teaching for transformative learning. In J. Branch, P. Bartholomew, & C. Nygaard (Eds.), *Case-based learning in higher education* (pp. 39-56). Oxfordshire, U.K.: Libri Publishing Ltd.

Hoeppner, A., & Reid, A. (2022). How voice students become professionals through active learning experiences. In K. Enomoto, R. Warner & C. Nygaard (Eds.), *Active learning in higher education* (pp. 35-62). Oxfordshire, U.K.: Libri Publishing Ltd.

Hørsted, A., & Nygaard, C. (2017). How to design a curriculum for student learning. In A. Hørsted, J. Branch & C. Nygaard (Eds.), *Learning-centred curriculum design in higher education* (pp. 97-120). Oxfordshire, U.K.: Libri Publishing Ltd.

Ip, T. (2017). Teaching academic writing against the grain: A project-based approach. In J. Branch, S. Hayes, A. Hørsted & C. Nygaard (Eds.), *Innovative teaching and learning in higher education* (pp. 293-306). Oxfordshire, U.K.: Libri Publishing Ltd.

Jaunzems-Fernuk, J. (2022). Tracking the mental well-being of pre-service teachers in post-secondary health methods courses. In K. Enomoto, R. Warner & C. Nygaard (Eds.), *Active learning in higher education* (pp. 289-318). Oxfordshire, U.K.: Libri Publishing.

Knowles, M. S., Holton III, E. F., Swanson, R. A., & Robinson, P. A. (2020). *The adult learner. The definitive classic in adult education and human resource development*. Taylor & Francis Ltd.

Kolb, D. A. (1984). *Experience as the source of learning and development*. Englewood Cliffs, N. J.: Prentice-Hall.

Kuh, G. D., Cruce, T. M., Shoup, R., Kinzie, J., & Gonyea, R. M. (2008). Unmasking the effects of student engagement on first-year college grades and persistence. *The Journal of Higher Education*, 79(5), 540-563

Lave, J., & Wenger, E. (1991). *Situated learning: legitimate peripheral participation*. Cambridge, U.K.: Cambridge University Press.

Lizzio, A., Wilson, K. L., & Simons, R (2002). University students' perceptions of the practice. *Studies in Higher Education*, 27(1), 27–52.

Marton, F., & R. Säljö (1976). On qualitative differences in Learning - Outcome and process. *British Journal of Educational Psychology*, 46, 4-11.

Matsushita, K. (Ed.) (2018). *Deep active learning*. Singapore: Springer.

McDermott, R. P. (1993). The acquisition of a child by a learning disability. In S. Chaiklin & J. Lave (Eds.), *Understanding practice: Perspectives on activity and context* (pp.269-305). Cambridge, U.K.: Cambridge University Press.

Merriam-Webster dictionary (2021). https://www.merriam-webster.com/dictionary/learning

Merseth, K. K. (1991). The early history of case-based instruction: Insights for teacher education today. *Journal of Teacher Education*, 42(4), 243-249.

Mizokami, S. (2018). Deep active learning from the perspective of active learning theory. In K. Matsushita (Ed.), *Deep active learning* (pp. 79-91). Singapore: Springer.

Nygaard, C., Brand, S. Bartholomew, P., & Millard, L. (Eds.) (2013). *Student engagement: Identity, motivation and community*. Oxfordshire, U.K.: Libri Publishing Ltd.

Nygaard, C. (2019). E-learning as a strategy for improving universitystudents' learning outcomes. In R. Evans & C. Nygaard (Eds.), *E-learning 1.0, 2.0, and 3.0 in higher education* (pp. 23-44). Oxfordshire, U.K., Libri Publishing Ltd.

Pahl-Wostl, C., Mostert, E. & Tàbara, D. (2008). The growing importance of social learning in water resources management and sustainability science. *Ecology and Society* 13(1):24 (online: no page numbers).

Piaget, J. (1936). *Origins of intelligence in the child*. London: Routledge & Kegan Paul.

Piaget, J. (1958). The growth of logical thinking from childhood to adolescence. *AMC*, 10(12).

Picard, M., & Guerin, C. (2015). Learning to research in the professions: Possibilities of discovery learning In C. Guerin, P. Bartholomew & C. Nygaard (Eds.), *Learning to research – Researching to learn* (pp. 105-123). Oxfordshire, U.K.: Libri Publishing Ltd.

Revans, R. W. (1980). *Action learning: New techniques for management.* London: Century Hutchinson (A Division of Random House Group).

Rigden, K. (2022). Using active learning to help retention rates for women in engineering through a virtual undergraduate mentorship program. In K. Enomoto, R. Warner & C. Nygaard (Eds.), *Active learning in higher education* (pp. 203-228). Oxfordshire, U.K.: Libri Publishing.

Ryan, R. M., & Deci, E. L. (2000). Intrinsic and extrinsic motivations: Classic definitions and new directions. *Contemporary Educational Psychology*, 25, 54-67.

Ryan, R. M., & Deci, E. L. (2009). Promoting self-determined school engagement: Motivation, learning, and well-being. In K. R. Wentzel & A. Wigfield (Eds.), *Handbook on motivation at school* (pp. 171-196). New York, N.Y.: Routledge.

Saeed, S., & Zyngier, D. (2012). How motivation influences student engagement: A qualitative case study. *Journal of Education and Learning*, 1(2), 252-267.

Schlechty, P. C. (2001). *Shaking up the schoolhouse.* San Fransisco, C.A.: Jossey-Bass Publishers.

Schooling, D. (2022). Teaching from the Native American Circle: a future campus-wide sustainability project as a catalyst for active learning. In K. Enomoto, R. Warner & C. Nygaard (Eds.), *Active learning in higher education* (pp. 319-341). Oxfordshire, U.K.: Libri Publishing Ltd.

Scriven, M. (1967). The methodology of evaluation. In R. W. Tyler, R. M. Gagne & M. Scriven (Eds.), *Perspectives on curriculum evaluation* (pp. 67-78). Chicago, I.L.: Rand McNally.

Shuell, T. J. (1986). Cognitive conceptions of learning. *Review of Educational Research*, 56(4), 411-436.

Skinner, B. F. (1936). *The behavior of organisms: An experimental analysis.* New York: Appleton-Century.

The Cambridge Dictionary (2021). https://dictionary.cambridge.org/dictionary/ english/learning

Thorndike, E. L. (1898). Animal intelligence: An experimental study of the associative processes in animals. *Psychological Monographs: General and Applied*, 2(4), i-109.

Thorndike, E. L. (1905). *The elements of psychology.* New York: A. G. Seiler.

Tinto, V. (2003). *Learning Better Together: The Impact of Learning Communities on Student Success*. Higher Education Monograph Series. Syracuse: Syracuse University.

Tyler, R. W. (1949). *Basic principles of curriculum and instruction*. Chicago, I.L., The University of Chicago Press.

Vygotsky, L. S. (1978). *Mind in society: The development of higher psychological processes*. Cambridge, M.A.: Harvard University Press.

Watson, J. B. (1913). Psychology as the behaviorist views it. *Psychological Review*, 20, 158-178.

Watson, J. B. (1930). *Behaviorism*. Chicago, I.L.: University of Chicago Press.

Chapter 2

How Voice Students Become Professionals through Active Learning Experiences

Anke Hoeppner and Anna Reid

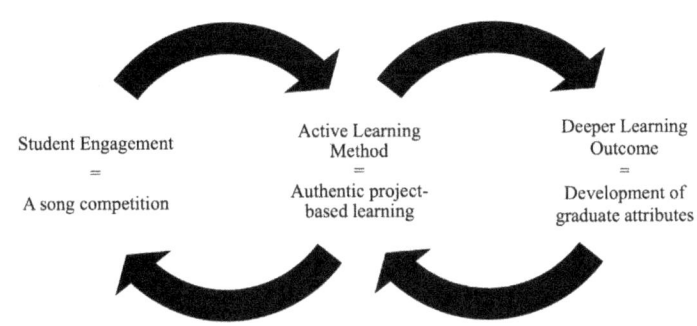

Introduction

With our chapter, we contribute to this book, *Active Learning in Higher Education*, by showing how we have used a song competition to engage students in authentic project-based learning to facilitate the development of graduate attributes in the context of professional preparation. In our context, we define active learning as a learning activity which encourages students to apply theoretical knowledge in activities that are authentic to the workplace of a singer and mirror what really happens in a singer's professional environment. As such, active learning allows us to meaningfully integrate different voice and music performance-related curriculum areas for a real professional outcome. Our case of active learning includes audition and competition experiences as precursors to the workplace audition. It also directs the students' thinking towards employment opportunities within the music performance industries other than performing directly as a singer.

Chapter 2

Vocal students at the Sydney Conservatorium of Music specialising in Western Art music study a variety of subjects in preparation for their future lives as professional singers. Including voice technical, music-theoretical, and stage performance skills, a considerable effort is directed towards the ability to sing and perform in languages other than their own. The popular song forms of the 18th – 20th Centuries provide a rich source of materials for young singers to develop their artistic voices. Based on German, French, Italian, and English poetry, it is a major challenge for students to acquire the facility to sing confidently in this most common set of Western Art song languages. An area of 'peril' for the pre-professional singer, and one that is difficult to address within the traditional classroom environment, is the combined application of the learned skills from different curriculum areas in an authentic performance situation in front of an audience. This is especially the case if the audience has knowledge of art song languages or are native speakers of the presented languages, but our remit is broader than that. Singers need to become familiar with the forms of work that are appropriate in their discipline. Young singers will compete for musical and monetary prizes in much the same way as young athletes. They will enter competitions where they will sing and be assessed for their vocal quality, and they will often be singing 'against' long term friends. Moreover, the singing competition is also a precursor to the workplace audition.

However, being selected to compete as a singer is only part of the equation. For performances to be seamless, a significant amount of background activity must occur – and this background activity can be a fruitful source of employment in the future during periods of limited vocal performance opportunities. Therefore, we determined to combine the competition with a most challenging class to help students understand the importance of the class and its importance in the context of the profession. We encouraged the students to process and evaluate their experiences relating to the song competition in an e-self-reflective questionnaire. The feedback we received by analysing the data from the questionnaires provides us with a rich source of information about how students value active learning and how it informs students' perspectives on their future professional workplaces. Reading this chapter, you should gain the following insights:

1. how integrating active learning into the curriculum design fosters students' employability thinking;
2. how active learning can inform students' perspectives on professional behaviours and communication;
3. how students value active learning in the context of a song competition.

Overview of main sections

This chapter has four main sections. In Section 1, we introduce the idea of employability thinking within the context of developing graduate attributes and how it led to the implementation of a song competition -as an active learning experience- into the course design for an entire undergraduate diction cohort. In Section 2, we detail the structure and organisation of the event and describe what the students accomplished. We finish this section with the questions from an e-self-reflective questionnaire which formed part of the course work and encouraged the students to reflect on their experiences. Section 3 analyses the quantitative and qualitative data we collected from the students' responses to the e-self-reflective questionnaire. In Section 4, we point to the limitations of this study and how we are planning to overcome them by collecting data from future diction cohorts on their journey through the undergraduate curriculum. We hope that the positive response to the first iteration of this active learning experience continues to challenge our students to creatively align other discipline areas to the professional work of a singer.

Section I: The background to active learning

The course curriculum for undergraduate vocal students focuses on developing voice specific skills. The subjects taught include voice lessons during which the students learn how to build and technically master their voices, music theory and oral skills. All these elements the students need to analyse and read music, including chamber music- for learning how to sing in small ensembles. Additionally, the students need to acquire performance skills to be able to both communicate the contents of their songs and how to behave in front of an audience. A significant skill for young singers is the ability to sing in the languages of the common set of Western Art music: German, Italian, French, and English. Yet, voice teachers do not have sufficient time to concentrate on specific language patterns (Bragger, 1975), onomatopoeia's sensory effects, and the intricate connections between poetic and musical structures. The students acquire these skills by immersing themselves in the theoretical and practical course content of diction studies. They learn the characteristic sounds of each language-specific to singing in conjunction with basic language and grammar rules. They also learn to read and write the International Phonetic Alphabet (IPA). Learning the IPA is akin to students learning their ABCs in year one at school. A written symbol is assigned to each sound from any language, such as vowels, consonants, consonant clusters, monophthongs, diphthongs and stresses. The students learn to read and write the IPA and transcribe sounds into IPA. Knowledge of the IPA allows students to recognise the sounds of the specific languages and helps them process, read, or sing with the dramatic and musical requirements intended by the poetry and composition.

At the Sydney Conservatorium of Music, voice students start learning German diction in semester one and Italian in semester two before encountering French diction in semester three and a rotation of the three languages in the remaining semesters until graduation. There is no specific course for English diction. The students are introduced to the principles of diction and the IPA using the German language. They then continue to add knowledge about the other languages as they progress through their curriculum. Each diction course is taught during 12 three-hour contact classes per semester using active learning methodology. The teacher introduces theoretical content combined with *"brief demonstrations and short, ungraded writing exercises followed by class discussion"* (Bonwell & Eison, 1991:6, see also Culic & Pavelea, Chapter 7 in this book) during the first two hours of class. A scheduled number of students then applies the learned content by singing their individual songs, with immediate feedback from the teacher during the final hour. The non-performing students observe this process. Considering that the German language has 14 vowel sounds, French 16, Italian 7, and English 15 (Adler, 1967), not to mention the different forms of consonant sounds, stresses, language patterns, and grammar rules, it is easy to imagine that the theory-rich teaching content in diction classes can be overwhelming.

This could be especially so for students with no prior knowledge of the taught languages and seemingly far removed from the students' idea of what it feels like to be a professional singer. The students face the challenge of understanding the influence of diction skills on the quality of their singing during their studies when their musical hearing and vocal techniques are not yet fully developed.

Consequently, the students are not fully aware of how the quality of their diction skills affects the immediate learning outcomes in the individual lessons with their voice teachers and future prospects of securing work in the highly competitive environment of a professional singer. We, therefore, extended Mitchell & Zigurs' (2009) idea of active learning as cited in Mitchell et al. (2017:23) as *"one time or ongoing student exercises that are introduced in the classroom to encourage student thinking and participation in an effort to engage students in the learning process"* to include Kolb's (2014:4) experiential learning model *"as the process that links education, work and personal development"* (see also Olson, 2022, Chapter 3 in this book). We intended to design an additional active learning project not with a focus on diction itself but on developing graduate attributes and directing the students' thinking beyond the classroom towards imagining how diction skills fit into the context of their future profession. We decided to create a learning space outside the classroom where the students would not 'imitate' future professional behaviours and actions but would deliver a real professional event in an authentic workplace situation.

The professional background of the German diction teacher informed the design for this active learning experience together with Chickering & Gamson's (1987:2) seven principles that reflect effective education practice for undergraduates. These are: *"(1) encourages contacts between students and faculty; (2) develops reciprocity and cooperation among students; (3) uses active learning techniques; (4) gives prompt feedback; (5) emphasizes time on task; (6) communicates high expectations; and (7) respects diverse talents and ways of learning"*. The teacher had extensive professional experience working for more than 30 years as a professional singer in the classical arts industry. In addition, the teacher had ten years of experience teaching voice and diction on a casual basis at the conservatorium. With such an abundance of lived professional experience, the support of the head of school, and the change to a full-time lecturing position, changes to the curriculum were implemented to include a real song competition as active learning. The song competition would create a competitive audition situation with the added pressure of performing in a foreign language in front of a native speaking audience akin to an authentic workplace audition in German-speaking countries.

However, there was a broader pedagogical approach. It is essential to support students in their professional aspirations and provide experiences where, as learners, they meet real professional experiences. Only a few students would reach the finals. The majority of participating students would not compete as singers but work in groups to organise and run the competition as a public event with outside audiences.

Scaffolded by Johnson and Johnson's (1989) cooperative learning model, team members work together, rely on each other, and hold each other accountable for all aspects of the song competition, including marketing, publicity, and ticket sales. By doing this, the students started the ongoing process of aligning their own needs with the needs of future audiences and employers:

- how do you get 'bums on seats';
- how do ticketing systems work;
- how do you write program notes;
- who is managing the stage;
- who is looking after the audience;
- could the associated activities be sources for future employment?

Other aspects of value were the opportunity to meet with students from other study years and listen to the auditionees' and finalists' performances, work together in teams, and feel pride in their accomplishments.

Active learning theory and methodology

There have been significant efforts to identify and develop graduate attributes across the tertiary education sector in Australia during the past 20 years in response to demands for readily employable graduates across a broad sector of industries, including the arts. Green et al. (2009) point to the difficulty of defining these attributes. Employability features strongly in the discourse by Andrews & Higson (2008), Munge (2009), Frawley (2017), and Rowe and Zegwaard (2017). Hinchliffe (2006), Barrie (2007), and Bennett (2009) explore the concept of lifelong learning and Killick (2009, 2018) and Jones and Killick (2013) that of global citizenship.

Barrie (2004) and Oliver (2011) explore graduate attributes extensively within the Australian context (as cited in Oliver & Jorre de St Jorre, 2018:822). The University of Sydney (2016) responded to the ongoing discussions by outlaying its graduate attributes for undergraduate education in the 2016-2020 strategic plan. The attributes are defined as: *"depth of disciplinary expertise…broader skills as in critical thinking and problem solving, oral and written communication, information/digital literacy, and inventiveness…cultural competence…interdisciplinary effectiveness…an integrated professional, ethical and personal identity…[and] influence."* (The University of Sydney, 2016 in Frawley, 2017).

An analysis of the curricula of 154 European art institutions in Austria, Germany, and Switzerland ties into the discussion about how to skill the future workforce for successful participation in the economy from an arts industry perspective (Bauer et al., 2011). Their study is motivated by the findings that while the arts contribute significantly to the European economies (Oakley, 2009, as cited in Bauer et al., 2011), the artists' share in the created income is not proportionate. The study shows that the institutions concentrate on developing artistic skills but do not efficiently equip the students with adequate levels of management skills to become economically successful participants within the economy. Bauer et al. (2011:639) conclude that *"knowledge of business administration, marketing, organization and knowledge about legal rights and duties should be included in any artistic education, regardless of the specific art discipline"*.

In her research about career development of Australian musicians, Bennett (2012) adds to the discussion from an Australian perspective. With an estimated contribution of over 3% to the gross domestic product in 2006 (Gulberg & Letts, 2005, cited in Bennett, 2012:65), the music sector significantly contributes to the Australian economy. The 2006 Australian census data report (Australian Bureau of Statistics 2006, cited in Bennett, 2012:69) shows that *"almost 1.1 million people in Australia had completed training in the arts or culture, and 1% of the population had completed some form of formal music training"*. While "80% of musicians teach, 70% perform and 30% run ensembles", almost *all musicians' work-portfolios included forms of self-employment*" (Bennett, 2008; Huhtanen, 2004; Metier, 2001, cited in Bennett, 2012:63). Bennett (2012:71) points to lost work opportunities within the complex employment structures of musicians because they have not or do not consider themselves having the necessary entrepreneurial business skills.

In contrast, employers appreciate arts graduates because of their transferable skill sets, including *"teamwork"* and the *"ability to work independently"*. The Australian Vice-Chancellors' Committee aims at increasing Australian higher education numbers to 60% (AVCC, 2003, as cited in Green et al., 2009:8). However, the effects of decreased expenditure per student challenge the implementation of those balanced vertical and horizontal program structures needed for graduates to develop the broad range of graduate attributes employers demand and expect from higher education (AVCC, 2003:9, as cited in Green et al., 2009:23). Bennett (2012:73) suggests that while teachers and music professionals understand the importance of developing business skills during tertiary education to maximise working opportunities after graduation, engaging the students with the subject in already busy curricula remains a challenge.

Reflecting on her body of research spanning 20 years about higher education and its ability to prepare employable and workforce-ready graduates, Bennett (2019:33) responds to the four challenges *"university funding; commitment to change by university staff; dealing with complexity; and building capacity"* as posed by the Australian Deputy Vice-Chancellors in their 2019 HERD-review. Bennett (2019:39) introduces the term *"employABILITY"*, focusing on students' development of cognitive and social 'abilities' as the foundation for lifelong learning and adaptability in unpredictable and fast-changing employment environments. This thinking can be developed using existing frameworks and curricula with minimal extra resources.

The optimisation of course designs with a strong focus on developing employABILITY thinking was the determining factor for us to apply active learning as the driver for implementing all aspects of musically preparing, organising, marketing, and running a song competition into the existing diction courses at the Sydney Conservatorium of Music. The Demant Dreikurs Scholarship Song Competition (DDSSC) was intended to give student vocalists a chance to sing Lieder in public, leading to a financial prize in the form of a scholarship. The scholarship was previously unaligned to any curriculum activity. We obtained and analysed students' feedback to find out how the participating students valued the active learning experience of the DDSSC. The findings add to the discussion about how active learning can contribute to students' development of graduate attributes and employABILITY thinking within existing curricula. In addition, the results from this study will be used to improve the efficacy of future iterations of this specific event and, with it, the intended learning outcomes.

The DDSSC provided the perfect opportunity to engage students in an active learning experience that mirrors future workplace structures. The pressures for the performers to prepare and deliver high-quality performances on time and the mechanisms involved to audition and perform, market, sell, and run the DDSSC for the participating student teams were authentic to real-life situations professional performers and arts organisations face in the marketplace. Participating students were all involved in German diction studies. Montgomery (2018) provides insight into how connections between voice and diction are made. The strong connections are made between the conceptions of vocal pedagogy and diction study where academic work and embodied practice cohere. However, the focus was on breath control, the positions of the mouth, tongue, resonance and projection, and the peculiarities of any particular language. Montgomery (2018) provides detailed diction technical knowledge but omits the exigencies of performance and communication. Although diction technical knowledge is critical for vocal preparation, it is often an uncontextualised activity. Wiewiora and Kowalkiewicz (2019:415) suggest *"the need to develop assessment practices that are contextualised, meaningful for students and closely linked to real-world challenges has been increasingly recognised in higher education"*. Moreover, Wiewiora and Kowalkiewicz (2019:416) continue by suggesting: *"Experiential learning provides exposure to authentic situations in which students can reflect upon and evaluate real-world scenarios, thus engaging in a more in-depth comprehension and application of knowledge. Authentic assessment is one that enhances experiential learning by utilising real-life challenges that students are likely to experience in the workplace."*

In their business context, Wiewiora and Kowalkiewicz (2019) gave students a scenario large enough and intricate enough to enable them to demonstrate the necessary skills to respond to the workplace situation. In addition, guided reflections were used to understand how students experienced applying knowledge to an authentic situation. Three things were found–a development in self-concept, knowledge of theory in context, and leadership. Self-concept included emotions, self-awareness, self-efficacy, self-regulation, and spiritual identity. Closer to our situation is the research undertaken by Johnson-Read et al. (2015), where they conducted three studies on the performance of Lieder. Like Montgomery (2018), the foci were on technical aspects of performance. *"Our broad interest was to investigate whether a set of principles for all genres and styles of singing could be available to reflect what performers do and to work toward well-defined guidelines to aid teachers and students"* (Johnson-Read et al., 2015:645. e15). A different approach to authentic learning situations is presented by James and Casidy (2018:401) where they advise: *"Students should be given tasks that develop and test the skills and practices that they will need in their future careers – tasks that mirror professional practice and test more than just rote memorisation. In response to these increased expectations, the topic of authentic assessments in higher education has attracted a significant amount of interest in the literature in recent years."*

However, they caution that there is a *"lack of empirical evidence supporting the relationship between authentic assessment and students' positive attitudes (i.e., satisfaction) and behavioural intentions"* (James & Casidy, 2018:402). Active learning involved in all aspects of preparing and running the DDSSC culminates in its public performance in front of a live and online audience. This public performance is authentic to live auditions and performances for professional singers, and we regard it as an authentic assessment for the students. In this chapter, we address the lack of empirical evidence supporting the relationship between authentic assessment and students' positive attitudes by analysing qualitative and quantitative data we obtained from an e-self-reflective questionnaire the students used to reflect on their experiences related to the DDSSC.

From the students' perspective, we explore the relation of learning using an active and, in our case, authentic learning environment and the professional skills that they encounter through the experience. The questionnaire was conducted online and included yes/no type questions. The students had unlimited space to elaborate upon their answers to these questions. The timeframe from distribution to the return of the questionnaire was eight weeks. Ethic's approval was obtained to ask for permission to access the quantitative and qualitative data at the end of the semester after diction marks were finalised to avoid feelings of coercion. A total of 38 students from the 48 strong diction cohort responded to our research invitation. The data in this chapter is based on the data from these questionnaires. The students reflected on the following questions:

- what study year are you in?
- what was the activity you were involved in?
- how much experience did you have in your activity prior to the event?
- did you learn something new and different?
- did you feel prepared for your activity?
- did you like your activity?
- do you believe your activity could be useful in your professional life after Uni?
- my team experience was…?
- were you proud to be part of the organisation of this event?
- what did you enjoy during the event?
- what advice do you have for the students who take over your activity in the next year?

Section 2: The case of active learning

The DDSSC took place in the form of a public recital. The event's planning, organisation, and execution involved the entire cohort of the undergraduate diction courses (from first-year to fourth-year tertiary students). Part of the active learning experience design was the e-self-reflective questionnaire the students used to reflect upon their experiences during the activity.

Diction classes typically have between 10-15 students in each year group. Traditionally the classes were face to face with supplemental e-learning activities. The students would learn to read and write the international phonetic alphabet, aspects of German grammar, and how the German language flows together with various compositions. The students perform for each other as a final in-class assessment in addition to writing assignments. The competition provided a completely different opportunity for the singers reaching the 'finals' to perform for a German-speaking audience and their peers from other study years. Non-finalist students would organise, market, run and present the competition professionally. In essence, the junior year students would support the senior students' performance with an expectation that they too will succeed in the competition.

Our pedagogical innovation allowed the students to experience how the at times dry and theory-heavy diction course content fits into the performance practice of a professional singer. Our pedagogical aim was not restricted to diction. The ability to apply specialised music and performance skills at a high interdisciplinary level determines the success of a singer in performance. Voice technical and acting skills and the music skills to communicate with the collaborative pianist and audience are part of the course work of voice students and are taught in separate classes. We stipulated that if the students see how diction fits into the professional practice of a singer, they extend this concept to include the course content from other classes.

The embodiment of the human voice and the many hours of daily practise it takes to develop vocal and performance skills can be all-consuming for students. We wanted the students to gain insight into non-voice related aspects of being a professional singer. We drew attention to stage management, ushering, program editing, marketing, and ticket sales. These non-voice related activities can be a fruitful source for future employments. We wanted the students to experience the impact of graduate attributes mentioned in the university's 2016-2020 strategic plan (Frawley, 2017:32) on creating, obtaining, and maintaining professional employment. Finally, we wanted the students to have fun by creating a platform for the whole cohort to meet, watch their peers perform, and work together towards a common goal.

An overview of how students work with active learning

Six finalist singers and two cover singers were chosen through an online audition process. All undergraduate students were eligible to audition.

All diction students who were not finalists were involved in the tasks concerning the organisation of this event as part of their course work. Each study year formed teams. Teams chose team leaders. The teams met at regular intervals outside of class hours and reported to the lecturer. The following tasks were assigned according to study year:

- first-year students were responsible for the direct contact with the audience and the jury during the event, including ushering and front of house duties, stage managing, and lighting. The students were introduced to the health and safety procedures by a volunteer staff member;

- second-year students were responsible for marketing and ticketing the event and producing introductory video clips of the finalists and cover singers. The screening of the video clips was part of the live event and introduced the finalists to the audience. A volunteer staff member instructed the students on using the Conservatorium ticketing system. Students developed and maintained the *DEMANT DREIKURS SCHOLARSHIP SONG COMPETITION* website and established the Facebook profile *DEMANT DREIKURS GERMAN SONG CONTEST*. Other student tasks included sourcing video and audio equipment and the subsequent filming, editing, and uploading of the event for online viewing;

- third-year students were responsible for researching and writing program note entries for a printed and online event program. The printed program notes were bilingual (German and English). Three students from this cohort performed as finalists in the event;

- fourth-year students presented the bilingual program under live performance conditions to a live and online audience, including native German speakers.

Given the multitude of tasks, the high level of teamwork involved to manage the tasks, and the different levels of student experiences before the specific learning activities, it was important to construct assessments in a manner that supported self-reflection and appeared fair to all student groups within the cohort (Hwong et al., 1993; Iyer, 2013). The DDSSC was a highly visible live event. We considered the impact of the high-pressure environment for the cohort of having the quality of the singers' performance on public display for an audience and fellow students. Other considerations included the quality of program notes and information on the website and social media, the filming and streaming of the event, the seamless flow of the event managed by the stage crews, and the communications with the audience managed by ticketing and ushering teams. In order to *"level the playing field"* (White & Fantone, 2010:476) and after reflecting on their active learning experiences in an e-self-reflective questionnaire with quantitative and qualitative open-ended questions, we assessed the students through the pass/fail system.

How we prepare and organise active learning

The active learning experience consisted of a *preparatory phase* that began in week one of the semester, the actual *competition* in week six, and the *reflection phase,* which ended with submitting an e-self-reflective questionnaire in week 14 of the semester end. The *preparatory phase* began with our first action of finding a date when the entire student cohort and an adequate performance venue were available. Finding such a time during study weeks was difficult at first. Our solution was to schedule the activity outside of the study week on a Saturday in week six of the semester. In addition, we scheduled a two-hour rehearsal in the evening before the event to allow the student presenters, ushers, and stage managers to familiarise themselves with the performance venue and set up the stage for the DDSSC on the following day. Including the dates in the course outlines meant that the students could keep these times free of other commitments. We optimised the teaching of other diction course content by including a higher proportion of self-assessment and content comprehension canvas quizzes to compensate for the extra time spent on the competition outside of class hours.

The concept of the competition was introduced and discussed in each class in week one of the semester. The classes then formed task teams and elected team leaders. A comprehensive schedule with clear deadlines for each task and regular meetings between the lecturer and team leaders was essential for monitoring progress or intervening in problematic situations. The student teams sourced IT equipment, e.g., cameras and microphones, and self-trained on using the equipment. All outside resources needed to be approved. The students reached out to and invited the German-speaking communities; we invited four Lieder experts and two representatives of the German communities to join the jury panel on the day of the competition. A Canvas module was designed to accommodate the submission of audition videos and as a communication platform. We invited expert staff to form an audition jury panel and chose six finalists and two cover singers from the audition entries. One hour of expert one-on-one tuition with the collaborative pianist was allocated to each singer, during which they rehearsed their competition repertoire. The students reached out to the German-speaking communities and the German Consulate to inform them about the competition to publicise the event and achieve ticket sales. The inclusion of the DDSSC in the general events calendar of the conservatorium made it possible to access resources for mentoring student ushers and stage managers by the relevant staff at the Conservatorium. An existing scholarship was aligned to the competition and supplied monetary prizes for the singers. Additional costs involved the purchase of a website domain, website building application, and the annual renewal fee.

Four vocal staff members and two representatives from the German-speaking communities donated their time and expertise as invited jurors on the day of the competition. The students set up a schedule for the day of the competition with the times and tasks for every team. Having a schedule helped to stay organised and on time before, during, and after the event on the day of the competition. All teams met for a briefing three hours before the commencement of the competition. The stage managers then set up the stage and back-stage areas, the greenroom facilities, the ticketing table, and the conference room for the jury. The presenters set up the lectern, sound system, and monitor for the PowerPoint presentation. The ushers prepared and cleaned the communication devices, greeted the jury and audience and controlled the flow of the audience members under COVID-19 restrictions. All finalists had a short rehearsal before the commencement of the competition to get acquainted with the acoustic conditions in the performance venue. All teams helped to reset the venue after the conclusion of the competition.

The competition was for the students the first live performance after a long period of online learning during a COVID-19 lockdown. The opportunity to meet and debrief in a relaxed atmosphere during the after-party was a vital part of the design of the learning activity and marked the beginning of the *reflection phase* for the cohort. We dedicated 30 minutes during the seminar in the following week for the students to discuss their experiences. The final task of the active learning experience was to reflect on their experiences in an e-self-reflective questionnaire. We purposefully did not include the questionnaire in the marked course assessments as we wanted to encourage reflection in a stress-free environment and avoid all feelings of coercion.

Section 3: The outcome

Student perspective

We wanted to know how the students experienced active learning by participating in the DDSSC. After obtaining ethics permission, we posted a research invitation to access the data from the e-self-reflective questionnaires. A group of 38 students responded to the invitation. The participants included 10 first-year, eight second-year, 10 third-year, and 10 fourth-year students. Of those participants, four students ushered, five students were involved in stage management, six students in ticketing and marketing, while four students produced introductory videos, filmed the event and built the website. Nine students wrote bilingual program notes, and 10 students performed as vocal finalists or presented the bilingual event. The following section describes the students' perspective of the DDSSC.

We wanted to know how much experience the students had in their assigned tasks prior to the commencement of the DDSSC (Figure 1) and if they learned something new or different through this active learning experience (Figure 2). More than half of the participants (52.5%) were familiar with some aspects of their student tasks and ranged their pre-task performance experiences from 'a moderate amount to a great deal'. Interestingly, most participants (79%) felt that they learned something new through their active learning experience of the DDSSC.

How Voice Students Become Professionals through Active Learning Experiences

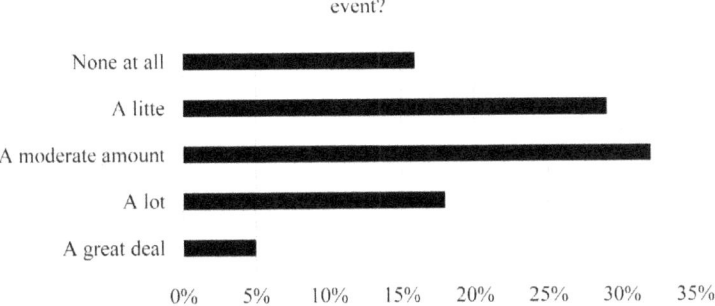

Figure 1: Participant experience levels prior to the DDSSC.

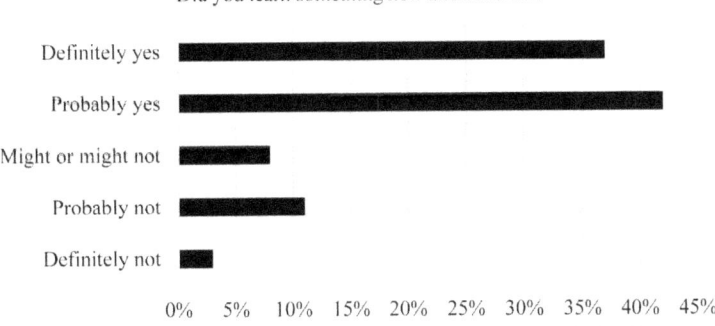

Figure 2: Participant response about gaining knowledge through their learning experience.

Interpersonal communication competencies, teamwork ability, technical (audio, visual, digital, research and formatting) skills, and the ability to adapt quickly to changed conditions emerging as salient themes from the cohort of students that felt they learned something new. The following quotes are indicative of the experiences of the ushering and stage-managing students:
- "I learnt how to manage people older than myself in a respectful way."
- "I did gain a better understanding of the workings of an entire professionally run production and how it runs along when everybody is working together as a well-oiled machine."

The students involved in media-related activities began to relate their gained technical media, programming, editing and research skills directly to their professional lives after graduating:

- "I learned some formatting techniques for programming, which I used for my own recital program."

The scope of experiences of the performing students was more diverse. Some students with prior entrepreneurial and performing experiences drew on their knowledge rather than learning something new:

- "I think as a performer, it is less an educational experience and more a performance/competition experience which is equally as fabulous, but perhaps we didn't learn as much as those in the other production areas."

Other performers appreciated the learning experience of performing to a live and a virtual audience and gained insight into other, untried avenues of performance.

We felt it important to know how well prepared the students felt for their tasks as this feedback would inform us for future iterations of the DDSSC (Table 1). The ushering and stage-managing first-year participants felt well prepared but experienced high levels of stress due to the unpredictable nature of their tasks. In contrast, the performing and presenting participants in years three and four did not find their experiences stressful. It is interesting that although feeling stressed, the first-year students liked their activities more than any other study year (Table 2). Being able to listen to and watch their peers perform, learning about the scope of activities involved in preparing and running such an event rather than only performing in it, the ability to work well in a team, and the challenge to perform in a different language in front of native speakers made the learning experience enjoyable:

- "It was fun to be a part of the running of the event and help out, as well as be able to hear the performers and get to know students in other years."

One participant was surprised to find presenting the event in a foreign language enjoyable:

- "It was interesting to be presenting an activity I unusually enjoy in a different language, as this changes the dynamic. I found that I had to be much more dedicated in my attention to inflection and tone, whereas normally I would probably wing it."

Did you feel prepared for your activity?

	Year 1	Year 2	Year 3	Year 4
Definitely yes	21%	21%	21%	37%
Probably yes	31%	23%	31%	15%
Might or might not	25%	0%	50%	25%
Probably not	50%	50%	0%	0%
Definitely not	0%	0%	0%	0%

Table 1: Participant response to the level of preparation for the DDSSC.

Did you like your activity?

	Year 1	Year 2	Year 3	Year 4
Neither like nor dislike	0%	60%	20%	20%
Like somewhat	22%	12%	44%	22%
Like a great deal	33%	17%	21%	29%
Dislike somewhat	0%	0%	0%	0%
Dislike a great deal	0%	0%	0%	0%

Table 2: Participant response to liking their learning activity.

Time pressure, dealing with an audience under COVID-19 restrictions, and inadequate or unreliable contributions from team members contributed to feelings of frustration:

- "…I found it frustrating that the responsibilities were shared inequitably among the members of the group."

A significant factor for integrating active learning into the diction course design was that we wanted the students to direct their thinking towards their professional lives after graduation. Finding out if the participants considered the learning activity useful in their professional lives after 'Uni' was interesting to us. We asked the participants for their feedback on a five-point scale. The student responses only inhabited three of the five points offered on the scale. The point *"very useful"* scored highest with an average response rate (across Years 1-4) of 42%, followed by *"extremely useful"* with 39.5% and *"moderately useful"* with 18.5% (Table 3). There were variations between the study years about why the students felt the active learning experience was useful. Financially supporting themselves through the newly acquired ushering and stage-managing skills was on the forefront of thinking for the participants of the first-year cohort as they found the experience:

- *"Helpful for when you don't have a vocal job."*

Further reasons why they found the experience useful were the ability to watch professional shows while on the job, a newfound appreciation for people working in this field of employment and gaining detailed knowledge of how a stage runs. The second- and third-year participants agreed that recording and media skills and the ability to maintain a professional digital online presence would be crucial in their working lives after Uni:

- *"Learning how to create a website is definitely a skill I will need, regardless of the career path I choose, but particularly for a career in music."*

The performing and presenting participants found the performance experience in a supportive environment a useful preparation for their future engagements in the industry:

- *"German-speaking is useful for any singer but having skills in presenting/hosting, particularly in an unfamiliar environment, is incredibly helpful; it mimics the stress of performing quite closely."*

Do you believe your activity could be useful in your professional life after uni?					
	Year 1	Year 2	Year 3	Year 4	Response rate
Extremely useful	20%	38%	70%	30%	39.5%
Very useful	60%	38%	20%	50%	42%
Moderately useful	20%	24%	10%	20%	18.5%
Slightly useful	0%	0%	0%	0%	0%
Not at all useful	0%	0%	0%	0%	0%

Table 3: Total participant response to the usefulness of the experience after graduation.

Employers appreciate arts graduates because of their transferable skill sets, including *"teamwork"* and the *"ability to work independently"* (Bennett, 2012:71). We considered the collaborative structure of the learning activities involving the DDSSC an opportunity for the students to reflect on their experiences working together in small teams. The majority of students valued their team experience as positive (Table 4). Only one student valued the experience as *'poor'*. The participants' team experiences were positive when high levels of communication and organisations were present:

- *"Communications and expectations were clear. We delegated different tasks to different people so that no one felt overwhelmed."*

The team experience was less positive, especially for the team leaders, when team members were not contributing equally to the set tasks:

- *"If I am completely honest, I did a disproportionate amount of the heavy lifting alone. We shared around the tasks equally in the beginning, however, it got to the point where I was worried that the project would not come together by the competition date. While this meant that I got to learn a lot, I feel as though it deprived others of learning these important skills."*

My team experience was?					
	Year 1	Year 2	Year 3	Year 4	Total student count
Excellent	33%	33%	20%	14%	15
Good	22%	11%	28%	39%	18
Average	25%	25%	25%	25%	4
Poor	0%	0%	100%	0%	1
Terrible	0%	0%	0%	0%	0

Table 4: Participants' response to how they value their team experience.

The high quality of the musical performances of the finalists and the knowledge of having contributed to the running of the event were the main reasons why 35 students from the participant cohort felt proud to have been part of the DDSSC. The ability to listen to and watch the finalists' performances, the experience of seeing how their contributions shaped the overall event, and the opportunity to meet and liaise with their peers from other study years made the event enjoyable. Equipment failure during the event and the perceived quality of the student-produced introductory videos contributed to why the remaining three students from the participant cohort did not feel proud to be part of the event.

We asked about peer advice for the students taking over next year's activities. The participants suggested detailed and early language preparation, clear communications within the teams, reaching out for support, and detailed planning as factors for capacity development.

Teacher perspective

The active learning concept of the DDSSC was grounded in the teacher's industry perspective and the university's focus on developing graduate attributes in the context of employability thinking. Vision, enthusiasm, and support from the school's leadership were the essential factors that allowed us to implement this activity. Breaking away from the teacher focused learning model raised the agency of both students and the teacher. The contact between the students and the teacher outside of the classroom and in an environment that mirrored a potential future workplace raised the levels of communications and trust in each other's abilities to be effective in a high-pressure environment. This had a lasting effect on the learning atmosphere in the classroom after the DDSSC. The students are less fearful of performing in front of each other, while the non-performing students engage better than before providing constructive feedback. There is an increased enthusiasm towards the coursework's theory-rich content after seeing it 'in action'. Independent student performance groups formed and reached out into the community with self-developed extra-curricular music programs. The level of performance confidence and experience among those students rose considerably and fed back into other curriculum areas such as individual voice lessons, stagecraft, and performance classes. The students bring diction, performance, and employability-related questions from those outside experiences to the classroom, contributing to a stimulating classroom environment.

Section 4: Moving Forward

Our study provides empirical evidence about students' positive attitudes in response to practice-based learning activities, as mentioned in James & Casidy (2018). However, it is appropriate to recognise the size of the participant cohort as a potential limitation. We address this limitation by following up our research investigation over the subsequent three iterations of the DDSSC. We are interested in learning if future data supports our current findings and how the students' perspectives change over the four years of their bachelor's degrees.

Extending our model to include other languages, such as Italian and French, would be interesting. However, lacking the financial resources for monetary prizes and paying casual staff prohibit us from doing so. In terms of future research, it would be helpful to include ideas of sustainability in the inquiry about active learning. This form of active learning in vocal studies is a first of its kind. Too often, diction studies, performance practice, and competition experience are worked on in isolation and usually in a traditional classroom. Using the impetus of a real competition, we aligned an active learning pedagogy with the discipline areas essential to professional work as a singer. The continuing funding for the competition enables us to extend this approach to vocal pedagogy into the future, possibly following graduating students' experiences into their professional careers.

Conclusion

Our findings support the idea that it is possible to foster the development of graduate attributes as outlined in The University of Sydney's 2016-2020 strategic plan (Frawley, 2017) by integrating active learning in the form of the DDSSC into an existing diction course for singers at the Sydney Conservatorium of Music. The characteristics of applied collaborative active learning described by Mitchell et al. (2017:28) as the ability to solve complex problems through teamwork and critical thinking support the development of these necessary attributes that prepare students for future employment in the music performance industries. Using active learning to integrate theory-rich requirements of a German diction course with the art of singing and the preparation and running of a song competition directs students towards seeing how the learned knowledge aligns with the requirements of a future workplace. Still, our remit was broader than placing German diction skills in the professional context. Although situated within the German diction course, only 50% of the students were involved in areas directly linked to language and diction skills. Under the pretext of German diction, we designed a learning activity to direct students' thinking towards other, non-voice related, professional employment within the music industries such as marketing, media representation, stage management, and ushering. Doing so, we responded to the earlier mentioned suggestions by Bauer et al. (2011:639) that *"knowledge of business administration, marketing, organization and knowledge about legal rights and duties should be included in any artistic education, regardless of the specific art discipline."*

Of the research participants, all found participation in the active learning experience useful for their lives after university, and the majority of the cohort stated they learned something new. The opportunity to learn audio, visual, digital, and word formatting skills, the ability to practise interpersonal communication skills working in a team and with an older audience, and the ability to react quickly to changing conditions emerged as salient themes why the students felt they learned something new. The students directed their thinking towards possible applications of the new knowledge within a professional context after graduation. Financial considerations and the opportunity to watch other performers were at the forefront of thinking for the students involved with ushering and stage-managerial tasks. The importance of creating and maintaining a professional digital online presence as part of managing their careers was noticeable in the thinking of the students associated with digital and marketing learning tasks. The opportunity to experience the stress of performing in front of a native speaking audience was a positive factor for the performing and presenting students.

In the context of the DDSSC, active learning made it possible to focus on students' cognitive and social development as the foundation for lifelong learning (Bennett, 2019:39). We agree that the students' thinking can be developed using existing frameworks and curricula. However, the collaborative character of active learning increased the workload for the faculty members through the process of implementing and monitoring this complex active learning project. Course ratings concern active learning classes, as millennials seem to prefer active learning (Therrell & Dunneback, 2015, cited in Mitchell et al., 2017:24). Still, they tend to give lower course evaluations (Martin, 2012, cited in Mitchell et al., 2017:24). So far, after the first year of data analysis, our findings do not share this concern. However, we will monitor the students' course evaluations over the four years of this longitudinal research study.

About the Authors

Anke Hoeppner is a Lecturer in voice and opera, Coordinator for diction and language studies at the Sydney Conservatorium of Music, The University of Sydney, Australia. She can be contacted at this email: anke.ryan@sydney.edu.au

Anna Reid is the Head of School and Dean of the Sydney Conservatorium of Music, The University of Sydney, Australia. She can be contacted at this email: anna.reid@sydney.edu.au

Bibliography

Adler, K. (1967). *Phonetics and diction in singing: Italian, French, Spanish, German* (NED - New edition). University of Minnesota Press.

Andrews, J., & Higson, H. (2008). Graduate employability, 'soft skills' versus 'hard' business knowledge: a European study. *Higher Education in Europe*, 33(4), 411–422.

Barrie, S. C. (2007). Academics' understandings of generic graduate attributes: a conceptual basis for lifelong learning. In P. Hager & S. Holland (Eds.), *Graduate attributes, learning and employability* (Vol. 6, pp. 149–167). Springer Netherlands.

Bauer, C., Viola, K., & Strauss, C. (2011). Management skills for artists: 'learning by doing'? *International Journal of Cultural Policy*, 17(5), 626–644.

Bennett, D. (2009). Academy and the real world: developing realistic notions of career in the performing arts. *Arts and Humanities in Higher Education*, 8(3), 309–327.

Bennett, D. (2012). *Life in the real world: how to make music graduates employable*. Common Ground Publishing.

Bennett, D. (2019). Graduate employability and higher education: past, present and future. *HERDSA Review of Higher Education*, 5, 31–61.

Bonwell, C. C., & Eison, J. A. (1991). *Active learning: creating excitement in the classroom*. Jossey-Bass.

Bragger, J. D. (1975). The teaching of music diction in departments of foreign languages. *The Modern Language Journal, 59*(1/2), 7–11.

Chickering, A. W., & Gamson, Z. F. (1987). Seven principles for good practice in undergraduate education. *AAHE bulletin, 3*(7).

Culic, L., & Pavelea, A. (2022). Enhancing students' interpersonal and leadership skills through an experience-based service-learning project: A case of active learning. In K. Enomoto, R. Warner & C. Nygaard (Eds.), *Active learning in higher education* (pp. 153–180). Oxfordshire, U.K.: Libri Publishing Ltd.

Frawley, J. (2017). *Graduate qualities – what are they and why are they important?* Teaching@Sydney. Retrieved from https://educational-innovation.sydney.edu.au/teaching@sydney/graduate-qualities-important/

Green, W., Hammer, S., & Star, C. (2009). Facing up to the challenge: why is it so hard to develop graduate attributes? *Higher Education Research & Development, 28*(1), 17–29.

Hinchliffe, G. (2006). Re-thinking lifelong learning. *Studies in Philosophy and Education, 25*(1–2), 93–109.

Hwong, N.-C., Caswell, A., Johnson, D. W., & Johnson, R. T. (1993). Effects of cooperative and individualistic learning on prospective elementary teachers' music achievement and attitudes. *The Journal of Social Psychology, 133*(1), 53–64.

Iyer, R. B. (2013). Relation between cooperative learning and student achievement. *International Journal of Education and Information Studies, 3*(1), 21–25.

James, L. T., & Casidy, R. (2018). Authentic assessment in business education: its effects on student satisfaction and promoting behaviour. *Studies in Higher Education, 43*(3), 401–415.

Johnson-Read, L., Chmiel, A., Schubert, E., & Wolfe, J. (2015). Performing lieder: Expert perspectives and comparison of vibrato and singer's formant with opera singers. *Journal of Voice, 29*(5), 645.e15-645.e32.

Johnson, D. W., & Johnson, R. (1989). *Cooperation and competition: Theory and research*. Interaction Book Company.

Jones, E., & Killick, D. (2013). Graduate attributes and the internationalized curriculum: embedding a global outlook in disciplinary learning outcomes. *Journal of Studies in International Education, 17*(2), 165–182.

Killick, D. (2009). Curriculum internationalisation: Identity, graduate attributes and 'altermodernity'. *Enhancing Learning in the Social Sciences, 2*(1), 1–33.

Killick, D. (2018). Graduates in/for a multicultural and globalising world. *On the Horizon, 26*(2), 72–78.

Kolb, D. A. (1984). *Experience as the source of learning and development.* Englewood Cliffs, N. J.: Prentice-Hall.

Mitchell, A., Petter, S., & Harris, A. (2017). Learning by doing: Twenty successful active learning exercises for information systems courses. *Journal of Information Technology Education: Innovations in Practice, 16*(1), 21–46.

Montgomery, C. (2018). The voice and diction connection: A diction instructor's approach to voice pedagogy. *Journal of Singing, 74*(3), 313–321.

Munge, B. (2009). From the outside looking in: A study of Australian employers' perceptions of graduates from outdoor education degree programs. (REFEREED PAPERS) (Report). *Australian Journal of Outdoor Education, 13*(1), 30.

Laguador, J. M. (2014). Cooperative learning approach in an outcomes-based environment. *International Journal of Social Sciences, Arts and Humanities, 2*(2), 46–55.

Oliver, B., & Jorre de St Jorre, T. (2018). Graduate attributes for 2020 and beyond: Recommendations for Australian higher education providers. *Higher Education Research & Development, 37*(4), 821–836.

Olson, H. (2022). Reflection towards excellence – empowering learners to become reflective practitioners. In K. Enomoto, R. Warner & C. Nygaard (Eds.), *Active learning in higher education* (pp. 63–82). Oxfordshire, U.K.: Libri Publishing Ltd.

Rowe, A., & Zegwaard, K. (2017). Developing graduate employability skills and attributes: Curriculum enhancement through work-integrated learning. *Asia-Pacific Journal of Cooperative Education, 18*(2), 87–99.

The University of Sydney (2016). *Strategic-plan-2016-20.pdf.* Retrieved October 18, 2021, from https://www.sydney.edu.au/dam/intranet/documents/strategy-and-planning/strategic-plan-2016-20.pdf

White, C. B., & Fantone, J. C. (2010). Pass–fail grading: Laying the foundation for self-regulated learning. *Advances in Health Sciences Education, 15*(4), 469-477.

Wiewiora, A., & Kowalkiewicz, A. (2019). The role of authentic assessment in developing authentic leadership identity and competencies. *Assessment & Evaluation in Higher Education, 44*(3), 415–430.

Chapter 3
Reflection towards Excellence: Empowering Learners to Become Reflective Practitioners

Hanna Olson

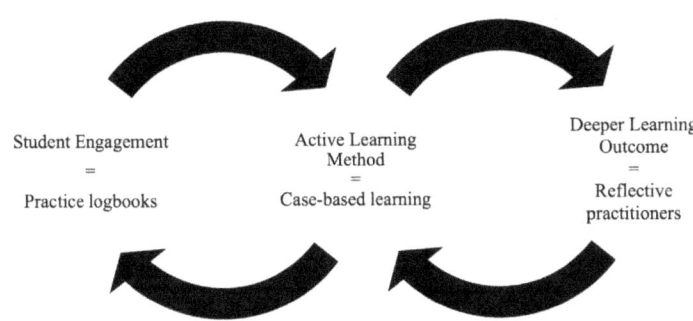

Introduction

My chapter contributes to this book, *Active Learning in Higher Education*, by showing how we have used practice logbooks to engage students in case-based learning to successfully educate them as reflective practitioners. Our active learning method through practice logbooks is used for students throughout their three years of study within the Bachelor of Oral Health (BOH) program at the Faculty of Dentistry, Te Kaupeka Pūniho, New Zealand's National Centre for Dentistry.

Active learning is a teaching approach to engage learners in their learning actively, rather than being passive recipients of 'unfiltered knowledge'. Active learning can be taught through the lens of reflective practice, using real-case scenarios in a clinical environment, which is well-suited for tertiary learners studying for a health professional degree. Through experience, new knowledge and skills are developed in a meaningful way, particularly when the experience is followed by reflective thinking (Zireva, 2021).

Already in the pre-clinical simulation context, before their first patient contact, students engage in the process of writing critical reflections after each pre-clinic session. This repetitive reflection exercise is performed daily, starting with simulation practice in their first year of study, then transferring to real patient clinics in year two. By the time students reach their third and final year, they have progressed their reflective writing competencies beyond simple reflective statements, now emerging to a higher order of reflective writing. In particular, final-year students enrolled in a health professional degree, who are utilising this learner-centred approach, should ultimately have become active learners, capable of describing the different layers of understanding, including tacit knowledge of their clinical performance. Eventually, they can now perceive the consequences of certain behaviours in the same way as an exceedingly well-rounded reflective health practitioner.

This chapter uses active learning as a methodology for implementing reflective practice in higher education; through the progression of routine daily reflection, students are actively involved in their learning process. Implementing active learning in a health professional undergraduate program can support the student journey by empowering students to become reflective practitioners. Through an active learning style designed to reach beyond basic knowledge and understanding, students will activate a deeper level of learning, including enhanced levels of communication skills. Successfully managed, these qualities will aid in students' ability to provide heightened patient care, which will be revealed as the chapter develops.

This chapter aims to provide insights into three specific areas:

1. how to outline critical reflection through a case-based active learning design;

2. how to implement teaching strategies and critical self-reflection;

3. staff and students' perspectives on being involved in the process of reflective practice.

Overview of main sections

This chapter has four main sections. In Section 1, I explain the background for incorporating an active learning design in higher education. In Section 2, I describe the rationale for exploring the use of reflective practice as part of active learning for students in health professional programs, along with giving practical guidelines. In Section 3, I document challenges for reflective practice and how they can be overcome, including students' views and the teacher's perspective. This is followed by Section 4, which explains how modification can be provided to engage students in any learning environment to start using and eventually master the active learning method of reflective practice.

Section 1: The background for active learning

Active learning is defined as a method of engagement in one's process of learning (Cattaneo, 2017; Kolb, 2014; Jonassen, 1991). Active learning strategy builds on prior knowledge and experience and is highly emphasised as a means for students to develop higher-order thinking (Zireva, 2021). The foundation for active learning was laid by well-known theorists such as John Dewey (Hickman et al., 2009), David Kolb (Kelly, 1997) and Kurt Lewin (Christie & De Graaff, 2017). Their learning theories emphasise learning through the transformation of experience into knowledge, skill, attitudes, values and emotions. This learning takes place through a cycle of concrete experience, reflective observation and abstract conceptualisation, with the final creation of knowledge through the transformation of experience (Healey & Jenkins, 2000; Kolb's Learning Theory as exemplified in Figure 1 in Section 2). In the process of learning, reflection becomes a means of transforming learning.

One barrier to the implementation of active learning, frequently mentioned in the literature, is the general perception that it is time-consuming for students and teachers alike. In active learning, students are required to be actively engaged in meaningful interactions in their learning processes (Prince, 2004), and teachers will need to provide constructive learning activities (Healey & Jenkins, 2000; Healey et al., 2014). However, since active learning draws upon previous knowledge and experience, it is vital to scrutinise students' prior understandings critically. To successfully introduce meaningful active learning processes, shortcomings in implementing an active learning approach must not be overlooked. For example, at the start of a course, a set of lectures on fundamental information of the specific underlying discipline or basic science component could be presented. Alternatively, students could be asked to fill out a knowledge-based questionnaire individually. That way, only topics that students did not fully understand, or if questions asked revealed to have a doubtful answer, would need to be addressed in class prior to moving forward with an active-learning scaffolded approach. Not only would a knowledge-based quiz reveal students' prior understanding and fundamental knowledge, but it would also resolve some of the more time-consuming challenges previously addressed with active learning. By allowing less time spent in a classroom, listening to the teacher explaining theory and concepts already known and familiar to students, more time could be allocated to the authentic exercise of active learning experiences.

The University of Otago has a set of principles for quality teaching, focusing on a quality learning experience where students are encouraged to take a deep approach to their learning, being actively engaged in the learning process (University of Otago, 2022). In contrast to the predominant content learning that the teacher would like to teach, commonly called a 'teacher-centred approach', active learning is usually referred to as 'student-centred', highlighting what students need to learn (Prosser & Trigwell, 1999). In the active learning methodology, the learner becomes more active than the educator, in which reflective thinking is anchored on all practices (Zireva, 2021). Therefore, by involving tertiary-level learners in meaningful activities through reflective practice, they eventually progress towards higher-order thinking (Zireva, 2021). Active learning strategies may also have a dedicated learning outcome to self-critique and self-assess, which is further discussed by Forasacco and Freire (2022, Chapter 4 in this book).

The engagement of critical thinking processes, where learners are practically engaged and make discoveries, will need to be repeated and allow for feedback (Holmes et al., 2015). One practical example of how critical thinking is being shaped through reflective practice with targeted feedback is within the undergraduate BOH program at the Faculty of Dentistry. Throughout their three years of study, learners enrolled in the program are encouraged to reflect on pre-clinical and clinical experiences they encounter by writing critically reflective journals. The skill of writing clinical reflections aligns with future professional standards (DCNZ). As oral health practitioners, they will be required to keep a professional portfolio to maintain an annual practising certificate. Therefore, developing skills in writing case-based reflections on patient interaction and clinical performance, already during their time of study, will enable learners to be adequately prepared to comply with these professional standards once they become registered oral health professionals.

Active learning theory and methodology

The framework of active learning theory stems from constructivism, where new knowledge is constructed and linked to previous knowledge and experience, previously highlighted by Hoeppner and Reid (2022, Chapter 2 in this book). According to this theory, learning is an act of social activity, integrating the magnitude of taking both sociocultural and individual constructions of knowledge into account in the learning process (Dewey, 1896). Some of the more eminent pedagogical approaches to constructivist theory are learner-centric when students find meaningful activities, understand certain behaviour, and ultimately perceive their learning environment to support their learning struggles (Enomoto et al., 2021).

In contrast to the more paradigmatic practice of didactic teaching, where higher education content material is being passively delivered from a podium in a lecture theatre, the process of active learning theory is where students become actively involved in the process of learning, which includes intellectual engagement (Zierva, 2021). This is sometimes referred to as learning by doing, with the additional layer of effective active learning design (Healey & Roberts, 2004). Active learning pedagogies are structured around problem-based, discovery-based, inquiry-based, project-based and case-based learning (Jonassen, 1991). These learning methods are based on elements of constructivism such as learner-centeredness, focus on process and content, use of interdisciplinary lessons, use of collaborative lessons, focus on student reflection, and importance of intrinsic motivation (Cattaneo, 2017).

Through reflective practice, students can immerse themselves into higher-order thinking because it involves both doing and thinking

(Ramsden, 2003). For example, after a clinical scenario with patient interactions, the student must understand what went well and not so well and critically reflect on their performance and practice experience. This, in turn, will enable learners to activate the necessary steps to take to enhance their clinical skills and further learning development.

Section 2: The case of active learning

The learning aims and objectives for clinical courses, where reflective practice is a central learning strategy, align well with the primary objectives of the University's 2013-2020 Teaching and Learning Plan (University of Otago, 2022) by:

- *promoting knowledge* – demonstrating advanced knowledge in specific areas of clinical dentistry as they relate to the practice or oral health therapy;
- *promoting understanding* – demonstrating the ability to critically review the literature in oral health;
- *promoting lifelong learning* – encouraging lifelong learning to provide a stimulating and high-quality learning environment which encourages students to challenge, critique and question knowledge about oral health;
- *enabling competencies* – demonstrating knowledge and understanding of the principles of safe clinical practice and their integration into the delivery of oral health care.

In simulation clinics, students are taught appropriate techniques and clinical procedures for planning, assessing, and caring for patients before their first patient contact. There are many steps for students to organise and think through, from the different perspectives of information gathering, such as uptake of a patient's medical history and clinical assessments until the stage of presenting a complete patient's care plan, prior to starting the actual treatment. It takes time for students to master these skills; this learning cannot entirely be taught from books or lecture materials during a classroom session. It has to be lived and experienced in the clinical environment by the students themselves (lived experience through project-based learning is further discussed by Schooling,

Chapter 13 in this book). Self-reflecting over their learning experience, through thoughtful thinking of how they would interact with and treat their patients, is a suitable way for learners to better understand the comprehensive task of care planning. By incorporating daily reflection, students learn to critically reflect on a specific incident, whether it be pre-clinical scenarios or patient interactions. This reflection on practice is characterised by allowing students to take on a learner-centred approach to their clinical training.

In their first year of study, students are introduced to writing reflective statements after completing each simulation task. This practice of reflection continues into their second year of BOH when students start treating real patients. In the student clinic, each student is guided under the supervision of a professional practice fellow registered with the Dental Council (NZ) as an oral health professional, who gives constant feedback on student performance alongside feedforward, specifically on how to manage a similar situation in the future confidently. Active learning is fostered within this clinical environment through a learner-centred, reflective approach. Students perform clinical assessments, create a care plan and treat patients under my (and other tutors') clinical guidance. An important aspect is the transparency of patient involvement for them to receive proper information and treatment options prior to commencement of care. Patients can make informed decisions to accept/decline care based on their understanding of all aspects. Therefore, each student's written care plan is discussed with the tutor and communicated and agreed upon with the patient before signing a consent for treatment.

An overview of how students work with active learning

Students within the BOH program are encouraged to reflect on their hands-on pre-clinical and clinical experiences critically. This entails the whole patient journey, starting with the initial assessment, including the patient's current concerns, medical, dental and social history, such as gathering medical conditions, medications, smoking and recreational history, dietary habits, oral home care regimen and clinical findings. After this comprehensive investigative exercise, the next step is for students to create a personalised oral health care plan to match each patient's individual needs. This plan is discussed with and later approved by a clinical tutor when completed. Not until the care plan has been discussed, approved and signed by the tutor is it presented to the patient. Hence, the care plan has the possibility of being scrutinised for further patient-clinician discussion and possibly revision before a final agreement is reached, following which the treatment can begin. This learning style of student-centred activities differs significantly from more traditional didactic teaching in a classroom or lecture theatre. Being actively involved in the process of learning encourages students to keep both motivation and interest high.

To provide a high standard of care for their patients, students have to consider their clinical findings and be made aware of a more holistic view of patient-centred care, including their wants and needs, by acknowledging and prioritising a patient's current concern. Moreover, the process of active learning is further enhanced when discussing patient cases in team meetings with classmates and clinical tutors prior to patients coming in for their appointments. After each clinical session, when students have been actively engaged in a specific patient case, they have another team meeting where students discuss potential incidents that may have occurred during the clinic that may have compromised the treatment. Additionally, these team meetings give the clinical tutor a chance to direct learner-specific feedback in a timely manner.

Immediately following each case-based scenario, students are encouraged to write a reflective statement relevant to an event that happened pertinent to that clinic. This statement could reflect anything they learned during patient interactions or care provision. If their patient cancelled or failed to attend their appointment, a possible learner reflection would be to critically think about how they can make it easier for their patients to attend appointments next time, or perhaps the 'no-show' was an act of miscommunication. By reflecting on suitable solutions to better communicate with their patients, students may find ways to avoid this 'no-show' from happening in future.

Students are provided with a physical hardcopy of a reflective journal called a logbook that they will bring to each clinical session. This logbook includes examples of statements to use as a guide to help them critically reflect on and write about their clinical sessions. The following questions, adapted from the three-step reflective framework by Hegarty (2011), are included in the journal:

- did I identify my goals for this session?
- was my preparation and conduct in accordance with professional expectations?
- was I prepared for the clinical tasks for this session?
- was my patient management appropriate?
- have I completed all sections of my patient file, written and electronic?
- have I managed the clinical tasks appropriately?
- what am I having difficulty with when undertaking the clinical task?
- what am I managing well when undertaking the clinical task?
- what strategies do I need to consider to improve my understanding of how to carry out the clinical task more effectively or efficiently?
- how did I achieve my goals for this session?

In addition to the daily practice of logbook entries of reflective statements in each year of their BOH studies, learners are required to write a reflective essay on a critical incident from their reflective journal. Where appropriate, students are to refer to research; a set minimum of academic articles is required for each cohort, starting with four articles in their first year and adding another two in their second year. Finally, in their last year of study, a minimum number of eight articles is required for reflective essay writing.

The following prompts and questions are exposed from within the logbook to help students comply with a structured format of writing reflective essays:

- read back over your reflective journal and select a particular incident that was significant for you;
- describe the context of the incident and the incident itself;
- discuss why the incident was significant;
- what were your thoughts, feelings, and concerns at the time, both personally and professionally?

Chapter 3

- what were the challenges you faced with this situation?
- how does this incident relate to your current knowledge?
- what went well? What would you do differently next time?
- how has this incident impacted on your clinical learning?
- how do this incident and your experience relate to current research?

How to prepare and organise active learning

This teaching method of case-based active learning design has some necessary preparatory steps. Learning material suitable to enhance active learning strategies through critical thinking and reflective practice is crucial to design case-based activities appropriately. First and foremost, learners will need to be exposed to Kolb's experiential learning cycle, as shown in Figure 1.

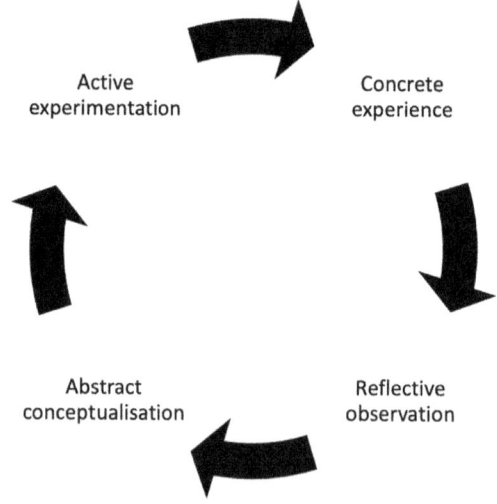

Figure 1: *Experiential learning cycle (adapted from Kolb, 2014).*

In this model, concrete experience refers to the activity experienced by the learner, for instance, when being exposed to a clinical scenario. Straight after the clinics, during the phase of reflective observation, the learner consciously reflects back. This is followed by abstract conceptualisation - when the learner conceptualises and processes the theory or model behind their clinical performance or observation. The last step in the model is called active experimentation and occurs when the learner is testing new theories and ideas for forthcoming clinics, such as providing strategies for care planning. As visualised in Figure 1, the experiential learning cycle is an ongoing process with non-specific entry or exit points. For each completed cycle, new learning concepts are constantly being developed, enhanced and acted upon (Healey & Jenkins, 2000).

After being exposed to the fundamentals of the experiential learning cycle, learners will need to understand that they are responsible for activating their learning. This is done by putting theory into action. Furthermore, active learning tends to be more self-directed as it moves towards independence. Thus, students' problem-solving skills are likely to be enhanced through discussions with peers and feedback from tutors. Interchangeably, problem-solving skills develop, and critical thinking occurs through service and experience. The more students engage in reflective practice, the more motivated they will become to remain active. Finally, it is essential to remember the most important aspect of all; internal motivation perpetuates active learning (Cattaneo, 2017; Zireva, 2021).

The structure of this particular reflection on practice has three main points, namely to describe, examine and articulate learning. At the start, students engage in a pre-clinical/clinical activity to describe the experience in terms of what, where, who, when and why? Next, to examine, students use prompts from their learning goals. These goals are divided into academic growth and personal growth. Combined, these goals represent articulated learning, answering questions such as 'What did I learn?', 'How did I learn it?', 'Why is this important?' and 'What will I do now because of it?'. The articulated learning draws the attention back to the initial experience of engaging in the activity by testing their learning and setting new goals (Healey & Jenkins, 2000).

In preparation for their reflective writing, students are taught and guided through the steps of critical reflection, which is done to give a reason for their decision or an event based on broader historical, social and political context (Hatton & Smith, 1995). Not only are students exposed to the method of active learning through didactic teaching, but active learning is also exemplified during tutorials and in team meetings. This enables students to think about and reflect on questions or thoughts that may emerge during pre-clinical/clinical sessions to fuel their tacit knowledge and activate learning. Students are guided through the practice of writing reflective statements and reflective essays by being provided with the following questions:

- why did I view the situation this way?
- what assumptions have I made?
- how else may I interpret the situation?
- what other action could I have taken?
- what will I do in the same situation next time?

After a thoughtful discussion, including prompts from the above-stated questions, learners are then guided through the process of writing a reflective essay. In preparation for this, the lecturer presents a guide to follow according to the general construction of an introduction, body and conclusion. The introduction includes the content of the incident and a brief discussion on why this incident was significant. The body incorporates thoughts, feelings, concerns and challenges they may have faced within the situation. Lastly, the conclusion involves evaluating the event; to include what specific learning occurred through this experience of active learning and possible changes that can be made in the future.

Section 3: The outcome

The outcome of incorporating this practice of active learning is formally evaluated once a year and informally evaluated throughout the academic year in the daily interactions of either case-based simulation practice or patient clinics. Students' daily reflective statements are read and commented on by a clinical tutor who has also been involved in the preparatory work or stages of actual patient clinics reflected on and explained by the student. Formal assessments on students' reflective essay writing skills occur in each year cohort. In this section, I report on students' commendations and teachers' perspectives on using reflective practice as a tool for active learning in students' journey to becoming reflective professional health practitioners.

Student perspective

Through active learning, students engage and take an active part in their learning with an increased learning cycle concerned with clinical skills and performance. While reflecting over past experiences, learners can think of ways to improve their patient interaction and clinical performance. This is exemplified in students' daily reflective statements and their yearly essay-writing assignment on reflective practice related to a critical incident. For example, in their reflective journal, students write blurbs on what methods they used to enhance their learning, whether it worked or not, along with a note on how to improve their clinical skills in the following session. For instance, novice logbook entries from junior students demonstrate a proactive stance to learning and that learning occurs when analysing and reflecting over clinical experience:

- *"Reflections help us to find our faults which have to be corrected and the ways to modify our skills to improve the clinical practice; therefore, this reflection helped me…to develop my professional skills."*
- *"It [reflective learning] encourages me to be a proactive learner, by learning to analyse clinical experiences rather than just getting through the session."*
- *"Written reflections allow me to think critically and reflect on my own progress to help overcome the challenges I have come across."*

Through reflection, some students have come to realise that learning happens as a result of changes in their attitudes and feelings:

- *"…reflection on cases can not only improve my learning but also unpack any personal feelings I may have in a professional manner."*
- *"Now that I am writing this reflection, I do realise that my attitudes and feelings towards such circumstances have shifted…These attitude changes are the most important outcome of my learning experience."*

Another student elaborated over the type of learning that reflective practice has brought about, considering knowledge and skills as well as professional growth:

- *"It is not only critical to reflect on positive and negative events but also to learn from the incident in order to be prepared for next time…*

> *Overall, through this experience, I have gained the necessary skills and knowledge that will allow me to achieve my goals. This is because I have learnt how to critically reflect sufficiently, which allows me to solve problems, make change, develop deeper understanding which can lead to professional growth and justify my actions."*

These junior students incorporated a constructive learning theory of reflective practice while observing senior students interacting in the patient clinic:

- *"I believe this situation was a constructive learning opportunity for me as I find experiential learning, such as the clinical aspects of the BOH course, the most effective way to learn…having the situation unfold right in front of my eyes helped me grasps skills and information that will be needed later in my degree, much faster than for example if it was taught in a tutorial…This will be important in the future when I have patients."*

- *"Over the last year, we have been taught about many clinical procedures and the theory behind them. However, only when I visited BOH3… is when I realised how to apply the knowledge and skills we have learned…Dealing with patients and their needs is best learnt when you are placed in an unexpected situation."*

Similarly to the above testimonies, most students argued that reflecting on an incident in the patient clinic would provide a learning experience for their future professional work. The below statements demonstrate that through critical reflections, students gain self-confidence in their clinical performance, which will lead to better patient care:

- *"A new understanding I have reached through this incident is practicing and reflecting on my mistakes are more likely to make me a better clinician, despite how I find it frustrating to not be adequate at a skill straight away. Reflection on my past mistakes allows me to see improvements in clinical practice and ways I can improve in order to provide the best possible care to patients."*

- *"My strengths throughout this experience was identifying my communication issues with children, recognising factors that influenced patient's behaviours and seeking out advice from a senior tutor. My weakness was maintaining confidence in an unfamiliar situation despite knowing*

I had proper training in my skillset. With more practices in experiences similar to this, I can assure myself I will not lack in self-confidence regarding communication and skillset."

Lastly, the excerpts below reveal how students let me in on their experiences and the developments of their thought process when writing reflective logbook entries. The following is an example of such a process, concluding that reflection is used as a tool to provide patient-centred care ultimately:

- *"Reflection required monitoring my goals, progress and practice through clinical sessions. Specifically, these reflections developed critical abilities. I found myself dedicating more time to reflect as I began to understand the significance of it to my professional development as a student and in the real world after I graduate. Throughout my journey, reflection has allowed me to be vulnerable and share my emotions and experiences that are difficult to convey to others considering the professional standards that have to be maintained in a clinical environment...As I continue to gain and enhance my clinical experience, I recognise the deeper meaning of critical reflection and the significance of it to ongoing professional development. By re-evaluating the experience and considering different approaches in response to the situation, it allows me to provide the best patient-centred care in the future."*

- *"It [this incident] has made me reflect and re-evaluate my progress over this year and what I can improve on in order to provide the best patient-centred care."*

Teacher perspective – reflections from clinical tutors

Early signs of student frustration are a somewhat regular occurrence observed by tutors, especially in their first and second years of study. Some students struggle quite a lot to write their first few reflective statements. This is usually overcome once they understand why this active learning style is essential and how reflective practice can assist them in becoming better clinicians. The active learning theory of reflective practice has shown to be important in assisting students in challenging themselves, making necessary changes, and strengthening their clinical performance yet, in a supportive, non-judgmental environment. Informal interactions and written comments from clinical tutors show an appreciation of students' reflective practice to improve their clinical skills. This is exemplified in the following comments:

- *"Student's logbooks provide a place for students to receive feedback and enable them to reflect on this feedback, they can then carry over successful skills to the next clinical session."*

- *"I have noticed students' clinical work improve after being given clinical feedback and allowing them to reflect on this."*

In addition to providing students with written feedback, some tutors also keep notes during clinical sessions where they write down individual students' performances on "what went well and what did not go well." If several students struggle with the same clinical skill, this can be brought up, ventilated and discussed with everyone in the team meeting at the end of the clinical session. Arguably, this would be a chance for students to learn from each other. They also learn from their own previous experience, and by reflecting on a particular scenario, students may change to a different approach next time to overcome obstacles in a similar situation:

- *"Often, the students will reflect on behaviour management if they have had a difficult child. We discuss ways of managing the child…or how we could have managed this better at the time."*

- *"The students often remember the techniques and apply with other difficult children that they may see."*

Although some of the junior students may have struggled to initiate writing formative reflective statements in their reflective logbooks, the practice of daily pre-clinical/clinical reflection has proved to be successful in the process of active learning from both the learners' and their clinical tutors' perspectives. In addition, having successfully completed three summative assessed reflective essays during their time of study, I am confident that each oral health student has successfully improved their clinical skills and academic performance by graduation. The majority of graduates have developed full competency of practice. They are ready to embrace their professional role as registered oral health professionals, willing and able to provide the best patient-centred care in their new career.

Section 4: Moving forward

Active learning is not a new phenomenon, as it has existed for some time, especially for adult learners in higher education settings. However, at universities -where active learning theories are being pedagogically enacted in a context such as BOH- for students straight from high school or otherwise new to higher education, this approach may seem a somewhat strange and unfamiliar practice. Therefore, I believe it would be wise to systematically introduce this active learning style of reflection on practice by following through with the step-by-step guide outlined in this chapter. By doing so, learners would be empowered to develop a sound approach to the active learning of clinical skills and performance with the ultimate goal of moving towards 'excellence through reflection'. Once the case of active learning has been properly introduced and used by the learners regularly, the intention is that this habit will also continue beyond their university studies.

Reflective practice can be incorporated as a motivating factor for learners in any health professional program and beyond. Students attending case-based clinical sessions urged to improve their clinical skills and performance could do exceptionally well by relating to the content in this chapter. Having said that, I would like to stress that writing critical reflective entries in a logbook is not just limited to a particular group of health care professionals; it can have much broader applicability. Incorporating reflective practice would take any student in any program at any level to a higher degree of learning by making small steps towards the reflective practice approach to activate higher-order thinking and a more profound degree of learning.

Conclusion

Throughout their three years of study, learners from the BOH program at the Faculty of Dentistry, Te Kaupeka Pūniho, New Zealand's National Centre for Dentistry, have been exposed to the concept of active learning by writing reflective statements from pre-clinical and clinical practice and performance. By reflecting on practice, learners have embraced the bigger picture of their future profession as they realise the importance of continuing to reflect on clinical practice in their careers post-university.

The students' comments strongly echo how their hands-on clinical skills are enhanced and actively learned and developed by themselves and through feedback from peers and clinical tutors to the highest standards through reflection on clinical skills and practice. Furthermore, learners have developed their critical thinking process through an active-learning scaffolded approach, enabling them to write high calibre reflective essays commensurate with their prior learning experience. This practice of active learning through reflection on practice has set the scene for students in becoming life-long learners and highly competent reflective practitioners.

Acknowledgements

The author wishes to express thanks to Ms Karen Hore for introducing her ground-breaking work of reflective practice into the BOH Programme during her terms of service as a professional practice fellow, as well as thanking Dr Susan Moffat, BOH Programme Convenor, for realising the importance and ongoing support for students' reflective practice in becoming reflective health care practitioners.

About the Author

Hanna Olson is a Lecturer, Deputy Convenor of the Bachelor of Oral Health Programme in the Faculty of Dentistry, and Programme Interprofessional Education (IPE) Convenor in the Department of Oral Sciences, at the University of Otago, New Zealand. She can be contacted at this email: hanna.olson@otago.ac.nz

Bibliography

Cattaneo, K. H. (2017). Telling active learning pedagogies apart: From theory to practice. *Journal of New Approaches in Educational Research*, 6(2), 144-152.

Christie, M., & De Graaff, E. (2017). The philosophical and pedagogical underpinnings of Active Learning in Engineering Education. *European Journal of Engineering Education*, 42(1), 5-16.

DCNZ (2022). Dental Council (New Zealand). Retrieved from: www.dcnz.org

Dewey, J. (1896). The reflex arc concept in psychology. *Psychological Review, 3*(4), 357-370.

Enomoto, K., Warner, R., & Nygaard, C. (2021). What drives teaching and learning innovations in higher education? In K. Enomoto, R. Warner & C. Nygaard (Eds.), *Teaching and learning innovations in higher education* (pp. 1-18). Oxfordshire, U.K.: Libri Publishing Ltd.

Forasacco, E., & Freire, J. (2022). Using co-designed technology-enhanced learning to develop postgraduate STEMM students' research communication competencies. In K. Enomoto, R. Warner & C. Nygaard (Eds.), *Active learning in higher education* (pp. 83-106). Oxfordshire, U.K.: Libri Publishing Ltd.

Hatton, N., & Smith, D. (1995). Reflection in teacher education: Towards definition and implementation. *Teaching and Teacher Education, 11*(1), 33-49.

Healey, M., Flint, A., & Harrington, K. (2014). *Engagement through partnership: students as partners in learning and teaching in higher education.* The Higher Education Academy, 1-78.

Healey, M., & Jenkins, A. (2000). Kolb's experiential learning theory and its application in geography in higher education. *Journal of Geography, 99*(5), 185-195.

Healey, M., & Roberts, H. (2004). Introduction-active learning and the swap shop. In M. Healey & J. Roberts (Eds.), *Engaging students in active learning: Case studies in geography, environment and related disciplines* (pp. 1-5). Cheltenham: Geography Discipline Network and School of Environment, University of Gloucestershire.

Hegarty, B. (2011). A framework to guide professional learning and reflective practice. Doctor of Education thesis, Faculty of Education, University of Wollongong, NSW. Retrieved from http://ro.uow.edu.au/theses/3720

Hickman, L. A., Neubert, S., & Reich, K. (Eds.) (2009). *John Dewey between pragmatism and constructivism.* Fordham University Press.

Hoeppner, A., & Reid, A. (2022). How voice students become professionals through active learning experiences. In K. Enomoto, R. Warner & C. Nygaard (Eds.), *Active learning in higher education* (pp. 35-62). Oxfordshire, UK: Libri Publishing Ltd.

Holmes, N. G., Wieman, C. E., & Bonn, D. (2015). Teaching critical thinking. *Proceedings of the National Academy of Sciences 112*(36), 11199-11204.

Jonassen, D. H. (1991). Objectivism vs. constructivism: Do we need a new paradigm? *Educational Technology Research and Development, 39*(3), 5-14.

Kelly, C. (1997). David Kolb, the theory of experiential learning and ESL. *The Internet TESL Journal, 3*(9), 1-5.

Kolb, D. A. (2014). *Experiential learning: Experience as the source of learning and development.* FT Press.

Prince, M. (2004). Does active learning work? A review of the research. *Journal of engineering education, 93*(3), 223-231.

Prosser, M., & Trigwell, K. (1999). *Understanding learning and teaching: The experience in higher education.* McGraw-Hill Education (UK).

Ramsden, P. (2003). *Learning to teach in higher education.* London: Routledge.

University of Otago (2022). University of Otago teaching and learning plan 2013-2020. Retrieved from https://www.otago.ac.nz/staff/otago027123.pdf

University of Otago (2022). Guidelines for teaching at Otago. Retrieved from https://www.otago.ac.nz/staff/otago027122.pdf

Schooling, D. (2022). Teaching from the Native American Circle: a future campus-wide sustainability project as a catalyst for active learning. In K. Enomoto, R. Warner & C. Nygaard (Eds.), *Active learning in higher education* (pp. 319-341). Oxfordshire, U.K.: Libri Publishing Ltd.

Zireva, D. (2021). Active learning: The panacea to miseducative practices in teacher education. In D. O. Lutsenko & G. Lucenco (Eds.), *Active learning - Theory and practice*[Working Title]. IntechOpen.

Chapter 4

Using Co-designed Technology-enhanced Learning to Develop Postgraduate STEMM Students' Research Communication Competencies

Elena Forasacco and Jorge Freire

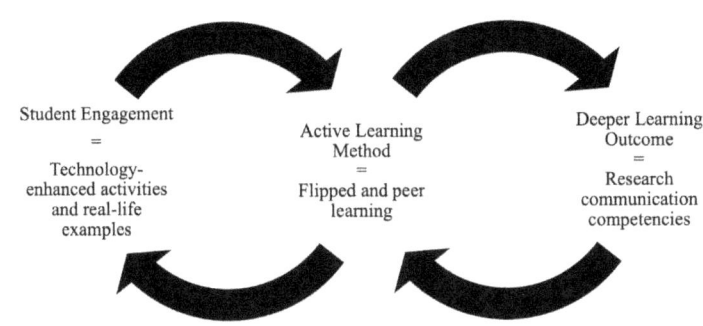

Introduction

With our chapter, we contribute to this book, *Active Learning in Higher Education*, by demonstrating how we engaged our postgraduate research and postgraduate coursework students in technology-enhanced activities and real-life examples using flipped and peer learning to develop their research communication competencies successfully. The students are STEMM master's and doctoral students (science, technology, engineering, mathematics and medicine) who participate in the Research Communication Programme at Imperial College London, U.K. The programme includes residential retreats, online and blended courses that aim to develop students' research communication competencies. The programme is based on active learning with asynchronous self-paced preparatory activities and synchronous live course activities. Teachers act as facilitators who promote the completion of asynchronous and online activities and peer-learning during synchronous activities (Ambrose et al., 2010; Gleason et al., 2011).

Since we work with postgraduate students who are adult learners with important working experiences and knowledge (Knowles, 1990), we define active learning as a tool to promote three aspects related to the way postgraduate students learn:

- interactions and exchanges of knowledge among peers (e.g. Bonk & Cunningham, 2012) to support social constructivism through the Community of Inquiry Framework (Richardson et al., 2012);

- engagement with content and real-life simulations for independent and authentic learning to help students set objectives and acquire knowledge by their own efforts, developing the ability for inquiry and critical evaluation (Candy, 1991);

- production and peer-assessment of resource files that support students throughout their master and doctorate (e.g. a version of a literature review for further development), and the new ideas developed by students through such activities should be something *"intelligible (understandable), plausible (reasonable) and fruitful"* (Hodson & Hodson, 1998:34).

Apart from focusing on the active learning method and its deeper learning outcomes for students, in our chapter, we also share examples of the co-design approach by which the teacher and the learning designer restructured the programme to be entirely based on active learning. Reading this chapter, you will obtain practical suggestions to:

1. develop courses based on active learning strategies to support the development of research communication competencies using technology-enhanced learning;

2. understand the teacher perspective (how to work with learning designers on the development of online and blended activities), and the learning designer perspective (how to work with teachers, students and other stakeholders in co-designing);

3. obtain the students' perspectives to enrich the discussion and provide suggestions to improve those strategies.

Overview of main sections

This chapter has four main sections. In Section 1, we give the rationale for using active learning based on students' needs and institutional and departmental guidelines. In Section 2, we explain how we developed an active learning fully-based programme, which includes blended courses, online courses and online residential retreats. We also show how we designed different active learning strategies based on the programme requirements and students' needs. Section 3 describes the students' perspectives on activities, their learning from the courses and the difficulties, and how we were able to (partly) overcome those difficulties during the design process. Section 4 outlines the outcomes of our active learning strategies based on the students', teacher and learning designer perspectives before we give practical recommendations to other teachers in Section 5.

Section 1: The background to active learning

The use of active learning at Imperial College London has been promoted since 2017 when the new 'Learning and Teaching Strategy' was published and included in the 'Digital Learning Strategy' and 'Blended Learning Design Strategy and Framework' of the Graduate School. However, since active learning is the most suitable approach to enhance the students' experience in the professional development context we work in (Webster-Wright, 2009), in 2015, we started the first phase to redesign the Research Communication Programme to apply active learning strategies. Within the Graduate School provision, developed in the last 15 years when the central Graduate School was created at Imperial, this programme is dedicated to developing postgraduate students' research communication competencies, with a special focus on dissertation and thesis preparation in compliance with the Imperial College Regulations. The Research Communication Programme has a doctoral provision, which includes a residential retreat and 11 courses complementary to courses delivered by the Centre for Academic English and by the Library, and a master provision with the online courses 'Preparing your literature review' and 'Preparing your dissertation'. The participation in all our courses is voluntary.

In 2019 we started the second phase that brought us to the development of the current design and activities, based on the key aim of the Graduate School's strategies: "*Enhance and develop a suite of blended, distance and face-to-face courses that promote active learning and inclusivity by exploring the affordances of technology-enhanced learning*" (Imperial College London Graduate School, 2019). This process had its major enhancement in 2020 due to the pandemic and the sudden need for online and remote active learning strategies. In this chapter, we focus on this second stage since it was the most meaningful part of the process.

The prompt for the redesign in 2015 was given by our students, who are both pedagogical co-designers and consultants, inputting their perspectives on learning, teaching, needs, preferences and priorities (Bovill & Felten, 2016). To us, the most striking comment was, and still is, related to a course delivered in 2015:

- *"I felt that just because I was a PhD student and not a more senior academic, I was being asked to perform somewhat childish activities. [...] I do appreciate the course is aimed at PhD students and not more senior academics, but my point is that I feel the course could benefit from changing its style to one where PhD students are treated with more maturity."*

Other comments related to the setting of the tasks: "*Some activities could involve more action than talking*", highlighting the importance of the feedback after activities: "*The good thing about this program was that we had a feedback session after every activity/task*". Some comments indicated the usefulness of working on activities related to their research projects: "*The activity which involved planning a project proposal with peers from a different discipline was the activity I felt I benefited most from*".

Based on those comments, the active learning strategies we included in our redesign were carefully discussed to tailor them to postgraduate students, designing asynchronous and synchronous activities that:

- support the master's and doctoral research process through the practice of competencies in real-life simulations;
- allow students to practise and self-assess their competencies, to focus on the specific competence they need to improve, to develop their own solutions and adapt their own strategies;

- follow a narrative and a constructive alignment;
- allow time for peer feedback and peer discussion over the activities.

During the redesign, the teacher's role was to begin the creative process of developing active learning strategies which could lead to the intended deeper learning outcomes. The success of the Research Communication Programme - measured by students' deeper learning outcomes - is connected to its importance for postgraduate research students and the meaningful active learning strategies designed thanks to the synergic collaboration of the teacher and the learning designer. The teacher, who is also the programme director, is responsible for the programme's success and has to ensure each course within the programme is meaningful and constructive for students.

The role of the learning designer was to make these processes tangible to create a sequence of connected asynchronous and synchronous activities that support a learner-centred approach (Agostinho, 2006; Ghislandi & Raffaghelli, 2015). Namely, the learning designer co-designed content and activities with the teacher and other stakeholders (such as students and supervisors) via a personalised approach: *"reviewing, editing, making recommendations, training, building learning objects, consulting, [performing] course reviews, quality assurance reviews and course deployment"* (Outlaw & Rice, 2015:1). This role considers the *"highly individualised and personal process"* teachers take to develop courses (McCurry & Mullinix, 2017:1), as well as teachers' digital capabilities and teaching and learning approach.

Active learning theory and methodology

Active learning is a suitable approach to teaching different subjects, including professional development (see Hoeppner & Reid, Chapter 2 in this book). This suitability is exemplified by Webster-Wright (2009), who notes that professional development is effective when based on learning that is continuous, active, social and related to the practice of students. The active learning strategies we use allow students to develop, practise, enhance and adapt competencies in a safe learning environment and promote the peer exchange of knowledge to enhance those competencies and develop solutions (Culic & Pavelea, 2022, Chapter 7 in this book; Ambrose et al., 2010; Smith et al., 2005). These strategies increase the students' motivation and engagement because they have realistic goals to achieve and allow students to use their knowledge during activities (Gleason et al., 2011).

Alongside theories on active learning, we based our redesign on the framework for adult learning (Knowles, 1990). According to this framework, learning is a cooperative process linked to the group and the learners' culture; adult learners can self-direct their learning and use their experiences and competencies during learning. These axioms make active learning effective and are shared with the principles of social constructivism (Vygotsky, 1978), which is the theoretical framework we have applied. This rationale was previously evidenced by Bonk & Kim (1998), who explained changes in the adult teaching and learning environment, whereby teaching as a transmission of knowledge has been replaced with teaching as an active, collaborative and learner-centred creation of knowledge that respects the adult learners' experiences.

Concepts underpinning the rationale of our redesign derive from the Community of Inquiry Framework (CoI), a collaborative constructivist model to promote and support online communities (Richardson et al., 2012), also used in the design of blended courses.

The main concepts of the social constructivism framework we considered are:

- learning is a developmental and dynamic process within which learners are actively involved (Adams, 2006);

- learning is a social process always in evolution (Aubrey & Riley, 2015);

- learning first happens among people, then it is internalised by each individual (Vygotsky, 1978); this happens when learning is considered *"as a sociocultural dialogic activity — a social constructivist or sociocultural approach"* (Bonk & Cunningham, 2012:26).

In parallel, we applied the following CoI principles:

- define an articulated, but simple, scaffolding approach to create and sustain a sense of community;

- courses and activities must promote trust and open communication among participants to maximise their engagement;

- support purposeful inquiry by setting clear expectations for each part of the course and activities, highlighting their applicability to a real-life context;

- promote critical reflection and meaningful interactions during activities, with structured and unambiguous instructions, prompts for individual and group reflection, discussion and feedback;

- motivate students to be active participants and ensure that inquiry moves to resolution by explaining the narrative of the course; ensure the assessment is congruent with the intended learning outcomes by asking participants to report back their learning from activities.

By combining the two sets of principles, we were able to redesign courses and active learning strategies that represent meaningful and useful experiences for students throughout their doctorate, which they had asked for with their comments (see Section 1), and to enhance their critical thinking, as also explored by Olson (2022, Chapter 3 in this book). Moreover, the application of those principles supported us to overcome the concerns we had when we started the course redesign: 1) how to develop meaningful online and asynchronous activities that are connected to synchronous activities; 2) how to engage and motivate students to complete online and asynchronous activities and 3) how to build and support prolonged online communities. In the following sections, we explain how we applied the principles above and how students engaged with and worked on activities.

Section 2: The case of active learning

The Research Communication Programme is attended by about 700 postgraduate students every year: to meet the students' demand, online courses are live for the whole academic year, blended courses have a duration of about 3 hours and are repeated about 10 times a year, and the retreat is delivered four times a year.

Our learning environment consists of non-homogeneous groups of students, at different career levels, master's and doctorate and with different scientific and cultural backgrounds. More than 50% of our postgraduate students are overseas students, mainly from the Far East and the Middle East countries. These differences might lead to non-homogeneous engagement during activities. For example, in some cases, we observed engaged students partly holding back during activities due to the low participation of other students; in other cases, engaged students were able to engage their reserved peers. Based on those reflections, we realised the need for inclusive and well-scaffolded active learning strategies to support and prepare all students to engage with all asynchronous, synchronous, and online activities and interact with peers. We aimed to provide students with active learning opportunities supporting:

a) a personalised learning experience that allows students to attend the course in stages, when they need to;

b) an accessible practice;

c) the completion of asynchronous and synchronous activities, which support the students' career;

d) the creation of a community of learners where student-teacher and student-student engagement are maximised.

An overview of how students work with active learning

The redesign of the programme allowed us to create and design diversified sets of active learning strategies to apply to online courses, blended courses and online residential retreats. Our active learning strategies are based on a flipped learning approach: before the class, we introduce concepts and give at least one activity for each learning outcome to allow students to practise and secure their learning; during the class, we use the time for active, practical and innovative applications of those concepts (Academy of Active Learning Arts and Sciences, 2018). This approach allows students more time to contact and reflect on new concepts (asynchronous moment), and in the synchronous moment, focus on discussion, reflection and feedback, and get a more personalised and valuable learning experience and deeper learning (Beattie et al., 1997). In this section, we explain how students work and engage with active learning in our courses through some examples (see Section 2 for details on activities).

In relation to active learning in online courses, we describe here how master's students work in the course 'Preparing your literature review'. We aimed to prepare an inclusive course suitable for all students, independent of their background and departmental requirements. Following consultations with supervisors from different departments, students and librarians, as part of the process of co-design, we decided to provide students with strategies to make the preparation and writing of their literature review more effective and efficient.

We designed different activities based on real-life examples, built following a scaffolding approach that allows students to build upon their competencies, practise while completing the course, and produce a draft literature review. Students 1) watch videos, animations and scenarios drawn from real life or research, where writing strategies are explained; 2) analyse guided and worked examples of literature reviews where writing strategies are applied; 3) answer quizzes with model answers and multiple-choice answers to verify their understanding, and use feedback to remediate any gaps; 4) apply those writing strategies on their own draft literature review by filling in provided templates that, combined, represent their draft literature review (Table 1).

	Draft your literature review – Template 1
	[If you cannot fill all the boxes now, add possible deadlines to help you with the time management]
Stage 1	Write the (provisional) title of your research project:
	Write your research question(s) and/or hypothesis:
	Write the keywords you use to find reading material related to your research question:
	Keyword 1:
	Keyword 2:
	Keyword 3:
Stage 2	What boundaries have you defined to select the reading material? Relate those boundaries to the evolution of your field.
Stage 3	What key points would you like to obtain by reading the material found using the keywords you defined above?
	Keyword 1 Key points
	Keyword 2 Key points
	Keyword 3 Key points
Stage 4	Based on the key points defined above, in your opinion, which organisation is the most suitable to prepare your literature review? Why?
Stage 5	Based on the organisation you are planning to use, prepare an outline of your literature review using Template 2.

Table 1: Example of a template students fill in while working on the online course.

As an example of active learning strategies designed for a blended course, here we use the 'Literature Review' course for doctoral students. We created a structured set of asynchronous activities that students complete independently and in their own time before the synchronous session: they have content videos to watch and practical tasks to complete in stages, based on their level of knowledge (any student from 1st year to final year can complete the tasks). As we clarify in the instructions, those tasks combined represent the skeleton of their literature review, which they can complete after the course while working on their research projects.

Students highly engage with both asynchronous and synchronous activities for a number of reasons. Synchronous activities consist of peer discussions and peer feedback on the asynchronous tasks: students are grouped by discipline, support each other with guided discussions and feedback, and define action points to improve their literature reviews. Along with the benefits of the content videos, they produce a skeleton of their literature review and exchange suggestions with peers working on similar projects.

As an example of active learning strategies created for a residential course, we use the two-day residential writing retreat for final year students. Students in their writing period feel isolated from their usual office community; this residential retreat gives a community to students. They no longer feel so isolated, which leads to an increase in their motivation and productivity.

Due to the pandemic, we created an online residential retreat consisting of 2.5 days of connected asynchronous and synchronous activities to support creating an online community of practice 'owned and managed' by students. In this context, students work on asynchronous active learning strategies essential to create trust and a sense of community. Those activities represent the space where students introduce themselves, meet and discuss before the synchronous part of the retreat. For the synchronous component of the retreat, activities promote group discussions and feedback sessions: students in their communities share their knowledge, competencies and expertise to support each other with their thesis writing (Table 2).

Asynchronous activities	Synchronous activities
Creation of trust: • introduce yourself to the whole group • talent bank: share your competencies and skills in a post and use the bank to ask for help from experts • suggestion box: share your suggestions	Creation of a group: • meet your group in the private Teams Class channel where meetings, resources and discussions can take place • define the working strategy of your group Work as a group during the retreat: • timetabled peer-feedback sessions, scaffolded by the 'Checklist for self-assessment' • peer-support to solve issues Maintain the community after the retreat: • 'open writing room' for meetings • forum/discussions in the Teams Class
Self-directed learning: • watch content videos that cover key introductory concepts • identify your needs using the 'Checklist for self-assessment'	Group learning: • Q&A sessions and group discussions about the videos • peer-support and peer-feedback based on their needs

Table 2: Example of connected asynchronous and synchronous active learning strategies used to create the community.

Our preparation and organisation of active learning

We applied a rationale to redesign the programme based on social constructivism, CoI and a framework for adult learning to overcome the (potential) concerns connected to blended, remote and online teaching approaches.

Since our courses are attended by students at different levels of their career, master's and doctorate degrees, we designed the new active learning strategies to facilitate the understanding of concepts using real-life examples and, importantly, the practice of those concepts through real-life simulations. For each course, we prepared:

- content videos with reflective questions throughout to prompt critical and active watching;
- at least one activity for each intended learning outcome organised into an asynchronous component, which students complete independently, and a connected synchronous component, based on group discussions and peer-feedback;
- detailed, simple and clear instructions for each component of activities;
- an email with general information, which teachers send to motivate students to complete the activities.

The success of these activities depends on the real-life examples and simulations used; the connection between asynchronous and synchronous components; their alignment with the intended learning outcomes; their importance for the students' development and career; the clarity of instructions (aims, timing, guidelines for individual tasks and group discussions and peer-feedback). Detailed instructions are essential to promote the students' participation: in online and blended courses, the teacher is not always present to clarify doubts and therefore, if students do not understand activities, they will not engage and complete them. Using the same examples as above, we explain how we prepared and organised effective active learning strategies.

When we designed the self-paced online course for master's students 'Preparing your literature review', we were concerned with the engagement in the course. When registering for online courses, our students expect passive sessions with videos to watch, resources to read, and semi-active sessions with multiple-choice quizzes to verify their general understanding (Sander et al., 2000). Our online course is the opposite: content videos and quizzes represent only 30% of the course.

Therefore, the main challenging objectives were to create a course based on active learning strategies that engage students, scaffold a complex process (writing a literature review), and facilitate students to apply the competencies developed to their own practice. To achieve these objectives, we organised the course into units (one for each learning outcome) that slowly moved from key definitions into the writing process of the students' literature reviews (Table 1). For each unit, we prepared content videos, case studies, scenarios brought to life by animations; model answer quizzes to give preliminary and general feedback on understanding; a glossary to clarify key terms; detailed instructions. In addition, we prepared meaningful and engaging activities based on worked examples: we provide students with literature reviews to analyse and templates to fill in to support them to write their own literature review in stages, in their own time. The scaffold created for this course is reflected in our institution's Blackboard module, the Virtual Learning Environment. We created a learning module for each unit that contained contextualised, connected activities.

In redesigning active learning strategies for blended courses, our main concerns were the definition of a clear and comprehensive scaffolding tailored to doctoral students, and the low completion rate for asynchronous activities. Resistance to asynchronous work can be expected from students (Tharayil et al., 2018) because doctoral students are busy with their research projects. They expect to learn and get specific support in a short period of time. We, therefore, carefully plan the asynchronous workload, focussing on the students' needs and preparing activities to support the enhancement of competencies with a maximum of 1 hour of asynchronous work.

This organisation makes students responsible for their own learning (asynchronous activities) and the learning of their peers (synchronous activities). Along with content videos to watch and short activities to apply critical thinking, we organised asynchronous activities around worked examples to facilitate the understanding of all students and templates students fill in to prepare their literature review in stages. We then planned connected synchronous activities, where students work in groups by discipline to peer-discuss their templates and receive discipline-specific support from their peers. This second aspect increases the students' engagement even more since, in this context, they are the experts in the field and reciprocally support their peers with their knowledge. The asynchronous activities are hosted in a dedicated learning module in Blackboard, while the synchronous sessions are delivered either in-person or remotely (in Microsoft Teams meetings).

Drawing on what we learned from the preparation of active learning strategies for online and blended courses, we designed the 2.5-day online residential retreat based on active learning. This process was particularly elaborate since we needed to create meaningful active learning strategies to build and support long-term online communities. The challenge, and goal, was to create a learning experience where students could benefit from the perspective of their peers and develop a sense of shared purpose and inquiry. A thesis is a unique piece of work, and the retreat is less focused on information acquisition and more on inquiry and active, social competency development.

Within the CoI framework, trust is essential for developing online communities. We, therefore, designed asynchronous preparatory activities to allow students to know each other and create trust before the retreat. Simple icebreaker activities give space to students to introduce themselves and their projects. In contrast, thematic activities support students to enter into the retreat mindset (e.g. sharing their competencies and suggestions in a matter of thesis) (See Table 2).

Due to the effectiveness of these asynchronous activities, once students join the synchronous component of the retreat, they are ready to work on their theses within their groups, and the retreat results in a space managed and organised by them. For the synchronous component of the retreat, we prepared active learning strategies to support students to work individually and collaboratively: videos and handouts containing writing tips and suggestions, and scaffolded instructions guiding peer-feedback, debriefs and reflective group discussion to share experiences and suggestions (see Section 3). Due to their effectiveness, these asynchronous and synchronous active learning strategies also support the continuity of the community in scaffolded 'Open writing rooms' where students can meet after the retreat, depending on their needs and the working practice they have defined within their group.

The practical organisation of the online retreat is a key part: we host it in a dedicated Teams Class, and its structure scaffolds the retreat. It represents the safe space students need. Each channel in Teams has a specific role: explaining the ethos and the focus of the retreat, containing the material and representing the platform for the asynchronous and synchronous activities.

Section 3: The outcome

Student perspective

At the end of each course, we collect students' feedback and comments to understand how courses and activities are perceived and obtain suggestions for improvement. After the Research Communication Programme redesign, we were keen on receiving and analysing feedback to understand if we could overcome our concerns.

As general feedback, all courses were well-received by students who emphasised their main learning points, such as how to read effectively, how to create a clear and flowing structure for a thesis, and the usefulness of the material to achieve the learning (*"Well structured"*, *"Templates were great"*, *"Useful handout"*, *"Pre-recorded videos and their reference lists"*).

Our first concern was about the meaningfulness of online and asynchronous activities and their connection to synchronous activities. Comments related to the blended course 'Literature review' highlighted the effectiveness of the active learning strategies applied, as individual asynchronous activities as well as support for synchronous peer-discussion: *"The pre-course activities were useful to start thinking about the topics and structure of my literature review. It was useful to discuss the pre-course activities with other students"*. Students also highlighted other positive aspects of activities: for example, the *"inclusiveness for all stages of research"*, which we needed to achieve due to the nature of our courses open to all doctoral students, independently from the subject, from first to final year.

Our second concern raised the students' engagement and motivation to complete online and asynchronous activities. Students reflected on the importance of activities for their learning as an indicator of their engagement. They also showed how important reflection and thinking time are while completing activities to benefit the most: *"Pre-course activities allowed me to sit down and really think about the structure of my literature review"* (blended course 'Literature review'). Interestingly, comparing the feedback of the in-person didactic version of 'Preparing your literature review' with the feedback for the new online course, results were better in the latter: 93% of students said *"the course met the learning outcomes"*; 89% of students *"felt they have developed a deep understanding of the course topic"*; 100% of students said *"the course encouraged me to think about the topic, form new ideas and understanding"*; and 96% of students said, *"the course encouraged me to manage my own learning"*. Despite the lack of written comments, these percentages provide the evidence we needed: students could not have achieved their learning if they had not engaged with the full set of activities. Their engagement probably also derives from the suitable technology used during the course, making it highly interactive and non-monotonous: 91% of students said: *"there is an appropriate mix of multimedia, text and other types of materials"*.

Our third concern related to using active learning strategies to create and support prolonged online communities connected to the online residential retreat. Students showed the effectiveness of those active learning strategies to create trust within groups and work as a group with their feedback. The following quotes synthesise the importance of group working while individually writing their theses, from different aspects:

- support against isolation: *"[The retreat] It's especially useful in times of hyper-isolation. Group work can be very useful because it provides a more intimate cocoon to share issues and stimulate each other."*
- a way to receive reliable advice: *"I really enjoyed the group work - great group, and the accountability was great. Wish it was longer!"*
- an opportunity to discuss with peers: *"Being able to have open discussions was also helpful."*
- a way to motivate each other: *"Keeping the [group] video call open really helped me stay motivated."*

Analytics seem to confirm the development of a community and the peer engagement within groups; for example, in the retreat held in January 2022, students wrote 87 posts in their group channels, which received 223 replies and 114 reactions through emoticons. Students attending this retreat still meet regularly for peer-feedback sessions and use the Teams Class to exchange peer suggestions.

Teacher and learning designer perspectives

An unexpected outcome emerged with our course redesign with new active learning strategies. Students engaged more in online and blended courses than with the previous in-person active learning strategies. With the previous format, courses had only synchronous active learning strategies: students had limited time to focus on and complete the tasks and have meaningful peer discussions. The newly designed blended courses allow students to have more time to work on asynchronous activities and get ready for the synchronous session and its activities. Online courses are self-paced, and students can work on the course in stages when they need to, for example, while writing their actual literature review.

From a teacher perspective, my main learning derived from the successful collaboration with my learning designer colleague: it was beneficial for me since we could understand similarities and differences between in-person active learning and online and blended active learning. This acquired knowledge allowed me to adapt my teaching competencies to our ambitious plan of redesigning the Research Communication Programme. Working on redesigning active learning strategies for online and blended courses taught me the importance of providing students with suitable scaffolding and a clear description of the type of activities to complete, workload implications and value they bring. Since I am not with them, they need detailed and clear instructions. As soon as they have doubts, they might lose their motivation and stop working on activities, leading to decreased engagement in synchronous activities.

A second learning point for us was the importance of the narrative between activities and the intended learning outcomes and their application: a straightforward story facilitates understanding. It motivates students to be active, especially when they can complete the course with a resource file that will help them during their doctorate, such as a literature review draft.

However, we also encountered issues, especially at the beginning of the redesign process: entering the mindset of online and blended courses, creating the narrative and preparing suitable scaffolding were not easy tasks for me since we have always been used to being in the classroom with students working on activities, ready to clarify doubts. Based on my learning points and issues, we plan to improve the scaffolding quality further and decrease my presence during synchronous activities accordingly for future courses. Students have already demonstrated they can take ownership of their learning and courses. Improved scaffolding should promote group discussions and facilitate peer exchanges even more: the learning will be more active, and my position in the classroom will be limited, as indicated in the principles of social constructivism (Copley, 1992; cited in Adams, 2006).

From a learning designer perspective, promoting active learning is challenging, particularly if learning experiences are co-designed; the opportunity to collaborate so completely, as was the case in the examples given here, is rare. The co-design approach worked because we could build trust and share risk and establish roles, responsibilities and workload carefully. In higher education, the educational technology course development model raises several obstacles to an approach based on active learning, as it puts too much pressure on teachers to design, develop, facilitate, assess and evaluate learning experiences without the required level of support, advice, training, guidance and resources. We had a unique opportunity to go beyond traditional approaches that do not facilitate valuing the teacher experience and the privilege of allowing the learning designer to collaborate and co-design (Quinn & Darby, 2021:34). We were also privileged not to be time and resource-poor and to have the ability to define goals, design, develop and iterate; to fail and learn.

Co-designing digital, active learning courses requires a research-informed approach and collaboration built on trust between teachers, students, stakeholders and the learning designer so that all students can benefit (Kumar & Ritzhaupt, 2017). In the initiatives outlined in this chapter, the course development process was structured to build trust and share risk by going through a process of planning (analysis of courses, student feedback, capabilities and needs, etc.); co-design (with students, teachers, stakeholders and the learning designer); development (the learning designer built digital artefacts, while gradually helping the teacher to build their digital capability to do so and handing over responsibilities); support for facilitation; and an organised process of piloting learning experiences, evaluating their success and redesigning them from the teacher, learning designer, student and stakeholder feedback.

From a joint teacher/learning designer perspective, the redesign was an active learning opportunity for us since we learned from each other while practising, and we socially constructed our learning through knowledge exchanges.

Section 4: Moving forward

The redesign of the Research Communication Programme positively affected students and us: students are considered as adult learners and have the agency of working on and learning during the courses, and we learned from the process, we forgot what active learning strategies were in place before our redesign, and we know that our active learning is beneficial from the students' feedback. From our perspective, there is no coming back. With our work and the positive response from students, we were also able to influence other teachers in the Graduate School who have evaluated the applicability of active learning to their blended courses.

Importantly, thanks to the acquired learning, we developed a 5-day online residential programme in partnership with Technology University Munich and Nanyang Technological University (Singapore). This programme, when in-person, is entirely based on active learning strategies to enhance intercultural and interdisciplinary teamwork and research communication competencies. When we started the design of its blended-online residential version, we used the experience from our online, blended and online residential courses to base it on active learning strategies. The following steps will be to improve this 5-day programme by implementing the synchronous active learning strategies; since students perceived those activities were not fully connected with the programme we will also create better scaffolding and narrative. We are also proud of this work since our international partners have implemented some of their courses based on the active learning model we developed for this programme.

From a student perspective, although sometimes they are reluctant to work before and during courses and still expect us to transmit knowledge to them, they have appreciated our active learning strategies and are getting used to them. In the future, we believe students will become more and more active since they see the extended benefits of activities for their research projects and future careers.

Conclusion

In conclusion, we believe that our newly redesigned active learning strategies' success lies in the synergic teamwork between the teacher and the learning designer of those courses. It is difficult for teachers and learning designers to have conversations both want to have; there tend to be disparities, asymmetrical power relationships, and a working model that does not favour developing active learning strategies. Co-designing helps break down some of those barriers and make active learning effective. We combined our knowledge and expertise and overcame issues and concerns, from the creation of 'the right activities' to the use of 'the right technology' to enhance engagement, create teaching and cognitive presences, and develop communities. To conclude our chapter, we have identified the below recommendations for other educators interested in online and remote active learning, transferable to any context.

As for the working practice:
- building trust between teacher and learning designer is the key to initiating an effective collaboration and designing meaningful active learning strategies, as for the sharing knowledge and expertise, as well as sharing risks;
- defining workload and working practice, as well as allocating tasks to support the design processes is essential;
- taking an iterative approach is key: design, develop, facilitate, assess and evaluate.

As for the teaching practice:
- the definition of a clear and simple scaffolding (aims of activities, timing, instructions for every stage of the activities) increases the students' engagement and motivates them to work and complete asynchronous, synchronous and online activities;
- building trust between students and teachers facilitates the creation of a community.

Co-design is slower, more complex and more resource-intensive, but designing for learning, taking in multiple voices, expertise, efforts and sharing risk ends up paying and producing a better learner experience.

About the Authors

Elena Forasacco is a Senior Teaching Fellow at the Graduate School at Imperial College London. She can be contacted at this email: e.forasacco@imperial.ac.uk

Jorge Freire is a senior learning designer who has worked in digital learning for more than a decade. He is a Digital Learning Producer at Central Saint Martins, University of the Arts London. He can be contacted at this email: jamdsf@yahoo.co.uk

Bibliography

Academy of Active Learning Arts and Sciences (2018). *Updated Definition of Flipped Learning. AALAS International.* Retrieved from https://aalasinternational.org/updated-definition-of-flipped-learning/

Adams, P. (2006). Exploring social constructivism: theories and practicalities. *Education*, 34(3), 243-257.

Agostinho, S. (2006). The use of a visual learning design representation to document and communicate teaching ideas. In L. Markauskaite, P. Goodyear & P. Reimann (Eds.), *Annual conference of the Australasian Society for Computers in Learning in Tertiary Education* (pp. 3-7). Sydney: Sydney University Press.

Ambrose, S. A., Bridges, M. W., Di Pietro, M., Lovet, M. C., & Norman, M. K. (2010). *How learning works. 7 research-based principles for smart teaching.* San Francisco, CA: Jossey-Bass. A Wiley Imprint.

Aubrey, K., & Riley, A. (2015). Lev Vygotsky. An early social constructivist viewpoint. In *Understanding & using educational theories* (1st ed., pp. 47-58). Los Angeles, CA: SAGE Publications Ltd.

Beattie, V., Collins, B., & McInnes, B. (1997). Deep and surface learning: A simple or simplistic dichotomy? *Accounting Education*, 6(1), 1–12.

Bonk, C. J., & Kim, K. A. (1998). Extending sociocultural theory to adult learning. In M. C. Smith & T. Pourchot (Eds.), *Adult learning and development: Perspectives from educational psychology* (pp. 67–88). Mahwah, N.J.: Lawrence Erlbaum Associates.

Bonk, C. J., & Cunningham, D. J. (2012). Searching for learner-centred, constructivist, and sociocultural components of collaborative educational learning Tools. In C. J. Bonk & K. S. King (Eds.), *Electronic collaborators. Learner-centred technologies for literacy, apprenticeship, and discourse* (pp. 25-50). Mahwah, N.J.: Lawrence Erlbaum Associates.

Bovill, C., & Felten, P. (2016). Cultivating student-staff partnerships through research and practice. *International Journal for Academic Development, 21*(1), 1-3.

Candy, P. (1991) *Self-direction for lifelong learning: a comprehensive guide to theory and practice*. San Francisco, CA: Jossey Bass Publishers.

Culic, L., & Pavelea, A. (2022). Enhancing students' interpersonal and leadership skills through an experience-based service-learning project: A case of active learning. In K. Enomoto, R. Warner & C. Nygaard (Eds.), *Active learning in higher education* (pp. 153-180). Oxfordshire, U.K.: Libri Publishing Ltd.

Ghislandi, P. M. M., & Raffaghelli, J. E. (2015). Forward-oriented designing for learning as a means to achieve educational quality. *British Journal of Educational Technology, 46*(2), 280–299.

Gleason, B. L., Peeters, M. J., Resman-Targoff, B. H., Karr, S., McBane, S., Kelley, K., Thomas, T., & Denetclaw, T. H. (2011). An active-learning strategies primer for achieving ability-based educational outcomes. *American Journal of Pharmaceutical Education, 75*(9), 1-12.

Hodson, D., & Hodson, J. (1998). From constructivism to social constructivism: a Vygotskian perspective on teaching and learning science. *The School Science Review, 79*(289), 33–42.

Hoeppner A., & Reid, A. (2022). How voice students become professionals through active learning experiences. In K. Enomoto, R. Warner & C. Nygaard (Eds.), *Active learning in higher education* (pp. 35-62). Oxfordshire, U.K.: Libri Publishing Ltd.

Imperial College London Graduate School (2019). *Digital Learning Strategy*. Unpublished internal document.

Knowles, M. (1990). *The adult learner: a neglected species* (4th ed.). Houston, Texas: Gulf Publishing Company.

Kumar, S., & Ritzhaupt, A. (2017). What do instructional designers in higher education really do? *International Journal on E-Learning, 16*(4), 371-394.

Imperial College London (2017). *Innovative teaching for world class learning. Learning and Teaching Strategy*. Imperial College London. Retrieved from http://www.imperial.ac.uk/media/imperial-college/about/leadership-and-strategy/vp-education/public/LearningTeachingStrategy.pdf

Intentional Futures (2016). *Instructional design in higher education: A report on the role, workflow, and experience of instructional designers.* Retrieved from https://intentionalfutures.com/static/instructional-design-in-higher-education-report-5129d9d1e6c988c254567f91f3ab0d2c.pdf

Lawless, K. A., & Pellegrino, J. W. (2007). Professional development in integrating technology into teaching and learning: Knowns, unknowns, and ways to pursue better questions and answers. *Review of Educational Research*, 77(4), 575–614.

Laurillard, D., Kennedy, E., Charlton, P., Wild, J., & Dimakopoulos, D. (2018). Using technology to develop teachers as designers of TEL: evaluating the Learning Designer. *British Journal of Educational Technology*, 49(6), 1044-1058.

McCurry, D. S., & Mullinix, B. B. (2017). A concierge model for supporting faculty in online course design. *Online Journal of Distance Learning Administration*, 20(2), 6.

Olson, H. (2022). Reflection towards excellence: empowering learners to become reflective practitioners. In K. Enomoto, R. Warner & C. Nygaard (Eds.), *Active learning in higher education* (pp. 63-82). Oxfordshire, U.K.: Libri Publishing Ltd.

Outlaw, V., & Rice, M. (2015). Best practices: Implementing an online course development & delivery model. *Online Journal of Distance Learning Administration*, 18(3).

Quinn, J., & Darby, F. (2021). *The learner-centered instructional designer: purposes, processes, and practicalities of creating online courses in higher education.* Sterling, VA: Stylus Publishing, LLC.

Richardson, J. C., Arbaugh, J. B., Cleveland-Innes, M., Ice, P., Swan, K. P., & Garrison, D. R. (2012). Using the community of inquiry framework to inform effective instructional design. In L. Moller & J. Huett (Eds.), *The next generation of distance education* (pp. 97-125). Boston, MA: Springer.

Sander, P., Stevenson, K., King, M., & Coates, D. (2000). University students' expectations of teaching. *Studies in Higher Education*, 25(3), 309–323.

Smith, K. A., Sheppard, S. D., Johnson, D. W., & Johnson, R. T. (2005). Pedagogies of engagement: Classroom-based practices. *Journal of Engineering Education*, 94(1), 87–101.

Strelan, P., Osborn, A., & Palmer, E. (2020). The flipped classroom: A meta-analysis of effects on student performance across disciplines and education levels. *Educational Research Review*, 30, 1-22.

Tharayil, S., Borrego, M., Prince, M., Nguyen, K. A., Shekhar, P., Finelli, C. J., & Waters, C. (2018). Strategies to mitigate student resistance to active learning. *International Journal of STEM Education*, 5(7), 1-16.

Vygotsky, L. S. (1978). *Mind in society: The development of higher psychological processes.* Cambridge, MA: Harvard University Press.

Wang, T. (2017). Overcoming barriers to 'flip': Building teacher's capacity for the adoption of flipped classroom in Hong Kong secondary schools. *Research and Practice in Technology Enhanced Learning, 12,* 6–17.

Webster-Wright, A. (2009). Reframing professional development through understanding authentic professional learning. *Review of Educational Research, 79*(2), 702–739.

Chapter 5

Partnering with Student Leaders: Active Learning through Integration of Peer Assisted Study Sessions into an Undergraduate Language Course

Kayoko Enomoto and Richard Warner

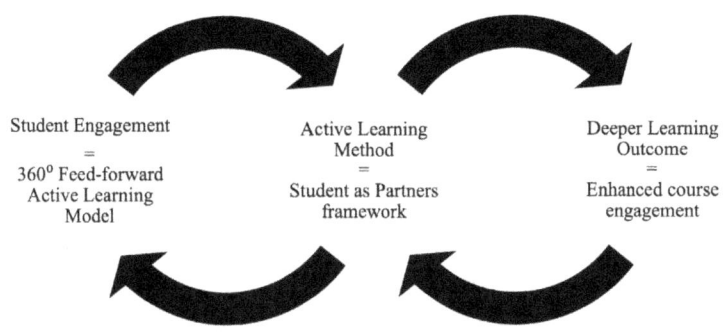

Introduction

With our chapter, we contribute to this book, *Active Learning in Higher Education*, showing how we use the Students as Partners framework to implement our 360° Feed-forward Active Learning Model that enhances students' course engagement, leading to deeper learning outcomes. This 360° Feed-forward Active Learning Model was implemented in partnership with a learning community of students. These students participated in Peer Assisted Study Sessions (PASS), an internationally accredited program, integrated into an undergraduate Japanese language course at the University of Adelaide, Australia.

PASS functions as a core dimension of our 360° Feed-forward Active Learning Model, which systematically provides a communication pathway for these Japanese language students and the teaching team (consisting of academic staff) to work together toward shared learning goals. PASS is attached to and supports certain selected courses as part of university academic support services, but it is peer-led by PASS student leaders, not by academic staff. Typically, students enrolled in a PASS-supported undergraduate course can voluntarily participate in weekly PASS sessions in addition to attending scheduled lecture and tutorial classes taught by academic staff. A trained PASS student leader leads such PASS sessions, and they facilitate interactive, supportive peer-learning, such as exploring content-related topics and discussing points of difficulty.

PASS as a program is situated within the framework of Students as Partners (Healey et al., 2014; 2016). This conceptual framework holds international sway in contemporary higher education and is not just confined to PASS. As the Wales Initiative for Student Engagement, as cited in Healey et al. (2014:12), identifies: *"One of the key reasons for developing a partnership approach is...that students should be active participants in the learning process, partnership is key to developing that participation"*. In the framework of Students as Partners, students function as active participants – active learners in their learning development. In active learning, students, instead of passively receiving external and quantifiable knowledge, are involved in creating their knowledge as active creators rather than sole consumers of course content. Prince (2004) points out that active learning requires students' engagement in their learning processes, which in turn requires the provision of both authentic and relevant learning activities. This necessitates students' metacognition - thinking about what they are doing and being able to demonstrate 'performances of understanding' (Perkins, 1999 as cited in Healey et al., 2014:37). Such performed understandings demand meaningful interactions, many of which involve active engagement between students in either a cooperative or collaborative sense. In other words, students are acting as partners in extending their learning.

In our 360° Feed-forward Active Learning Model, such a partnership between students is extended to the students' partnership with the teaching team, which is enabled through PASS student leaders. The 360° Feed-forward Active Learning Model systematically embeds and co-creates an effective, timely communication pathway that connects the teaching team with students' realities and voices every week through the PASS student leader (Figure 1).

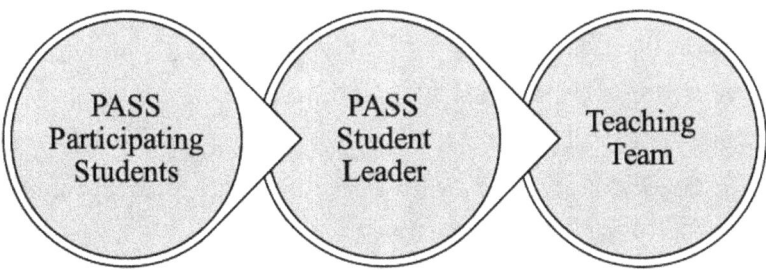

Figure 1: Communication pathway from students to teaching team effected by the 360° Feed-forward Active Learning Model.

Thus, the Students as Partners framework provides the pedagogical underpinning in our model, which will be outlined in more detail in Section 2.

Reading our chapter, you will gain the following three insights:
1. how partnering with PASS student leaders can be successfully enacted in an undergraduate language course;
2. how the model can increase PASS student attendances and student engagement through active learning;
3. how the model is sufficiently flexible to be operated in different modes of course delivery: face-to-face, hybrid and fully online contexts.

Overview of main sections

In Section 1, we provide a background briefly interrogating the concept of active learning, followed by a discussion of the Students as Partners conceptual framework where PASS is situated. Then, in Section 2, we describe the particular context of our case of active learning in a second-year Japanese language course. This is followed by Section 3, in which we demonstrate relevant comments as evidence to show the effectiveness of our 360° Feed-forward Active Learning Model. In Section 4, we discuss possible ways to improve the existing model and possible future implementations in other course contexts before we conclude our chapter.

Section 1: The background to the 360° Feed-forward Active Learning Model

Our 360° Feed-forward Active Learning Model, to be outlined in detail later in Section 2, sits within the conceptual and theoretical boundaries of active learning. Nonetheless, it needs to be noted that the term active learning itself has no collectively held definition (Prince, 2004). However, as Børte et al. (2020) observe, there are terminological parallels through which cognate concepts are explained and developed. Indeed, active learning can cover a wide range of learning scenarios and terminology, yet common to all of them is the guiding principle of engaged and questioning actions on the part of students to develop their understandings.

Fitting within these broader active learning conceptual parameters are i) collaborative learning (O'Donnell & Hmelo-Silver, 2013) and ii) cooperative or peer learning (Boud & Cohen, 2014). In collaborative learning, small groups of students work with a common focus in mind (perhaps a group assignment), whereas cooperative or peer learning - sometimes interpreted as a variety of collaborative learning - is typified by students working together on a task, though being assessed individually (Børte et al., 2020; Healey et al., 2014; Prince, 2004). Notably, with active learning in these various guises, students do not passively accept knowledge as a given and quantifiable. Instead, they engage with it, including questioning its validity and contextual applicability, to create their version of knowledge (Enomoto et al., 2022 in Chapter 1 in this book). Indeed, PASS could be seen to exemplify this aspect of active learning, with students and PASS leaders working cooperatively. Crucially, in both collaborative and cooperative/peer learning environments, there is active learning occurring when students are interacting rather than acting alone (Prince, 2004). Active learning is also evidenced in problem-based learning (Hørsted & Nygaard, 2017; Schwartz, 2013), where the context and motivation are precipitated by using problems as learning tools of themselves, involving self-directed active learning and very frequently some form of collaborative and/or cooperative learning (Børte et al., 2020).

As teachers, it is upon us to provide active and thought-demanding constructive learning experiences (Perkins 1999 in Healey et al., 2014), perhaps engaging students' 'multiple intelligences' (Gardner, 2009) if we are to see a shift in student engagement which could lead to a better understanding (Enomoto et al., 2022, Chapter 1 in this book). As Healey et al. (2010) note, this teaching for understanding focus necessitates students to move through what can be termed 'performances of understanding' towards more complete subject comprehension. Within their model (Figure 2), we can see four major activities that mirror the cyclical nature of experiential learning (Kolb, 1984) and inform student performances of understanding. Those activities are 'experience', 'reflect', 'generalise', and 'test'. These 'performances of understanding' are not solely the prerogative of students developing their individual learning. Instead, as Healey et al. (2014) identified, they are likely to effectively function in a Students as Partners scenario, such as in PASS. Such partnerships should be regarded as processes towards deeper learning outcomes.

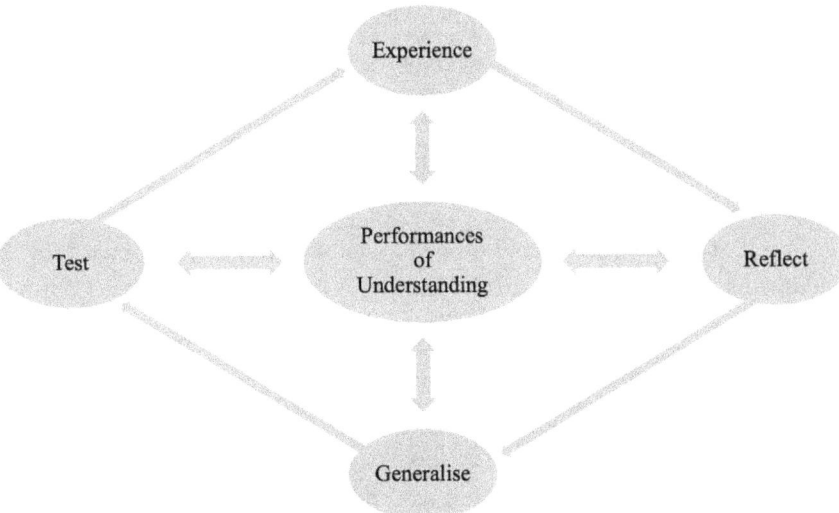

Figure 2: Performances of understanding in an active learning approach (Adapted from Healey et al., 2010:3).

Chapter 5

Active learning in the Students as Partners framework

PASS has both its theoretical and pedagogical origins in this broader Students as Partners framework to facilitate active learning. Acting as such, students can work as active co-constructors of their learning, concerning both the desired learning outcomes of the particular course and (oft times) broader study skill development transferable to other courses. This conceptual framework of Students as Partners in learning is nothing new. Yet, it has been a powerful driving force internationally, informing both institutional policy and pedagogy in the early decades of the twenty-first century, with a correspondingly rich and varied literature (Bernstein, 2018; Bovill et al., 2016; Bovill, 2017; Gravett et al., 2020; Healey et al., 2014; Nygaard et al., 2013).

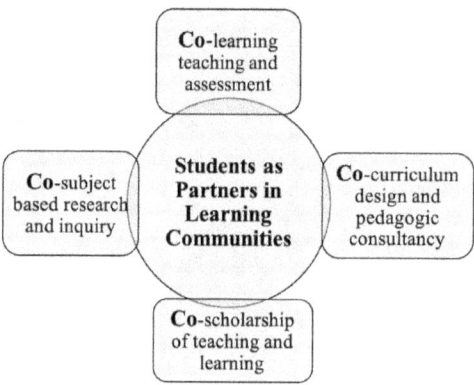

Figure 3: Students as Partners in learning communities in higher education (adapted from Healey et al., 2014:25).

Within the parameters of the Students as Partners framework in the learning and teaching processes, many strands have been succinctly synthesised (Healey et al., 2014) into four main interlinked partnership learning communities. Figure 3 shows that partnered learning has a broad area of scope, and one would assume the potential to be a powerful force in many aspects of higher education. Yet, as previously noted, it is requisite to acknowledge that not all elements of students as partners in learning involve active learning. Still, as will be outlined in Section 2, the active learning element is intrinsic to this conceptual framework. Following Healey et al.'s (2014:25) Students as Partners framework, Figure 3 provides us with four major 'partnership learning communities', in which we can locate PASS within all of the quadrants.

Utilisation of Peer Assisted Study Sessions (PASS) as part of the whole course

At this juncture, we outline the conditions determining the need for PASS development in an Australian higher education context (many such conditions being of international relevance), define PASS and determine its purpose. The conditions precipitating PASS development in Australia were outlined in the seminal Bradley Review (2008), which recognised and promulgated significant changes in student cohorts, particularly an increase in students from lower socio-economic backgrounds and international students. The often poorly met needs of such students required the development of interactive programs to help improve their academic performance and, in the broader sense, to help students undertake the cultural shift to the academic demands required of a higher education environment. PASS emerged at our university from within these 'shifting sands' of changing student cohorts as a systematised active learning-focused way in which successful students could become paid PASS leaders. These student leaders have to meet strict selection criteria to become able to lead and facilitate the learning of peers, working within the Students as Partners framework. To apply to become a PASS leader at many Australian universities, students must meet a required minimum Grade Point Average set by the university and have completed the course they wish to lead with a high grade. Typically, to qualify as a PASS leader, students must also pass an interview, undertake online training modules (approximately 6-7 hours of work), and participate in an interactive PASS training program.

In the higher education sector, PASS functions at the course-based level and, as Zaccagnini et al. (2017) point out, PASS is often aligned to what might be deemed 'high-risk' courses. These courses are considered high risk owing to their level of perceived difficulty, high fail rates or gatekeeper courses for student advancement to other courses, typically but not exclusively at undergraduate level. In addition, PASS is often attached to large first-year core courses, but this is not always the case, as can be seen in our particular PASS context.

The purpose of PASS is to assist students in gaining a deeper understanding of their course material, maximise their grades, and further develop their academic skills. PASS addresses the 'how' and the 'what' to learn through PASS leaders' (or peer-mentors) interactions with PASS attending students. Thus, PASS sessions contain course content specific coverage and allow for the *ad hoc* development of study skills. One of the positives of these scenarios is hierarchical with the *"absence of a 'formal and expert' teacher who gives answers in a didactic fashion"* (Dancer et al., 2015:1811). Students can feel less cowed by asking study-related questions to PASS leaders than perhaps they might of their lecturers or tutors. Thus, as van der Meer and Scott (2009) note, PASS can help students develop the foundational habits for life-long learning.

There are constants between the different PASS set-ups, one of which is that the selected PASS leaders work with students who attend voluntarily, relevant to high-stake/risk courses. Where PASS is linked to such courses, a variety of studies, noted by Connolly-Panagopoulos (2021), have indicated positive outcomes for the associated student cohorts. There were positive correlations between PASS and increased subject knowledge in the findings of Green (2018) and Dawson et al. (2014), with the latter also observing greater rates of student retention, as did Hermann-Werner et al. (2017), who also noted improved academic achievement and pass rates, as a result of PASS. Such increases in academic achievements were also found by Dawson et al. (2014) and Spedding et al. (2017). As Connolly-Panagopoulos (2021) states, such positive attainments could indicate an active learning shift that PASS promulgates. PASS student leaders lead and encourage peer discussions to shift away from a grade-based surface learning focus towards a deeper learning focus (Capstick et al., 2004; Garcia-Melgar et al., 2021).

Furthermore, PASS with an appropriate organisational structure, including properly qualified and trained PASS leaders, can encourage students to embrace an active approach to learning. This can result in student participation in knowledge construction with their peers, rather than via a hierarchical pathway, as was reported in Morrison (2006:5): *"I like that PASS is not a lecture…you are involved in the learning. PASS is really helping me understand more"* (PASS student) and *"…Students own and operate PASS. They are not the spectators. They are the stars in their own show"* (PASS leader) and *"…PASS was interactive…Having things explained and the challenge of explaining concepts to others forces you to cement your own knowledge"* (PASS student). Such positive comments are conducive to both the creation and the ongoing development of any active learning approach – in our case, the 360° Feed-forward Active Learning Model, which we outline in Section 2.

In addition, PASS has further benefits for both students and the PASS leaders themselves. A study by Lockspeiser et al. (2008) established that PASS leaders maintained both a greater likelihood than academic teaching staff of predicting areas of difficulty in the students' course materials and conceptualising why an idea or theory might prove to be perplexing to students. This, the authors named 'cognitive congruence'. As Brown et al. (2016) note, such congruence allows PASS leaders to include manageable language and 'pitch their material' to meet students' comprehension levels. The students have greater cognitive congruence with PASS leaders than with their lecturers and tutors; identifying PASS leaders' comprehension of subject-related content as nearer to their own.

Aligned to the concept of cognitive congruence is that of 'social congruence', which considers the PASS leaders' interpersonal skills and abilities to provide an active learning environment that allows for the unfettered interchange of ideas (Chng et al., 2011 in Brown et al., 2016). Essential for the success of any PASS scenario is a positive balance of the social and the cognitive, whereby two-way interactions between PASS leaders and students operate both on a similar cognitive level and, in terms of social congruence, the PASS leaders provide the conditions for student confidence and discussion to flourish. The study by van der Meer and Scott (2009) reiterates the importance of the social aspects of PASS when they found that although students placed a high value on both PASS content and learning skills development, they attached equal weight to the effectiveness of social integration - a sense of belonging and becoming part of a community of practice.

Yet, the philosophy and enactment of PASS are not without their controversies and problems. In the first instance, the jumping on board of the PASS 'bandwagon' by many universities - both nationally and internationally - could be cost-driven rather than philosophically determined. In such instances, PASS implementation is more likely to be tokenistic (Zaccagnini et al., 2017) as PASS is comparatively cheap to implement, given it employs academically successful undergraduate students (at a lower rate of payment) than that paid to academic staff. Moreover, even when there is funding for PASS, it can be limited by how results-driven a university is. This is exemplified in the work of

Connolly-Panagopoulos (2021:4), who reasons that *"institutional funding is aligned with strategic drives which are, in turn, often informed by quantitative measures such as academic attainment"*. Notwithstanding evidence correlating PASS with enhanced academic achievement (Spedding et al., 2017), it could be contended that qualitative measures of student achievement are not as impactful in securing PASS funding. Moreover, as identified by Huijser et al. (2008), the intangible benefits [such as social integration] of PASS are more challenging to study [and therefore justify] than the quantifiable academic results to which university management can more easily relate.

Problems can also occur because PASS can be created in different ways in different higher education institutions, with various other constructs and reporting lines. To exemplify this, a recent study by Connolly-Panagopoulos (2021) argues for the centralisation of PASS leader training at the whole university level rather than managed at the faculty level. To help justify her position, she draws upon the work of Garcia-Melgar et al. (2021), who argue that PASS leaders may not be able to recognise the requirement to facilitate the learning of material as opposed to merely teaching it, owing to the results of PASS leaders receiving insufficient training, which can vary in quality between universities. Muddying the waters further are student (and sometimes institutional) perceptions that PASS functions as a deficit model. From such a deficit perspective, PASS is just for at-risk students, which can include English as an additional language international students from very different academic cultural experiences and expectations (Warner & Enomoto, 2021), rather than functioning as an active and partnered learning community from which all germane students could obtain benefit. This student at-risk perception could go some way to at least partially explain why some PASS sessions are characterised by low attendance rates and indeed was the major defining explanation in Allen et al.'s (2019) findings. Certainly, without students' participating in PASS sessions, none of the benefits of PASS can be realised.

In our particular PASS context, since its initial iteration in 2017, increasing attendances has been a significant objective. To achieve consistently high PASS attendances each week, we recognised it was imperative to promote students' perception of PASS as an integral part of the whole course rather than as remedial academic support solely for struggling students. Therefore, in the design of our 360° Feed-forward Active Learning Model to be outlined in the next section, it was essential to feed-forward to all students each week the clear relevance to the weekly content of actively participating in each upcoming PASS session.

Section 2: The case of active learning

This active learning case is situated in a second-year Japanese language course, Japanese 2A, at the University of Adelaide, an Australian research-intensive university. In 2017, Japanese 2A began receiving PASS academic support, funded by the university. As a general rule, high attrition, high fail rate or large first-year courses are prioritised to receive PASS support to help improve student retention. However, in the case of Japanese 2A, this rule did not apply. This course was explicitly nominated for PASS support because of its marked leap into more complex language content from first-year basic Japanese. This was done with the recognition that language students require practical experiences of actually using the target language through active learning activities, just as science students do through their laboratory practicum. Furthermore, it has been shown that more time is required for language students (who are native speakers of English) to learn non-cognate character-based languages (such as Japanese) than cognate languages such as German (Goodman et al., 1989). In this regard, Japanese is one of the most time-consuming languages for (English-speaking) Australian students to study at university.

Therefore, in this context of Japanese 2A, maximising students' course engagement through active learning stands paramount in its course delivery. To do so, we identified that the Japanese 2A teaching team must be proactive, swiftly responding to students' evolving needs to support their active language learning. This is so that second-year students do not drop out but continue learning Japanese, as the course content becomes progressively more complex from Week 1 to Week 12. One practical way to be proactive is to systematically embed an effective communication pathway connecting the teaching team with students' realities and to hear their voices (Figure 1). Drawing on the Student as Partners framework (Healey et al., 2014), such a need to be proactive stimulated and resulted in our design of the 360° Feed-forward Active Learning Model (outlined below) - through partnering with PASS Student Leaders.

Japanese 2A PASS is peer-led by a qualified PASS Student Leader who successfully completed the required interview, online PASS training module, and in-person interactive training program to be selected as a PASS Leader. Thus, the selected PASS Leaders, who had previously completed Japanese 2A with a high grade, are deemed to possess appropriate language content-specific knowledge and necessary generic skills, including communication, time management, and leadership skills, fundamental to successfully leading PASS sessions. PASS runs typically for one hour per week for 11 weeks at the university, starting from Week 2 of a 12-week semester. In addition, in the case of Japanese 2A, PASS Leaders have also run two or three additional test review PASS sessions because participating students often request them.

PASS Student Leaders do not teach fellow students like tutors. Instead, they facilitate interactive peer learning as peer mentors in their weekly PASS. In Japanese 2A, between 2017 and 2019, the corresponding PASS was delivered face-to-face in the physical classroom environment. However, at the beginning of the 2020 pandemic, as all teaching activities were quickly pivoted online at the university, PASS sessions were also forced to move online with very short notice. Unsurprisingly, the 2020 PASS Leader was initially apprehensive about their capacity for facilitating online PASS and concerned about poor attendance once their PASS sessions moved entirely online. Then, in 2021, a hybrid delivery mode was adopted for running PASS by the university. This was to allow those students who were unable to come to the campus (such as offshore international students and students with health reasons) to synchronously participate in the same PASS session via Zoom with on-campus students. Similar to the 2020 PASS Leader's situation, the hybrid delivery mode challenged the 2021 PASS Leader to swiftly upskill their capabilities for running in-person PASS with on-campus students in a physical room whilst including off-campus students into the room via Zoom using a laptop.

Likewise, Japanese 2A tutors faced the same challenges as the PASS Leaders. In the particular 2020-2021 pandemic context, it became crucial for the course coordinator to build a mutually supportive partnership with PASS Leaders and Tutors. Thus, since 2017 and through the pandemic, the 360° Feed-forward Active Learning Model has evolved progressively to strengthen a mutually supportive partnership further.

The model addresses two objectives: 1) to enable realistic anticipation and proactive addressing of not just content-related difficulties but also student experience, and 2) to provide the Course Coordinator, Tutors and PASS Student Leader with a heightened sense of cohesion and mutual support as one team.

An overview of how our model works to facilitate active learning

Our 360° Feed-forward Active Learning Model builds upon the work of Zaccagnini et al. (2017), which foregrounds the importance of meaningful and regular interactions between PASS student leaders and course coordinators as enabling strategies for running successful PASS. As Figure 4 shows, central to this cyclic model, consisting of three dimensions, is the concept of 'feeding-forward', enabling student voices in each dimension to feed forward into the immediately following dimension in the cycle. The Course Coordinator collaboratively enacts the cycle in the Lecture (Dimension 1), the Tutors in Tutorials (Dimension 2) and the PASS Student Leader in weekly PASS sessions (Dimension 3).

In the specific instance of 2020-2021 Japanese 2A, Dimension 1 involved students' watching the pre-recorded grammar lecture asynchronously, whilst Dimensions 2 and 3 involved students' either physically attending or 'Zooming' in for the synchronous tutorial and the synchronous PASS. In Dimension 1, the Course Coordinator asynchronously delivered the weekly grammar lecture video introducing new grammar points to be learned during a particular week. Unlike an interactive in-person grammar lecture, the challenge for students was to form an instant connection with the new grammar and to feel able to actively use it, watching the video.

Therefore, to bring about active learning through feeding forward into the subsequent synchronous tutorial, the Course Coordinator (in Dimension 1) relayed to Tutors (in Dimension 2) potential areas of difficulty and misunderstanding on the new grammar points and how students could interactively practise constructing their own sentences in the tutorial. Following this feed-forward, the Tutors reviewed and checked such areas of difficulty by facilitating interactive language learning activities, often utilising (humorous) pictorial scenarios to facilitate students' active learning in the tutorial. The effectiveness of such active learning activities was demonstrated in the student evaluation of teaching (SET):

- "…*The tutorials were very interactive, as we all worked together to answer questions and translate.*"; *Tutorials are engaging and allow for a variety of questions and ideas to be considered in and amongst a group setting, whether online or face–to–face.*"; "*I don't think I would ever choose a zoom tutorial over an on-campus one, but…Sensei [Tutor] kept the tutorials as interactive and engaging as they would be in person.*" (SET, 2020)

- "*[Tutors are] very interactive and encouraged student participation whenever possible*"; *[Tutor] always made classes really fun and engaging. I always felt comfortable speaking up in her class*"; "*I really enjoyed the tutorials this semester. They were always really fun and engaging.*" (SET, 2021)

The Tutors also introduced new vocabulary items and kanji characters, using realia and pictorial materials in preparation for the following week, noting the level of students' confidence with new vocabulary and kanji in their tutorial to feed-forward to the PASS Leader from Dimension 2 to Dimension 3.

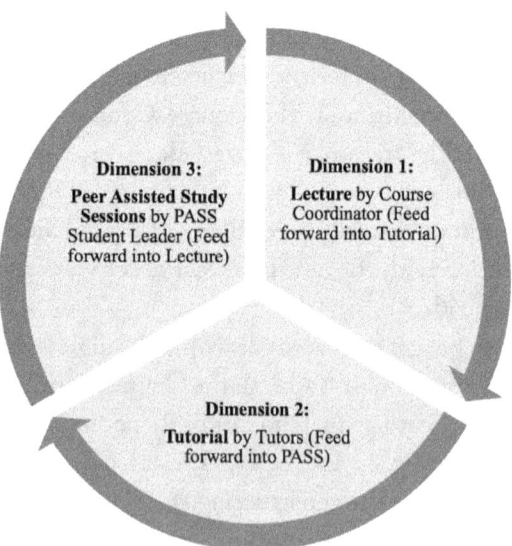

Figure 4: 360° Feed-forward Active Learning Model.

After the synchronous tutorial, the Tutors (in Dimension 2) communicated to the PASS Leader (in Dimension 3) the areas students struggled with during their tutorial so that the PASS Leader could anticipate possible questions that participating students might ask or possible items that they might want to work on in that particular week's PASS session. The PASS Leaders consolidated students' active use of grammar points by i) answering participants' questions, facilitating oral/written practice in the forms of questions and answers, conversation scenarios, and translation exercises. They also facilitated practising vocabulary and kanji, for example, using Kahoot quizzes so that all students can equally and actively participate regardless of being on-campus or off-campus.

After the synchronous PASS, the PASS Leader (in Dimension 3) emailed the Course Coordinator (in Dimension 1) a brief reflective observation report (often in dot points) describing what they noticed about those students who came to that particular week's PASS session. Such reports tended to contain helpful information on the areas of difficulty and weaknesses that should be followed up in the subsequent week's lecture recording (Dimension 1) and the voices of participating students. For example:

- *"…I asked students what they struggled with the most for test 2, and they found the particles, kanji, and not knowing the context of the very last questions."* (2018 PASS Leader's email)

- *"There was still some slight confusions regarding when to use 〜てから, 持っています in regards to possession, the translation of 〜ましょうか and also some general mix-up between 借りる [to borrow] and 貸す [to lend]."* (2019 PASS Leader's email)

Significantly, such observation reports also contained various descriptions of active learning that took place during their PASS sessions. For example:

- *"I found the students responded to this prompting [=a question in Japanese] really well and ended up taking their conversations in some creative directions."* (2020 PASS Leader's email)

- *"We did the usual Kahoot which focused on kanji, vocab & grammar…I told them to ask follow up questions and create a conversation out of the q&a and then bring one interesting point back to the main group to discuss. It was quite a fun exercise, and it was interesting to see how creative the students got with their language skills."* (2021 PASS Leader's email)

As an essential organisational requirement, the Course Coordinator sent timely reminders (as course announcements) each week via the Canvas learning management system, clearly highlighting the relevance of attending PASS to the weekly content, promoting students' perception of PASS as being a relevant active learning part of the whole course. To bring about such students' perception of PASS, rather than sending identical reminders every week, it was imperative that each weekly reminder clearly pointed students to specific content areas of that week, explaining how consolidating those areas in the upcoming PASS session would help them understand new grammar points in the following weeks:

- *"I regularly attended PASS sessions...These sessions were a huge help to stay on top of my studies week to week."* (SET, 2020)

Furthermore, our 360° Feed-forward Active Learning Model, through partnering with the PASS Leaders, also made it possible for the Course Coordinator to indirectly but proactively seek students' authentic input into Dimension 1 through the PASS Leader (in Dimension 3). Participating students' voices helped the course coordinator create lecture recordings so that students felt able to form an immediate connection with the new grammar, leading to their active learning. For instance, students' voices were relayed via the PASS Leader to suggest that one lecture be broken into digestible mini-lectures, each covering just one grammar point with real-life, interesting (humorous) examples and checkpoint translation exercises, which was swiftly implemented for the following weeks.

- *"I found the lectures to be very interesting and engaging"; "[videos contain] clear explanations of grammar points with useful examples and interesting lectures."* (SET, 2020)
- *"[the course coordinator] makes her teaching interesting by incorporating real-life examples in her videos"; "They provide lots of explanations and examples...in video lectures to help us learn complex grammar."* (SET, 2021)

Thus, this feed-forward cycle updates and connects the entire teaching team with students' learning-related realities every week, thus enabling a proactive response to their issues in a timely manner, in so doing, enhancing students' course engagement through active learning. At the same time, the model also provided the Japanese 2A team with a heightened sense of cohesion and mutual support, which will be demonstrated in the following section.

Section 3: The outcome

Perspectives of participating students' and PASS Student Leaders

The effectiveness of the 360° Feed-forward Active Learning Model on Japanese 2A PASS attendances is clearly evidenced by students' high and steady weekly attendance since its first iteration in 2017. Between 2017 and 2021, Japanese 2A has consistently achieved the highest attendance amongst all PASS-supported courses in the Faculty of Arts. There was no apparent decrease in Japanese 2A PASS attendance seen in the pandemic learning context of 2020 and 2021. Indeed, Japanese 2A saw the highest numbers of attendances among a total of 20 courses supported by PASS in the Faculty in Semester 1 in 2020 (70 attendances) and in 2021 (88 attendances), suggestive of increased student engagement. This was despite Japanese 2A being a comparatively small course with only around 80 enrolled students. By way of comparison, a large first-year course with approximately 750 enrolled students saw attendances of less than 10.

Similarly, 15 out of 20 PASS-supported courses saw under 20 attendances in Semester 1 in both years. As we discussed in Section 1, these small attendances, regardless of course enrolment sizes, are not uncommon across many universities (Allen et al., 2019). In this respect, this 360° Feed-forward Active Learning Model could be implemented in other PASS-assisted courses to increase student attendance and course engagement through active learning.

We consider two primary reasons for our feed-forward active learning model's high and steady weekly attendance. Firstly, as we discussed in Section 1, our model promotes students' cognitive congruence (Lockspeiser et al., 2008; Brown et al., 2016) in the peer-learning context of

PASS. As a result, students feel 'safe' when making mistakes in front of peers and receiving help from them, engaging in active learning:

- *"[some] are super on top of the course content and were very helpful in helping other students."* (2020 PASS Leader's email)
- *"I've noticed the pronunciation of ない [negative verb] form is a bit difficult for some students, so I've been making everyone articulate everything properly and getting other people to help correct mistakes. I think this is helping as I saw some improvement in pronunciation by the end of the session."* (2021 PASS Leader's email)

Secondly, our model similarly promotes students' social congruence (Chng et al., 2011 as cited in Brown et al., 2016), notably, a sense of belonging. Through the PASS Leader, participating students felt their voices were being heard, thus enriching their student experience. Offshore and onshore international students especially valued such social congruence. To evidence this, the 2021 PASS Leader reported:

- *"Offshore students expressed that the opportunity to interact with domestic students enhanced their overall university experience."*
- *"Many offshore students enjoyed talking to their classmates [in PASS sessions] outside of lectures/seminars."*
- *"International students also enjoyed practising both Japanese and English during PASS sessions."*

With both cognitive and social congruence being built within the PASS sessions, students saw themselves as equal to others in a non-hierarchical learning environment (Dancer et al., 2015; Morrison, 2006). In this non-hierarchical PASS environment, they could feel more comfortable sharing observations or problems and asking the sort of questions they would not necessarily share with the Course Coordinator or Tutors. The following PASS Leaders' email reports indicate students' feeling able to openly express their opinions and feelings, thus engaging in active learning. At the same time, these reports also demonstrate active learning on the part of the PASS Leader in developing their reflective capacity for taking initiatives.

- *"They [students] said they struggled with that [grammar-related] section in the test, but more importantly, would like to continue with the*

> *oral practice. So in the future, I will split my sessions into two parts - the first part a full grammar review and revision, and the second part will be used for speaking practice with great focus on q&a."* (2020 PASS Leaders' email)

- *"I observed how fast students can read Hiragana, and most students are alright, while some take a bit longer with Katakana...Students expressed positive feedback with the dictation exercise, so I might incorporate it into future sessions."* (2021 PASS Leader's email)

These reflective observations and suggestions indicate that our PASS Leaders function as 'co-curricular designers' within the Students as Partners framework by Healey et al. (2014) in Figure 2. Moreover, the 360° Feed-forward Active Learning Model helped the PASS Leaders successfully respond to the pandemic-induced challenges of running fully online (in 2020) and hybrid (2021) PASS sessions. Despite being forced to move fully online or hybrid delivery with very short notice and being initially concerned about their skill sets and capacity to deliver in this radically different pandemic environment, both 2020 and 2021 PASS Leaders achieved by far the highest attendances in the Faculty. PASS Leaders made this possible because they also felt supported by and a sense of belonging to the entire teaching team.

- *"7 people attended [PASS] - a lot were regulars...One student seemed quite behind. They hadn't looked at the ta-[verb]form and struggled to use some forms...I thought I'd flag this as I was a bit concerned."*; *"[Student A] has come to every PASS session so far, and I can definitely see his confidence and speaking skills improve so far. He's been a joy"*; *"[Student B] hasn't attended my [PASS] sessions before but was very engaged and happy to contribute. It was great having him."* (2020 PASS Leader's email)

- *"[Student C] showed interests in participating with other students as well! ...the material I provided during the session was relatively easy... but it was apparent that [Student C] did struggle with some of the translation exercises and will need extra practice for the oral test."* (2021 PASS Leader's email)

In this way, the PASS Leaders developed their generic skill sets and reflective capacity for reflective observations, initiatives, and suggestions transferable to their future contexts in academia and/or the workplace. For example, they took the initiative to ascertain how they could best engage participating students, whether on-campus or off-campus, in active learning utilising Kahoot quizzes to practise vocabulary and kanji characters. In so doing, they gained research and time management skills to prepare for their PASS sessions and improved their digital skills using Japanese.

Teacher perspective – our reflections

Since Japanese 2A first received PASS support in 2017, the Course Coordinator has worked closely with PASS Student Leaders and Tutors as 'partners', implementing the 360° Feed-forward Active Learning Model. In the previous five iterations of the model, all partners have contributed significantly to the course delivery, enabling the course coordinator to respond proactively to students' evolving needs and voices. As a result, each of the partners has provided invaluable input into the current design of the model as a teaching team member, progressively developing the feed-forward model to best enhance students' course engagement through active learning. In 2020, our partnership in implementing the 360° Feed-forward Active Learning Model was recognised by a University Commendation for Excellence in Teaching - Team Award - recognising our outstanding contribution to the student learning experience.

The unprecedented pandemic recently forced Japanese 2A students to learn one of the most complex, time-consuming languages - Japanese - in the fully online and hybrid environments in 2020 and 2021, respectively. For the Course Coordinators and Tutors, the thought of engaging language students without physical interactions was daunting and overwhelming initially. The PASS Leaders were similarly concerned about poor attendance once their solely face-to-face PASS sessions moved online or hybrid. Moreover, many Japanese 2A students were apprehensive about their capacity for learning Japanese online. This type of initial anxiety with pivoting between online and offline learning spaces is also discussed by Swann (2022, Chapter 10 in this book) and also by Jaunzems-Fernuk (2022, Chapter 12 in this book). In such a challenging pandemic context of learning and teaching, being proactive in responding to students' voices has become more imperative than in the previous years for all the partners involved in the course delivery. Indeed, our model systematically effected a communication pathway connecting the teaching team with students' realities and to hear their voices (Figure 1): "*[The best aspect of this course is] lots of effective communication between students and staff*" (SET, 2020); "*The content was difficult, but all teachers helped in making learning the content easier by giving us advice*" (SET, 2021). Thus, this 360° Feed-forward Active Learning Model can work effectively in all modes of course delivery: face-to-face, fully online and hybrid.

Section 4: Moving forward

Thus far, in its five-year iteration, our 360° Feed-Forward Active Learning Model has shown great promise, particularly regarding high and steady attendance in PASS sessions. Yet, as with any other program or course, in Japanese 2A, there is the desire for further consolidation (at the very least), coupled with both improvement and growth with regard to our feed-forward active learning model. We need to discover what elements or strategies could be further enhanced or put into place whilst incorporating elements and strategies that are not yet occurring.

In terms of Japanese 2A PASS attendance, we need to see if there are ways in which the already high attendance levels could be improved yet further. Student 'buy in' at the beginning of any PASS-supported course is crucial. Such buy-in could be improved if the students could see greater institutional buy-in to the value of PASS. Such institutional buy-in could be validated clearly through course coordinators spruiking PASS in their course descriptions and announcements. Likewise, during the first lecture, they could promote students' perception of PASS as an integral part of the whole course, not as optional remedial academic support. Such spruiking would be more likely to be successful if it were part of a larger (pre-semester) orientation program of events strategising the importance and value of active learning on the part of students. This orientation program could stress the great value the academic culture holds on working with peers and help mitigate a shift from the traditional model of perception of didactic learning coming from the teacher. Instead, it could focus on learning being a collective effort.

Such foundational stress on the importance of cooperative active (as opposed to reactive) learning could also i) help mitigate some students' perceptions that PASS is a deficit model, and only for those with problems or ii) encourage greater attendance by students who attend just a particular PASS session to help them pass a test or review what went wrong in a test. Thus, a future challenge is to explore how we can effectively encourage our students to move away from such a remedial or deficit mindset.

Another possible way of increasing attendance at PASS sessions is to examine ways in which the social benefits (van der Meer & Scott, 2009), including social congruence (Chng et al. (2011) as cited in Brown et al. (2014) of attending, could be foregrounded. Our 360° Feed-forward Active Learning Model does seem to be providing a safe space for social integration and expression, as demonstrated by some of the comments in Section 3. However, these students are already participating in this PASS, so we need to foreground ways of attracting more students in the first instance, using these social elements as levers to do just this. As outlined in the paragraph above, buy-in from the institution through course coordinators is essential to reinforce these social benefits. Such benefits could form part of the benefits and value of an active-learning push in the orientation program of events and in the spruiking of PASS by course coordinators and tutors.

However, we need to remain mindful of why so many PASS sessions are poorly attended in some courses, which is not uncommon across many universities. Students, especially those from non-traditional backgrounds, are often time-poor. Many of them have to work part-time to fund their living expenses during their studies. This need to work can apply particularly to students from lower socio-economic backgrounds and some international students. That is not to say that such students are necessarily disengaged with learning. Regardless of their backgrounds, serious students are likely to look favourably upon any strategy or activity that could extend their learning. Yet, perhaps, optional PASS sessions are not the highest priority in their continuing academic survival.

Due to the pandemic, the version of PASS in Japanese 2A has been delivered in two ways: in 2020, entirely online, and in 2021 in a hybrid mode. Encouragingly, neither form of delivery has resulted in an apparent drop in PASS attendance compared with the face-to-face versions of PASS run between 2017 and 2019. Future pandemic-induced uncertainties demand that we continue with the hybrid mode. However, it is more than pragmatics that ensures the continuity of the hybrid mode. While forcing a move to the online space, the pandemic has enabled us to address the issue of inclusivity better. Giving students the option of attending a synchronous PASS session online can be made possible when medical circumstances beyond their control do not allow them to participate in PASS in person.

A significant challenge for us now is adopting and implementing the 360° Feed-forward Active Learning Model, initially in other language courses, particularly those with low PASS attendance. The pandemic has also forced other PASS-supported language courses to adopt fully online and hybrid versions, yet, much lower attendance rates have characterised these PASS versions than in Japanese 2A. It would appear that the delivery mode was not a causal factor as the high and steady attendance in Japanese 2A attests.

Conclusion

In this chapter, we have presented the 360° Feed-forward Active Learning Model, which provides conditions for active learning to occur. The model enabled students' voices to feed-forward in weekly course delivery cycles, thus maximising their active learning and empowering our students as 'partners' in their learning and in our course content delivery. Regardless of face-to-face, online or hybrid modes of delivery, this model has had a positive and sustained impact on student PASS attendance throughout its five-year iterations since 2017. Moreover, the model has also brought about a strong sense of partnership in the entire teaching team: the Course Coordinator, Tutors and PASS Leaders, providing the team with a strong sense of cohesion and collegiality as equal partners, as clearly indicated through the comments in Section 3. Therefore, adopting and implementing this model enabled us to realistically anticipate and proactively and swiftly address content-related difficulties and student experience whilst also providing ourselves with an enhanced sense of interconnectedness and mutual support as one team.

Acknowledgements

The authors wish to express their thanks to the past PASS student leaders - Rebecca Leung, Kate Pressler, Josephine Ocampo, Jarrel Alansalon and Amanda Gunawan; the tutors - Miwako Takasawa, Ryoko Toden and Keiko Nakao, for their invaluable support and contributions to the implementation of the 360° Feed-forward Active Learning Model.

About the Authors

Kayoko Enomoto is a Senior Lecturer, Head of Asian Studies and Director, Student Experience in the Faculty of Arts at the University of Adelaide, Australia. She can be contacted at this email: kayoko.enomoto@adelaide.edu.au

Richard Warner is an Adjunct Lecturer in the School of Education in the Faculty of Arts at the University of Adelaide, Australia. He can be contacted at this email: richard.warner@adelaide.edu.au

Bibliography

Allen, P. J., Tonta, K. E., Haywood, S. B., Pereira, R. M., & Roberts, L. D. (2019). Predicting peer-assisted study session attendance. *Active Learning in Higher Education, 20*(3), 249-262.

Bernstein, D. A. (2018). Does active learning work? A good question, but not the right one. *Scholarship of Teaching and Learning in Psychology. 4*(4), 290–307.

Børte, K., Nesje, K., & Lillejord, S. (2020). Barriers to student active learning in higher education. *Teaching in Higher Education. 25*, 1-19.

Boud, D., & Cohen, R. (2014). *Peer learning in higher education: Learning from and with each other*. Abingdon, Oxon.: Routledge.

Bovill, C. (2017). Breaking down staff-student barriers: moving towards pedagogic flexibility. In I. M. Kinchin & N. Winstone (Eds.), *Pedagogic frailty and resilience in the university* (pp. 151–61). Rotterdam: Sense.

Bovill, C., Cook-Sather, A., Felten, P., Millard, L., & Moore-Cherry, N. (2016). Addressing potential challenges in co-creating learning and teaching: overcoming resistance, navigating institutional norms and ensuring inclusivity in student-staff partnerships. *Higher Education, 71*(2), 195–208.

Bradley, D., Noonan, P., Nugent, H., & Scales, B. (2008). *Bradley Review of Australian Higher Education: Final Report*. Canberra, ACT: Department of Education, Employment and Workplace Relations, Commonwealth of Australia.

Brown, K., Nairn, K., van der Meer, J., & Scott, C. (2014). "We Were Told We're Not Teachers…It Gets Difficult to Draw the Line": Negotiating roles in Peer-Assisted Study Sessions (PASS). *Mentoring & Tutoring: Partnership in Learning*, 22(2), 146-161.

Capstick S., Fleming, H., & Hurne, J. (2004). *Implementing peer assisted learning in higher education: the experience of a new university and a model for the achievement of a mainstream programme*. Peer Assisted Learning Conference Proceedings, Bournemouth University, U.K. Retrieved from https://www.bournemouth.ac.uk/sites/default/files/asset/document/capstick-fleming-hurne.pdf

Connolly-Panagopoulos, M. (2021). Centralisation: Placing Peer Assisted Study Sessions (PASS) within the wider work of learning developers. *Journal of Learning Development in Higher Education*, 21, 1-22.

Dancer, D., Morrison, K., & Tarr, G. (2015). Measuring the effects of peer learning on students' academic achievement in first-year business statistics. *Studies in Higher Education*, 40(10), 1808-1828.

Dawson, P., van der Meer, J., Skalicky, J., & Cowley, K. (2014). On the effectiveness of supplemental instruction: A systematic review of supplemental instruction and peer-assisted study sessions literature between 2001 and 2010. *Review of Educational Research*, 84(4), 609-639.

Enomoto, K., Warner, R., & Nygaard, C. (2022). Passive learning and active learning in higher education: their underpinning learning theories and consequences for teaching and assessment. In K. Enomoto, R. Warner & C. Nygaard (Eds.), *Active learning in higher education* (pp. 1-34). Oxfordshire, U.K.: Libri Publishing Ltd.

Garcia-Melgar, A., East, J., & Meyers, N. (2021). Peer-assisted academic support: A comparison of mentors' and mentees' experiences of a drop-in programme. *Journal of Further and Higher Education*, 45(9), 1163-1176.

Gardner, L. (2009) Multiple approaches to understanding. In K. Illeris (Ed.), *Contemporary theories of learning* (pp. 129-138). Abingdon, Oxon.: Routledge.

Goodman, D. S., Marr, D. G., Brown, C., Stoddart, M., & Beresford, M. (1989). *Asia in Australian Higher Education: The Ingleson Report*. Canberra: Australian Government Publishing Service.

Gravett, K., Kinchin, I. M., & Winstone, N. E. (2020). 'More than customers': Conceptions of students as partners held by students, staff, and institutional leaders. *Studies in Higher Education*, 45(12), 2574-2587.

Green, J. L. (2018). Peer support systems and professional identity of student nurses undertaking a U.K. learning disability nursing programme. *Nurse Education in Practice, 30,* 56-61.

Healey, M., Flint, A., & Harrington, K. (2014). Engagement through partnership: students as partners in learning and teaching in higher education. *The Higher Education Academy,* 1-78.

Healey, M., Flint, A., & Harrington, K. (2016). Students as partners: Reflections on a conceptual model. *Teaching & Learning Inquiry, 4*(2), 8-20.

Healey, M., Solem, M., & Pawson, E. (2010). Introduction. In M. Healey, E. Pawson & M Solem (Eds.), *Active learning and student engagement: International perspectives and practices in geography in higher education* (pp. 1–7). London: Routledge.

Hørsted, A., & Nygaard, C. (2017). How to design a curriculum for student learning. In A. Hørsted, J. Branch & C. Nygaard (Eds.), *Learning-centred curriculum design in higher education* (pp. 97-120). Oxfordshire, U.K.: Libri Publishing Ltd.

Huijser, H., Kimmins, L., & Evans, P. (2008). Peer-assisted learning in fleximode: Developing an online learning community. *Journal of Peer Learning, 1*(1), 51–60.

Jaunzems-Fernuk, J. (2022). Tracking the mental well-being of pre-service teachers in post-secondary health methods courses. In K. Enomoto, R. Warner & C. Nygaard (Eds.), *Active learning in higher education* (pp. 289-318). Oxfordshire, U.K.: Libri Publishing.

Kolb, D. A. (1984). *Experiential learning: Experience as the source of learning and development.* Eaglewood Cliffs, N.J.: Prentice-Hall.

Lockspeiser, T. M., O'Sullivan, P., Teherani, A., & Muller, J. (2008). Understanding the experience of being taught by peers: the value of social and cognitive congruence. *Advances in Health Sciences Education, 13*(3), 361-372.

Morrison, K. (2006). Peer Assisted Study Sessions supporting student engagement and quality learning in economics and business, *Synergy, 24,* 3-6.

Nygaard, C., Brand, S., Bartholomew, P., & Millard, L. (Eds.) (2013). *Student engagement – Identity, motivation and community.* Oxfordshire, U.K.: Libri Publishing Ltd.

O'Donnell, A., & Hmelo-Silver, C. E. (2013). Introduction: What is collaborative learning? In C. E. Hmelo-Silver, C. A. Chinn, C. K. K. Chan & A. O'Donnell (Eds.), *The international handbook of collaborative learning* (pp. 1–15). New York: Routledge.

Prince, M. (2004). Does active learning work? A review of the research. *Journal of Engineering Education, 93*(3), 223-231.

Schwartz, P. (2013). *Problem-based learning.* New York: Routledge.

Spedding, J., Hawkes, A. J., & Burgess, M. (2017). Peer assisted study sessions and student performance: the role of academic engagement, student identity, and statistics self-efficacy. *Psychology Learning & Teaching, 16*(1), pp. 144-163.

Swann, S. (2022). Constructing the employable graduate through active learning projects. In K. Enomoto, R. Warner & C. Nygaard (Eds.), *Active learning in higher education* (pp. 229-262). Oxfordshire, U.K.: Libri Publishing Ltd.

van der Meer, J., & Scott, C. (2009). Students' experiences and perceptions of peer-assisted study sessions: Towards ongoing improvement, *Journal of Peer Learning,* (2), 3-22.

Warner, R., & Enomoto, K. (2021). An innovative assessment method to evaluate independent learning and academic writing skills. In K. Enomoto, R. Warner & C. Nygaard (Eds.), *Teaching and learning innovations in higher education* (pp. 209-232). Oxfordshire, U.K.: Libri Publishing Ltd.

Zaccagnini, M., O'Sullivan, S., & Stephen, M. (2017). *Moving beyond tokenism: Defining and strengthening the relationship between PASS leaders and subject coordinators for enhanced outcomes* [Poster Presentation]. HERDSA. Sydney, NSW, Australia.

Chapter 6

Impact of Learning Space Design on Students' Experiences in an Active Learning Classroom

Selin Üst and Orçun Kepez

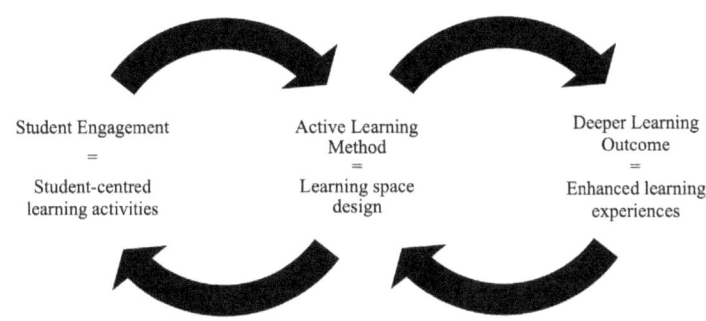

Introduction

Our chapter contributes to this book, *Active Learning in Higher Education*, by showing how we have used learning space design to engage students in various student-centred learning activities leading to a deeper learning outcome in the form of enhanced learning experiences. The learning space is the Steelcase-KHAS Active Learning Center (henceforth referred to as ALC), implemented in 2015 at the Cibali Campus of Kadir Has University. The ALC was designed with research-informed design guidelines within the scope of a research project that collaborated with Steelcase Education and Polyvision. The main aim of this research project was to understand what roles spatial aspects of the learning environment play in the experiences of the learning community (Kepez, 2018). The research-informed design guidelines (Salama, 2015; Sanoff, 1994) followed to realise the learning space were:

- supporting the learning community to explore and discover new pedagogies that fit best to their needs through affordances;
- providing desired privacy when needed; and
- giving control to the user to maximise environmental comfort.

The ALC is an active learning environment enabling numerous classroom layouts with moveable furniture. The walls, comprising ceramic-steel surfaces, can be used as screens for projection, boards for writing on and magnetic boards for attaching visual materials. Several electrical sockets around the room, some of which are on the floor, are installed for providing easy access to laptops and other electronic devices. In addition, the furniture configuration in the space can be changed to meet the needs of various courses. All these affordances in an active learning classroom enable the learning community to explore and discover even new experiences that we try to document and understand.

Each learning community member has a distinct need to define and maintain personal and interpersonal boundaries in the classroom. Even in traditional classrooms, previous research documents that students choose different seats and rows based on their privacy needs (Kaya & Burgess, 2007). In the ALC, the wheeled furniture, the presence of writing surfaces and individual boards, access to power outlets support members of the learning community to locate themselves based on their privacy needs without any concern over lack of access to classroom resources.

Previous research has indicated that the lack of control on environmental comfort increases users' stress levels, resulting in reduced performance (Cohen et al., 2013; Bilotta et al., 2018). To help prevent this from becoming an issue, our ALC is equipped with independently operable lights for optimal user control; users also can control various use scenarios in terms of Heating, Ventilation, and Air Conditioning (HVAC) and openable windows. With these qualities, it can be best described as a microecology that shapes classroom behaviour through the affordances it provides (Gibson, 1979; Johnson et al., 2018; Kepez & Üst, 2020).

Reading this chapter, you will gain the following insights:
1. what are the spatial attributes that can lead to enhanced learning experiences and deeper learning outcomes;

2. how to develop critical thinking skills within the existing curriculum through active learning strategies; and

3. how to design future learning environments that respond to different learning communities' diverse and unique needs.

Overview of main sections

The chapter has four main sections. In Section 1, we introduce the concept of active learning and active learning classrooms. In Section 2, we analyse the ALC as a case study, reviewing student feedback on spatial attributes of the learning environment. In Section 3, we elaborate on the outcomes of the active learning environment. In Section 4, we describe the resources and the leadership for implementing similar projects with success before concluding our chapter.

Section 1: The background for active learning

Adopting a research-informed approach (Salama, 2015; Sanoff, 1994) in its design, the ALC is designated for students from different university faculties. Students who received education at this centre were requested to share their experiences through open-ended surveys. This chapter is based on the post-occupancy evaluation of the ALC by analysing the students' written feedback about their active learning classroom. The same research team used the textual analysis of open-ended responses previously in the post-occupancy evaluation of another learning environment – a design studio. It was found to be effective by providing a discreet medium where students can freely and anonymously express their feelings about the learning environment (Kepez & Üst, 2017).

Active learning theory and methodology

Since the mid-1990s, alternative classroom models encouraging students to be active participants in the learning environment have emerged. Although there has been a growing number of publications on active learning, these have focused on the pedagogy rather than the spatial dimension of active learning. However, the rise of virtual learning during the COVID-19 pandemic (da Vinha, 2022, Chapter 8 in this book; Sezginalp & Üst, 2021), which has benefitted from active learning pedagogies, increases the significance of in-class behaviour and physical design of the space.

Already, in North America, these spatial dimensions of active learning have attracted some attention. There have been three major pioneer projects in higher education focusing on the effects of space on students' learning: SCALE-UP (Student-centred Active Learning Environment for Undergraduate Programs), TEAL (Technology Enabled Active Learning) and Active Learning Classrooms. North Carolina State University developed the SCALE-UP project to facilitate interaction among students working on activities. SCALE-UP consists of round tables sitting three teams of three students, surrounded by whiteboards and a teacher station located in the middle of the space (Beichner & Saul, 2003). Like SCALE-UP, TEAL, which the Massachusetts Institute of Technology operates, aims to create a dynamic learning environment full of round tables for small group works, multiple projectors, whiteboards accompanying each table, and a podium that helps to monitor all around the space (Lee et al., 2018). Finally, the Active Learning Classroom, operated by the University of Minnesota, offers a student-centric learning environment that takes the focus away from the teacher. It is furnished with moveable furniture so that the configuration of the furniture within the space can be changed according to the needs of different classes (Baepler et al., 2016). The catalyst for all these approaches was the growing need to engage the millennial population of students in crowded entry-level classes by offering pedagogies with special spatial requirements (Ruffo, 2008). Defined as digital natives, this new student population requires alternative pedagogies for engagement (Rue, 2018; Hernandez-de-Menendez et al., 2020).

Active learning encourages students to think about what they are doing and perform meaningful learning activities (Bonwell & Eison, 1991). It can be defined as any teaching method that includes the essential elements of student activity and participation in the learning process (Prince, 2004). Defining the conventional 'industrial' model of education as a kind of passive learning approach, Scott-Webber (2012) pointed out that more versatile design of learning spaces needed to be used instead of 'a row by column' seating to encourage new ways of learning for the future success of the students. In fact, there is demand from the student population of interest to have different types of classroom configurations when they were asked to assess or design their own (Kepez, 2018; Kepez & Üst, 2020). Active learning pedagogy moves beyond applying new learning methods that support student engagement and extends to considerations of spatial requirements; the latter may often be overlooked. Assessing learning outcomes of active learning rarely discusses the spatial requirements of the 'reported' classroom behaviours. Thus, our case study will demonstrate the learning space design features enabling active learning based on students' reflective analyses of their learning experiences.

Section 2: The case of active learning

The chapter is based on the evaluations by 79 students from various faculties of Kadir Has University, whose classes were held in the ALC. The ALC, the subject of this study, was established by transforming a traditional classroom into an active learning classroom in 2015 (Figure 1). The ALC has been an industry-specific research project carried out by an interdisciplinary research team. It contains easy-to-move furniture to enable change of room configuration depending on the needs of the courses, personal mini whiteboards, and special ceramic steel surfaces appropriate for projecting, hanging posters with magnets, and writing (Figure 2). Far from being just a flexible learning environment designed to address the spatial requirements for the needs of the new generation, the ALC is, in fact, a multidisciplinary pedagogy lab. Thus, we were motivated to analyse the impact of design features on students' behaviours within the space.

Students worked in nine different classes conducted in traditional classrooms in the first half of the same semester and the ALC in the second half of the Spring Semester. The switch occurred after introducing the classroom features to faculty members teaching in the ALC. The main idea is to adapt their courses to the new learning environment. Thus, this study assumes that the transformation from traditional pedagogies to active learning will be naturally occurring rather than imposed. Before the semester, we use a systematic method to determine which courses are offered in the ALC. Firstly, we list the courses delivered by the full-time teaching staff. Secondly, we shortlist the courses that do not exceed the capacity of the space and thirdly, we send an invitation to these faculty members to ask them if they would volunteer to teach there. Final selections mainly were made also to ensure diversity among faculties and departments.

Figure 1: Traditional Classroom before conversion to an active learning classroom.

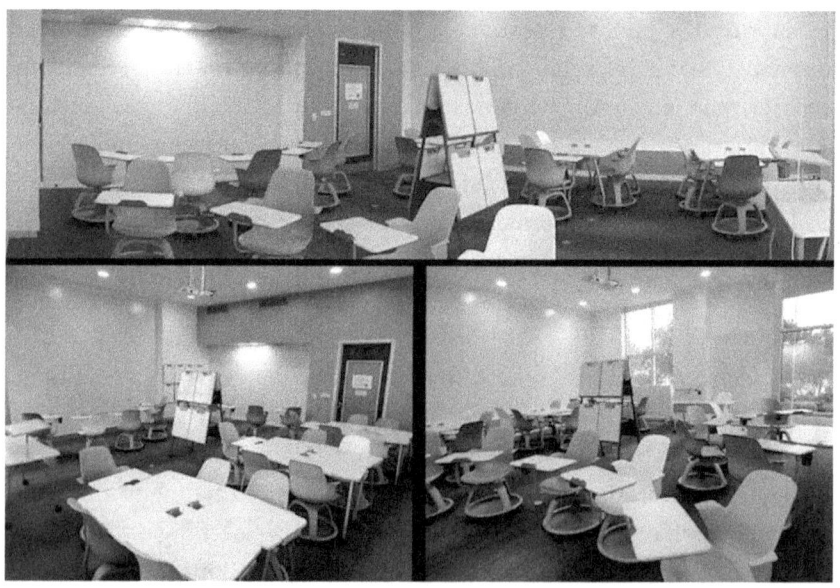

Figure 2: The ALC with different configurations.

Afterwards, teachers are introduced to the new classroom features and the concept of active learning when they are invited to conduct their lectures in ALC. A booklet containing visual guidelines that display the main possible classroom configurations for different purposes is also placed on the teachers' desk and introduced to all teachers at the beginning of the semester (Figure 3). Through collegial and informal communication, all teachers are given the opportunity to approach the research team whenever they need help, have questions, or just want to share their ongoing experiences.

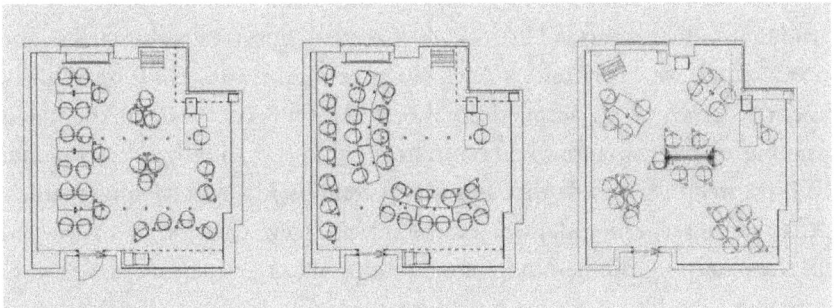

Figure 3: Examples of the ALC with different classroom configurations.

Every student and teaching staff member was expected to evaluate the ALC at the end of each semester. As part of these evaluations, students responded to surveys on their experience in the facility, and teaching staff shared their feedback about the courses through informal interviews. The collected data were kept confidential, and evaluations were carried out anonymously. We focus on the open-ended evaluations on the facility by the students who attended their courses in the ALC in the 2016-2017 spring semester. No criterion has been specified in the open-ended question: 'Please share your suggestions and opinions about the ALC'. Students were only asked to write down their learning experiences about this new facility. It helped students concentrate on their experiences rather than focusing on leading questions and answers. When questions have no such focal point, they enable the collection of data concerning individual and collective experiences as well.

Section 3: The outcome

Students' outcomes

For this chapter, the texts that were produced independently by 79 students were evaluated through content analysis as a qualitative research methodology. With content analysis, the aim is to conduct in-depth analyses of the studied content (in our cases texts) and arrive at the main concept and its relevance through defining emerged thematic parts (Creswell, 2002, 2009). The collected texts were submitted by the students who responded to the open-ended question voluntarily. The texts, which were written in Turkish, were then translated into English, and two researchers scrutinised the students' texts. Due to the small number of participants, the researchers worked manually with the data to interpret the content through the systematic identification of themes. After each researcher identified different emergent themes, they reviewed all the emerging themes and resolved any conflict. All these themes were compared, and each group was given a specific title based on different concept observations. Lastly, a more detailed analysis was carried out on the texts which were categorised under these common titles with the aim to arrive at unnoticed concepts and their relevance.

The content analyses revealed that students relied on their past learning experiences when discussing their new learning experiences. Those reported experiences fell into two main categories: 1) individual and 2) collective. Reported individual experiences had two subtitles: 1a) privacy and 1b) ergonomics. Collective experiences also had two subtitles: 2a) flexibility and 2b) appropriateness of the ALC for various activities (Figure 4).

Impact of Learning Space Design on Students' Experiences

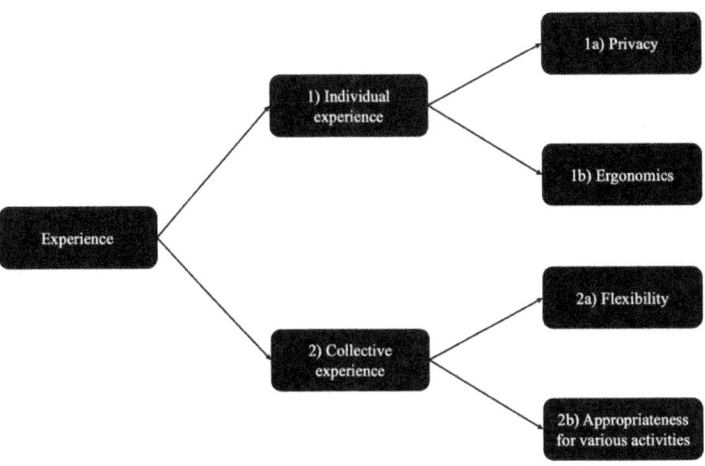

Figure 4: Themes emerging from content analysis.

1a) Privacy

In learning environments, students seek to control their interpersonal boundaries to negotiate their social contact within the physical environment (Sommer, 1969; 2002; Gifford, 2007; Kaya & Burgess, 2007). In the classroom, every student has a distinct need for a degree of privacy. Seat selection (based on the seat location- front row through to the back, and position in the row) and classroom configuration has become a point of interest when studying the privacy needs of students (Kaya & Burgess, 2007). Based on the congruent findings of the literature, it seems evident that some students claim a particular seat and row, indicating a strong tendency for privacy as a factor in classroom environments.

Based on their self-reports, the privacy needs of students were covered by being able to maintain their social distance. This was not only when they stood but also while they were seated, being able to be alone to focus on learning activities when they needed and being able to freely design their individual or group learning environment by placing the furniture of their choice wherever they want. Students stated:

- *"With its moveable and modifiable features, the classroom enables students to have discussions or to communicate with others more*

Chapter 6

> *conveniently, or to study and, more importantly, to produce individually whenever needed."*

- *"Students can sit in groups with their friends, or can have personal furniture to interact with others."*

- *"Although we are all together in the class, we can have a space to move individually and to design the best learning environment for ourselves."*

1b) Ergonomics

Ergonomic and more comfortable furniture allows students to concentrate on lessons and leads to more active participation (Bullard, 2009; Cornell, 2003; Knight & Noyes, 1999). Participants in this study came from classrooms with fixed row seats or stools (some wheeled, some not) without back support. Several complaints had been received about "static" classroom environments with non-ergonomic furniture. Thus, when exposed to the ALC, positive feedback was received about the comfort of the chairs, giving a hint on the desire for comfort in static parts of the classes. Students reported:

- *"Very comfortable. It is very convenient for those with back pain like me."*

- *"Comfortable furniture prevented me from getting distracted."*

- *"Ergonomic and comfortable furniture prevented me from getting bored, of course, due to body aches."*

This reported comfort responds to a basic need that was not met before. The chairs were designed to deliver comfort by supporting healthy posture, ease of use, mobility and functionality (storage area under the seat, coffee cup holder, tablet/mobile phone holder in the adjustable desk attached to chairs). The tables were also moveable, height-adjustable and had accessories for pens, storage systems for mini-boards and support group arrangements by design. With all these features of the furniture and other design elements of the ALC, the ergonomic needs of the learning community were planned to be covered to the extent that is greater than just comfort. However, when students arrive at the space with their strong need for physical comfort that is mostly associated with health, other factors that support ergonomics were overshadowed.

2a) Flexibility

'Flexibility' refers to the affordances embedded by design to the ALC, explored and discovered by the learning community. Moveability (of the furniture, mini whiteboards), operability (of the HVAC, windows), selectability (of the electrical outlets, colours of the seat, seating type, lighting level of the room) are the main affordances that were designed and used actively in the classroom. In one of several studies on the effects of the studio on learning and teaching, Taylor (2009) asserts that it provides flexibility for both teachers and students, and thus, improves the experiences of both parties when a traditional classroom is converted into an environment consisting of mobile furniture and chairs. Students referred to the flexibility of the classroom by mentioning the moveable furniture, the wall system and mini whiteboards.

- *"Thanks to mobile furniture, we can have much better group studies and become more active. We have the freedom to move in the classroom thanks to the furniture."*
- *"It is a great advantage to have mobile furniture that can be adjusted according to different seating plans."*

Their comments highlighted the opportunity to have different furniture configurations with ease, leading to freedom of movement in the classroom and design group work. Other students commented:

- *"It is a well-done arrangement to have furniture that can be easily moved. It brings great convenience and freedom of movement."*
- *"Having boards all around us made it way easier for us to work in groups. It gave me a sense of freedom."*

They also mentioned that the flexibility of the ALC contributes to their creativity in developing ideas, fostering a positive mood and increasing productivity. Students shared their excitement:

- *"Because we are in need of writing and drawing something all the time, these walls of boards made the lessons much more fun."*
- *"Thanks to the writable walls, we could use each and every corner of the classroom more productively."*
- *"I believe that mini-whiteboards will highly contribute to the development of new ideas."*

Also, there were only a few negative student comments on the flexibility of the ALC, which derive from inevitable individual preferences:

- *"It is hard to reach the upper parts of the continuous board system."*
- *"Being mobile makes it difficult to concentrate on the lesson. That's why I prefer the fixed furniture."*
- *"The movable furniture creates a lot of focus points in the classroom, which disrupts the concentration of the students."*

2b) Appropriateness for various activities

'Appropriateness of the ALC for various activities' refers to meaningful student-centred learning activities that occurred by discovering the affordances in the learning environment. This can be better explained by sharing a teacher's observation of in-class behaviour, where students naturally use ceramic steel walls contributing to their collective experiences. However, it was also observed that they also used ceramic steel walls spontaneously for problem-solving when they were 'expected to listen and watch' their teacher. Obviously, there is a distinction between these activities in their contribution to the collective learning experiences, nurturing the idea that flexibility does not always lead to 'appropriate' in-class behaviours. Since switching between different furniture configurations was very easy, all classes could use the space effectively. Students strongly identified the student-centred activity of reshaping the classroom as functionally beneficial:

- *"The classroom enables us to move more freely. Thanks to the mobile furniture, we are able to take positions according to the type of classes."*
- *"With its adaptation to different course requirements, it creates a different space perception, and thus, helps us break down our prejudice that it is boring to be in courses, and awakens our curiosity."*
- *"It helps to be able to customize the in-class environment and to have user-friendly furniture. It is beyond a conventional class arrangement. It is highly appropriate for working in groups during group assignments."*

Teacher perspective - my reflections

Teachers whose courses were moved to the ALC in the middle of the semester reflect on their experiences during and post semester in the form of informal interviews. All teachers mentioned positive comments throughout the semester in both impromptu conversations and their end-of-year informal interviews. Similar to students, they liked the features of the classroom. One teacher commented, *"I looked forward to my course in [the] ALC"*, and another commented, *"It's so nice that students can make groups with ease during my class"*. However, not all of them benefited from these features during their experiences. Coming from traditional classrooms, most of the teachers continued with the same syllabus that they were already used to. Although the potential of the classroom was explained to them in detail, a booklet for main configurations was provided, and their participation in this study was organised at the beginning of the semester, only two among all nine courses were held with active learning pedagogy by the same professor who had former experience.

Teachers reported an increase in student engagement during the class and decreased absenteeism. The teachers also mentioned that even in traditional formal engineering courses conducted in the ALC, students moved into the classroom freely to use ceramic steel walls when they were expected to sit and listen. Moreover, sometimes students carried conversations without raising hands first, disrupting the formal tone of the lecture. Obviously, students felt free to move and be active participants in these courses when teachers were not ready.

Section 4: Moving forward

The ALC grew an interest in our community as an exemplary learning space where many faculty members contacted us to teach there mainly because of its appealing physical qualities. Combined with KHAS University's newly adopted project-based teaching model, the ALC serves as an experimental environment where different disciplines can teach first-year core courses. However, we witnessed that based on the course design and teachers' attitude towards the university's approach, the use of the ALC may differ from one teacher to another, varying in traditional and active learning configurations. That said, without training faculty members, any ALC can function only as another classroom, limiting its potential to faculty members' personal intuition in teaching.

When teachers explore different teaching opportunities suitable for their courses, they will be driven by different experiences and put effort into organising their classroom environment. Thus, it can be said that the design of an ideal learning experience is based on designing a collaborative learning experience in which all the members of the learning community are involved and work together. Unlike a traditional classroom setting where the teacher is the centre of the knowledge, everyone in an active learning classroom acts in an enabling capacity to the best of their ability. Obviously, making this happen in an institution requires intrinsic motivation from a community supported with expertise, mentorship, time and spatial requirements for this kind of training. Engagement of student leadership for a successful transformation of active learning curriculum is an effective method in face to face, hybrid and online education (Enomoto & Warner, 2022, Chapter 5 in this book). Moreover, universities should provide budget allocation for new learning spaces and freedom to explore active learning pedagogies in the learning community. Needless to say, in a growing neoliberal 'publish or perish' culture, the contributions of teachers to their served learning community must be treated equally when compared to the weight given to other scholarly activities.

Conclusion

This case study of an active learning environment was based on the individual open-ended responses of students after their first semester in the ALC. The content analyses first revealed that feedback from students was shaped by their past experiences and their comparison with the new ones in the ALC. The reported experiences fell into two main themes: 1) individual experiences and 2) collective experiences - both of which had two subtitles. The individual experiences were grouped into two subcategories: 1a) privacy and 1b) ergonomics. Collective experiences were grouped into two subcategories: 2a) flexibility and 2b) appropriateness of the ALC for various activities.

The themes, especially individual experiences reported from this study, can be used in future assessment instruments developed for this

ALC. The achieved privacy level in an ALC is often overlooked in the readily established instruments that focus on flexibility and diversity of pedagogies potentially applied. The open-ended comments revealed that the inherent need for privacy does exist even when working with groups. Our study showed that ergonomics is often associated with the comforts of the sitting experience and posture health. Ergonomics as a concept is loaded with the comfort of the furniture and the supportiveness of all environmental attributes (such as light level and acoustics). From a designers' perspective, there are maybe too many ergonomic-related variables that are difficult to perceive by the end-users. For future studies, ergonomics should be unpacked and disseminated further within the context of critical environmental features.

Our conclusion encompasses the learning community and the designers of learning environments for active learning. For the learning community, it is important to be open to new possibilities in active learning classrooms. Decision-makers of the learning communities, in our case the university administration, should provide resources for both teachers and the students, including training programs, mentorship from experts, and assessment tools. For students, in this case, they should demand new pedagogies that can be easily applied in an active learning classroom by effective use of all features that they are aware of. Finally, the designers who will design future active learning classrooms must recognise that those pedagogies are dynamic and ever-changing. Thus, they have to follow alternative design strategies, such as participatory design, involving all learning community members.

Acknowledgements

We would like to thank the students and the teachers of Kadir Has University for their participation in this study. We would also like to thank Steelcase Education and PolyVision for their generous grants for realising the Steelcase Active Learning Center at Kadir Has University.

Chapter 6

About the Authors

Selin Üst, PhD, is an Assistant Professor in the Department of Interior Architecture and Environmental Design in the Faculty of Architecture and Design at Ozyegin University, Istanbul, Turkey. She can be contacted at this email: selin.ust@ozyegin.edu.tr

Orçun Kepez, PhD, served as an Associate Professor in the Department of Interior Architecture and Environmental Design in the Faculty of Art and Design at Kadir Has University, Istanbul, Turkey. He can be contacted at this email: orcun.kepez@icloud.com

Bibliography

Baepler, P., Walker, J., Brooks, D., Saichaie, K., & Petersen, C. (2016). *A guide to teaching in active learning classrooms: History, research, and practice.* Sterling, Virginia: Stylus Publishing, LLC.

Beichner, R. J., & Saul, J. M. (2003). *Introduction to the SCALE-UP (student-centered activities for large enrolment undergraduate programs) project.* Proceedings of the International School of Physics "Enrico Fermi," Varenna, Italy. Retrieved from http://www.ncsu.edu/per/scale-up.html

Bilotta, E., Vaid, U., & Evans, G. W. (2018). Environmental Stress. In L. Steg, A. Van Den Berg & J. De Groot (Eds.), *Environmental psychology: An introduction* (pp. 36-44). BPS Blackwell.

Bonwell, C. C., & Eison, J. A. (1991). *Active Learning: Creating Excitement in the Classroom. ASHEERIC Higher Education Report 1.* School of Education and Human Development, George Washington University, Washington, D.C.

Bullard, J. (2009). *Creating environments for learning: Birth to age eight.* New Jersey: Merrill.

Cohen, S; Evans, G. W.; Stokols, D., & Krantz, D. S. (2013). *Behaviour, health and environmental stress.* Springer Science and Business Media.

Cornell, P. (2003). The impact of changes in teaching and learning on furniture and the learning environment. *New Directions for Teaching and Learning*, 92, 33–42.

Creswell, J. W. (2002). *Qualitative inquiry and research design: Choosing among five approaches.* Thousand Oaks, California: Sage.

Creswell, J. W. (2009). *Research design: Qualitative, quantitative, and mixed methods approaches* (Third Edition). Thousand Oaks, California: Sage.

da Vinha, L. (2022). Fostering active learning online using interactive video lectures. In K. Enomoto, R. Warner & C. Nygaard (Eds.), *Active learning in higher education* (pp. 181-202). Oxfordshire, U.K.: Libri Publishing Ltd.

Enomoto, K., & Warner, R. (2022). Partnering with student leaders: Active learning through integration of Peer Assisted Study Sessions into an undergraduate language course. In K. Enomoto, R. Warner & C. Nygaard (Eds.), *Active learning in higher education* (pp. 107-134). Oxfordshire, U.K.: Libri Publishing Ltd.

Gibson, J. J. (1979). *The ecological approach to visual perception.* New York, N.Y.: Psychology Press.

Gifford, R. (2007). *Environmental psychology: Principles and practice.* Colville, W.A.: Optimal Books

Hernandez-de-Menendez, M., Escobar Díaz, C. A., & Morales-Menendez, R. (2020). Educational experiences with Generation Z. *International Journal on Interactive Design and Manufacturing (IJIDeM), 14*(3), 847-859.

Johnson, A. W., Blackburn, M. W., Su, M. P., & Finelli, C. J. (2018). How a flexible classroom affords active learning in electrical engineering. *IEEE Transactions on Education, 62*(2), 91-98.

Kaya, N., & Burgess, B. (2007). Territoriality: Seat preferences in different types of classroom arrangements. *Environment and Behavior, 39*(6), 859-876.

Kepez, O. (2018). The Steelcase Active Learning Centre as a community design centre. In K. Enomoto, R. Warner & C. Nygaard (Eds.), *Innovative teaching and learning practices in higher education* (pp. 179-200). Oxfordshire, U.K.: Libri Publishing Ltd.

Kepez, O., & Üst, S. (2017). Post occupancy evaluation of a transformed design studio. *İTÜ AZ, 14*(3), 41-52.

Kepez, O., & Üst, S. (2020). Collaborative design of an active learning classroom with high school students and teachers. *Archnet-IJAR: International Journal of Architectural Research. 14*(3), 525-541.

Knight, G., & Noyes, J. (1999). Children's behaviour and the design of school furniture. *Ergonomics, 42*(5), 747–760.

Lee, D., Morrone, A. S., & Siering, G. (2018). From swimming pool to collaborative learning studio: Pedagogy, space, and technology in a large active learning classroom. *Educational Technology Research and Development, 66*(1), 95-127.

Prince, M. (2004). Does active learning work? A review of the research. *Journal of Engineering Education, 93*(3), 223-231.

Rue, P. (2018). Make way, millennials, here comes Gen Z. *About Campus, 23*(3), 5-12.

Ruffo, J. A. (2008). "Millenial" or "Net Generation" students and their impact on the development of student-centered facilities. *Planning for Higher Education* 37(1), 5.

Salama, A. M. A. (2015). *Spatial design education: new directions for pedagogy in architecture and beyond.* Farnham Surrey, England; Burlington: Ashgate.

Sanoff, H. (1994). *School design.* New York: Van Nostrand Reinhold.

Scott-Webber, L. (2012). Institutions, educators, and designers: wake up!, *Planning for Higher Education*, 41(1), 265-277.

Sezginalp, P., & Üst, S. (2021). Adapting to the Living Space in the First Interior Design Studio. *Journal of Design Studio*, 3(1), 97-106.

Sommer, R. (1969). *Personal space: the behavioural basis of design.* Englewood Cliffs, N.J.: Prentice-Hall.

Sommer, R. (2002). Personal space in a digital age. In R. B. Bechtel & A. Churchman (Eds.), *Handbook of environmental psychology* (pp. 647-660). New York: John Wiley & Sons.

Taylor, S. S. (2009). Effects of studio space on teaching and learning: Preliminary findings from two case studies. *Innovative Higher Education*, 33(4), 217–228.

Chapter 7
Enhancing Students' Interpersonal and Leadership Skills through an Experience-based Service-learning Project: A Case of Active Learning

Lorina Culic and Anișoara Pavelea

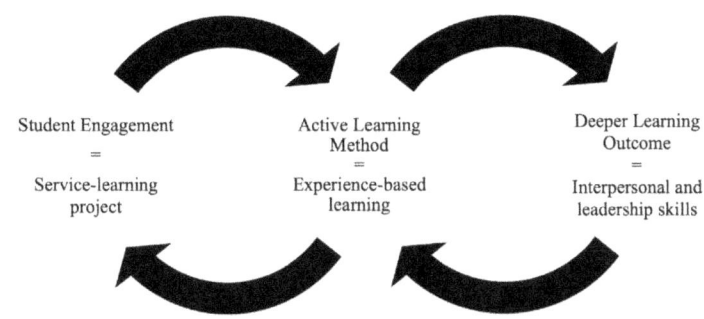

Introduction

With our chapter, we contribute to this book, *Active Learning in Higher Education*, by showing how we have used experience-based learning to engage students in a service-learning project to enhance their interpersonal and leadership skills. Our active learning case takes place in an undergraduate Interpersonal Communication course for first-year students majoring in Communication, Public Relations and Advertising from the Faculty of Political, Administrative and Communication Sciences at Babes-Bolyai University in Cluj-Napoca, Romania. Due to the global COVID-19 pandemic, the course took place entirely online through weekly course meetings over 14 weeks. Working in an online setting allowed us to observe which variables positively or negatively affect active learning (Han et al., 2021). In the chapter, we discuss the implication and extent of adapting a university course to an active learning environment. We also analyse the implications of the service-learning online course as a pedagogical approach for students' increased community engagement and a tool for developing and acquiring interpersonal and leadership skills.

Active learning is often seen as *"an instructional method that engages students in the learning process"* (Prince, 2004:223), in contrast to the traditional lecture. We consider active learning a method that encompasses a variety of learning activities in which teachers encourage students to build knowledge through their own experience (Kolb, 1984). Active learning promotes student engagement and allows the teacher to introduce a diverse range of activities into the traditional lecture (Bonwell & Eison, 1991; Prince, 2004) to make learning more interactive. Thus, active learning brings about multiple benefits, as it:

- engages students cognitively, behaviourally and emotionally (Hollingsworth & Lewis, 2006);
- increases students' satisfaction with their individual and group learning processes (Hyun et al., 2017);
- develops high-order thinking skills and involves group work (Freeman, 2014);
- promotes collaboration among students and enhanced reflection (Isaías et al., 2021); and
- enables students to relate learning to career goals and reflection on life (Han et al., 2021).

As well as being mentally arousing and challenging, active learning is *"an iterative, dialogical and collaborative student-centred approach"* (European University Association, 2019:3) that has influenced other learning approaches, including problem-based learning (Barrows & Wee, 2007), the flipped classroom (Prober & Khan, 2013), and action learning (Dilworth, 1996).

Encompassed under the umbrella of active learning, service-learning is often seen as a transformative methodology (Mezirow, 2000; Rodríguez-Izquierdo, 2021). Service-learning enhances classroom knowledge through experiential learning in different real-life community settings that facilitate students' interaction with community partners (Brand et al., 2019). In addition, service-learning combines community or public service with structured opportunities for learning, offering students *"the opportunity to explore the connections between the theoretical realm of the classroom and the practical needs of the community"* (Heffernan, 2001:2). At the core of service-learning is the idea that cognitive, affective, and moral growth are inseparable and that a student's ability to analyse situations and material actively and to reflect upon experiences is critical to building their active citizenship, personal accountability and social responsibility.

In actuality, service-learning provides a framework for interaction between the students, community and society, conducive to collaboration and personal, civic and academic development. Although the practice of service-learning is widespread internationally, such active learning pedagogy is limited in Romanian universities, with only a few such universities implementing service-learning projects that focus on learning outcomes and course creation in disciplines like psychology or social work (Rusu et al., 2015; Rusu, 2020). It is hardly unexpected that this methodology has received little coverage and visibility among active learning practices. This is because adopting service-learning is a complex process that requires much time and dedication from universities and teachers to identify and coordinate with community partners in terms of implementation and coordination of service-learning projects.

By reading this chapter, you will gain insight into:

1. the important role of service-learning in higher education;
2. ways in which participants may work during a course to develop a service-learning perspective; and
3. how to organise an online service-learning project, and what online instruments to use for teaching.

Overview of main sections

This chapter has four main sections. In Section 1, we discuss the context of using active learning in a university environment and the strengths and advantages of a service-learning methodology for improving students' interpersonal skills. Section 2 describes the online course's content and organisation based on the service-learning methodology. Section 3 details the outcomes of the active learning process concerning students' experiences and evaluations, teachers' perspectives and lessons learned. Finally, Section 4 outlines the challenges of using experience-based active learning in a university and online environment and recommends future improvement before we conclude this chapter.

Section 1: The background to active learning

The idea of using a service-learning project came from a presentation we (the authors) attended in a private school in Cluj. There, a New Horizons Foundation member held a presentation on the benefits of this methodology. The New Horizons Foundation is a NGO organised *"to help individuals accomplish their charitable objectives in religious, educational, scientific, benevolent and health-related activities"* (New Horizons Foundation, 2022:NP). The idea sparked in our mind that if kindergarten and school children can develop service-learning projects, so can our students.

Our university strives to be recognised as a world-class university, encompassing three academic missions: i) didactic, ii) research-development-innovation and iii) relationship with society. Based on our university's mission, we first conducted a pilot project in 2020, asking our students to design a service-learning project from scratch. The experience of the New Horizons Foundation gave wings to the first experience with service-learning projects with the CLAYSS Foundation and Impact Clubs, international extracurricular community involvement clubs. The CLAYSS Foundation is a Latin American NGO with the mission *"To contribute to the growth of a fraternal and participative culture in Latin America through the development of educational, social engagement projects"* (CLAYSS, 2022:NP).

We had the opportunity of implementing service-learning projects in a setting that treasures and encourages community development and civic involvement, curricular innovation, and university-industry partnerships through collaboration projects. Such collaborations included private and public institutions, NGOs, associations and foundations, with formal and non-formal education, corporate social responsibility campaigns, and community development projects. Combining all three missions, our class on interpersonal communication emphasises the importance of developing students' knowledge, attitudes, skills, and values.

Based on the previous experience with students in the first wave of the COVID-19 pandemic, we had to rethink our strategy and adapt it to the new online format of the class. We found it particularly relevant to start the class with a comprehensive presentation on service-learning methodology, with examples from New Horizons projects and testimonials from students who have previously attended the class.

Active learning theory and methodology

Building on the constructivist views of Piaget (1936) and Vygotsky (1978), with a focus on Kolb's (1984) experiential learning theory, stating that individuals actively construct their knowledge through prior knowledge and direct experiences, we have implemented an active learning approach in higher education. Students, in this case, are not only involved in what they are doing but are also asked to reflect upon their experience and develop metacognitive abilities (Bonwell & Eison, 1991). They build their knowledge, based upon their zone of proximal development, through concrete experience, reflective observation, abstract conceptualisation and active experimentation. However, under Bonwell and Eison's (1991) broad definition, active learning falls under a wide spectrum of learning activities (from very simple 2-minute pauses to complex case studies, simulations and gamified activities) and learning strategies, such as experiential learning, learning by doing and service-learning and so forth (Chi, 2009). Such diverse pedagogies are why we consider active learning more of an approach than a method.

Our class was designed as a collaborative learning experience, using the CLAYSS service-learning five-step model (Sosa Rolon, 2020):

1. motivation;
2. diagnosis;
3. project design and planning;
4. implementation; and
5. closure and multiplication.

As Regina and Ferrara (2017:14) observe, this is an *"innovative means of applying academic subjects, acquiring competencies and skills, and modifying attitudes"*. Starting from a student-centred approach, valuing feedback from students, we opened the class with an informal needs assessment at the beginning of each semester, indicating that only 6% of the students have had previous service-learning experience during college, and 39% have participated in some form of volunteering or NGO experience.

For the past eight years, we have tried different teaching methods and pedagogical approaches, different types of assessment (multiple-choice tests, oral exams, written assignments, research projects and portfolios), each presenting an array of advantages and disadvantages. Yet, service-learning seems to be the most suitable framework, meeting all our expectations for the educational process. Service-learning projects represent an invitation to reading about existing community problems, encouraging students to reflect upon the community problems and issues, their place in the world and their contribution. Service-learning combines service to the community with personal learning objectives, empowers students to concentrate on their learning process, and allows them to identify and assess their skills in real-life situations realistically. This methodology goes hand in hand with the class objectives revolving around familiarising students with the main concepts and theories in social psychology, reflecting upon how we think, feel, and act in social contexts. We encourage students to observe the surrounding reality actively, ask questions, use critical thinking, and learn to understand the uniqueness and diversity of each person.

Our Interpersonal Communication class, grounded in social psychology, is designed for first-year Communication, Public Relations and Advertising students from the Faculty of Political, Administrative and Communication Sciences at Babes-Bolyai University in Cluj-Napoca, Romania. The main topics include: social perception and cognition, interpersonal relationships, stereotypes and discrimination, and prosocial behaviour. It is the only class where students can experience service-learning projects. The department focuses on research and project-based learning. Students are encouraged to undertake both individual and group research projects during their first year, followed by second-year corporate social responsibility campaigns, event planning, public relations and public health campaigns, or marketing and advertising strategies.

Section 2: The case of active learning

The mandatory undergraduate Interpersonal Communication course in Semester 2 utilises active learning and has 235 students majoring in Communication, Public Relations and Advertising. However, students must carry out a service-learning project for ten weeks. The first weeks are dedicated to familiarisation with the service-learning methodology and theory, the presentation of success models from students from previous years, and identifying the service-learning project topics.

A first-year students' profile from the Communication, Public Relations and Advertising specialisation is that of a student who is a digital native depicted in Parker and Igielnik's (2020) Generation Z profile. They characterise such a native as follows:

- increased digital skills;
- interest in content creation and social media editing and management;
- egalitarian values and prone to activism;
- openness to experiences;
- inclination towards improving verbal and written communication skills; and
- increased English language skills.

Even if they are endowed with digital skills and have communication and research skills, first-year students have not encountered service-learning contexts in other subjects or the need to work in real-life team contexts by implementing communication campaigns. Thus, this is the major challenge of this active learning framework.

Due to the pandemic, all the Interpersonal Communication course classes were held weekly, on Zoom, during the second semester, from February to June 2021 (See Table 1). Students attended a two-hour lecture and two-hour seminars organised in 10 groups of students, totalling 235 first-year students. The mean age of the students was 19.8 years (SD = 1, range [18, 25]), from which 71% were females. They were divided into small groups of 4-5 members, in alphabetical order. Still, they were allowed to freely choose one of 4 goals from the UN 2030

Agenda for Sustainable Development Goals (SDG), according to their interests, values and preferences, as Moely et al. (2008) recommend, and the topic of the project to be implemented for the next ten weeks. The faculty teaching staff closely supervised them (Celio et al., 2011). The UN goals count 17 directions of direct intervention that aim to end poverty, hunger and inequality, take action on climate change and the environment, improve access to health and education, build strong institutions and partnerships, and more (United Nations Development Group 2015). From the 17 directions of interventions, students chose to concentrate on five primary UN goals, distributed among the 45 teams of students in our class as follows: 44% - quality education, 17% - climate action, 14% - gender equality, 14% - sustainable cities and communities, and 11% - reducing inequalities (to be detailed further in Section 3). Focusing on these five goals, tied to course content, has facilitated and shortened students' decision-making, offering them a clear framework.

Students had access to all class materials (including Handbook, PowerPoint presentations, videos, previous service-learning projects, books and articles, charts and graphs) on Google Drive. A course calendar was provided to students (See Table 1).

Week	Topic	Recommendations	Resources	Tools
W1	Course overview: Assessment criteria	*Present the course's major topics and discuss the evaluation criteria.* (e.g. 30% written exam, 70% service-learning project activities, including class participation, weekly tasks, final project, project presentation)	Handbook Syllabus	Zoom

Week	Topic	Recommendations	Resources	Tools
W2	Previous project presentations: Motivation	*Provide examples of service-learning projects and invite experts to the class (e.g. Second-year students' service-learning presentations and New Horizons Foundation interview)*	Project presentations, Videos	Mentimeter Canva, PowerPoint
W3	CLAYSS methodology	*Discuss service-learning methodology (steps) and set project topics*	CLAYSS Handbook, Calendar, service-learning case-studies books and articles	Mentimeter
W4	Diagnosis 1: Community needs assessment	*Identify the problem and run the diagnosis. e.g. interviews with the community members and stakeholders*	Community map, Problem Tree Exercise, Media Analysis	Google Street View, Whiteboard Mentimeter
W5	Diagnosis 2: Formative assessment 1	*Identify community partners and draft the communication strategy*	Community map, Community photos, Websites	Jamboard, Whiteboard, Mentimeter
W6	Project design and planning	*Design project's activities, resources, and calendar*	SMART objectives, Gantt Chart	Google sheets
W7-11	Implementation/ activities: Formative assessment 2	*Monitor the implementation of the projects. Provide feedback to students and scaffolding*	Project management workbook	Excel, Discord, Zoom, SNS

Week	Topic	Recommendations	Resources	Tools
W12	Closing and multiplication: Final assessment	*Make sure students thank partners, synthesise the outcome and outputs of the project and disseminate the results*	Media project dissemination	Google Drive, SMS analytics
W13	Project presentations: Final assessment	*Offer students feedback and encourage participation*	Celebration Photos Peer evaluations Evaluation grid	Zoom, PPT, Canva, Prezi, Kahoot
W14	Evaluation evaluation of students' community: i) service self-efficacy and civic attitudes and skills ii) course & seminar evaluation	With a six months follow-up	Survey, Institutional Assessment	Google forms

Table 1: Course overview.

The service-learning approach proved to be quite innovative for students. They were challenged to apply their skills in real-life settings (see Hoeppner & Reid, 2022, Chapter 2 in this book) while helping others and constantly reflecting on the experience. Scaffolding was provided to students over time and when appropriate (such as identifying topics, socio-demographic profiling examples, tutorials, offering examples of community resources, suggesting types of exercises and resources, formal recommendations for collaborations and NGO contacts). The students stated that time management, team conflict, and project management were the most challenging tasks. For some of them, these projects have been the first actual contact with NGOs or other institutions, which emphasised their individual responsibility in implementing a group project. We tried throughout the whole semester to encourage students to make connections between what we studied in the Interpersonal Communication class and other subjects, such as research methods, nonverbal communication, ethics and academic writing.

Implementing service-learning projects is user-friendly and could be translated into other classes. The CLAYSS handbook (Regina & Ferrara, 2017) offers a clear methodology, and the impact of service-learning methodology on students are multiple:

- increased self-efficacy (Gerholz et al., 2018);
- life skills (interpersonal, leadership ability, social self-confidence, critical thinking skills, conflict resolution skill, and understanding national and community problems) (Astin & Sax, 1998);
- changes in beliefs and stereotypes, developing prosocial behaviour, civic responsibility, reporting greater satisfaction with service-learning courses, the teacher, reading assignments and grades (Berson & Younkin, 1998).

An overview of how students work with active learning

Students were encouraged to go through the materials at their own pace. Second-year students gave examples of previous service-learning projects and provided several additional resources, including NGOs contact lists, examples of good practices, and service-learning associations.

Given the management framework of the CLAYSS project and the course calendar, weekly meetings were suggested to students, and the progress of their work was discussed weekly in our Zoom sessions. Students had the opportunity to ask questions, provide feedback to colleagues, ask for teacher feedback, and debrief encountered obstacles. With an emphasis on active learning, we worked on stimulating students' engagement by using in courses and seminars:

- 2-minute pauses;
- think-pair-share and short writing exercises (community resources map, SMART objectives, list of partner organisations, Gantt charts);
- debates;

- class discussions and opinion polls;
- provocative pictures;
- decision-making activities; and
- visual learning.

Special attention was given to the reflection phase, encouraging students to be strategic in following their learning objectives. Each online meeting was an invitation for students to reassess the project's feasibility, schedule, resources needed, skills developed and need to be flexible and adapt to new situations. Students were free to choose (for example) the type of beneficiaries, their number, community partners, project time frame and activities.

Moreover, as the service-learning approach recommends, students had to set personal learning goals and identify sets of skills that they would like to develop and observe and return to them through the project activities carried out. To work through all these stages, students had to consult with their teams, go through the seminars' practical exercises, and apply them in solving the requirements of their service-learning project. Also, the seminar teacher had a consultative, coordinating, and clarifying role, each team being able to request a consultation when they had any ambiguities.

How we prepare and organise active learning

The service-learning project activities were organised over ten weeks. The first weeks of the course were dedicated to reading and comprehending the CLAYSS handbook (Regina & Ferrara, 2017) and previous service-learning projects presentations to understand the task and project models better. Among the methods used in the first stages of the service-learning project design, we utilised:

- direct observation in the community;
- individual interviews with community members recorded by students;
- participation in local council meetings and media analysis;
- short videos provided by The New Horizons Foundation (2017); and

- different international organisations that provided examples of service-learning projects.

In addition, we also utilised:
  - photos, maps and Google Street View for capturing the community problems;
  - online platforms with public notifications to the town hall;
  - Excel charts and Gantt charts for establishing a project timeline and schedule;
  - Mentimeter for anonymous answers and games; and
  - Zoom and Discord for weekly project meetings.

All of the support materials were offered with the role of inquiring and analysing, developing ideas, creating solutions and evaluating. They were made available to students on the course Drive platform to browse and access at their own pace and have all the materials at hand.

Section 3: The outcome

Student perspective

We saw a total of 45 teams and projects delivered and presented at the end of the semester. The service-learning projects varied in the amplitude of beneficiaries, from a minimum of 5 beneficiaries to a maximum of 95 beneficiaries, with an average of approximately 29 participants per project. Moreover, students collaborated with 41 institutions, NGOs, community associations or public experts, professionals and public figures.

Students had the opportunity to opt for a direct service-learning intervention based on face-to-face interaction with the beneficiaries or indirect intervention, working on broad issues through awareness and educational campaigns on the chosen topics. Most projects had a local or national intervention, while only a few had an international approach, working with beneficiaries from two countries.

At the end of the semester, students had the opportunity to discuss and evaluate their service-learning project experience and involvement in a debriefing and feedback session organised with the course and seminar teachers. Also, students had two anonymous instruments to evaluate the course: an institutional questionnaire for evaluating the course and the seminar, with online completion on the university platform and a Google Form questionnaire offered at the end of the semester, composed of closed and open questions and two scales: the community service self-efficacy scale (CSSES) (Reeb et al., 1998) and civic attitudes and skills scale (CASQ) (Moely et al., 2002). One assessment was optional and one included in the course requirements, both assessments taking place before students could find out their project and course grades, for a more objective evaluation.

An evaluation of the major themes of the projects shows us that they are grouped into five categories (Figure 1):

Educational campaigns 44%

- awareness campaigns about mental health with topics such as identifying depression and stress, increasing motivation, combating procrastination in students, addressing positive thinking, promoting sex education in young people, developing critical thinking skills or useful digital skills in pandemic period;

Environmental and climate action 17%

- projects promoting the community involvement in cleaning actions planting trees and flowers, promoting green means of travel;

Gender equality 14%

- combating stereotypes and prejudices and reducing gender and sexual orientation discrimination;

Sustainable & involved communities 14%

- supporting local entrepreneurship, local tourism and volunteering activities;

Reducing inequalities 11%

- combating ethnic discrimination and social inequalities.

Figure 1: Service-learning project topics.

To find out how this course learning experience was perceived, we focused on four dimensions encompassed in the surveys' open-ended questions:
1) what did the students learn about themselves?;
2) what did they learn about the community?;
3) what was the most fulfilling project experience?; and
4) what was the most negative experience?

1) What did the students learn about themselves?
On the first dimension, students' self-evaluation shows a better understanding and awareness of their skills, reporting better teamwork skills:
- *"I have learned that I can contribute to the effectiveness of teamwork by decision making and applying persuasion techniques to maintain the team spirit. I learned that I can be a good task manager, and I have learned that I like to help the community. I feel happy and energised when I can be useful to the community."*
- *"I have learned that I prefer teamwork only when there is a good organisation and that positive feedback gives me a sense of well-being and makes me want to continue what I do."*

Further, students developed to some extent project management skills (planning, management, coordination) that they can employ:
- *"I can learn something in a very short time, that I have enough patience, that I can coordinate a team to a small extent."*
- *"I learned that I can take on more responsibilities and accomplish them step by step in an organised way."*

There was also evidence of team responsibilities and leadership:
- *"How to be a leader, organise activities and be accountable for certain mistakes."*

Moreover, students reported improved written, oral and online communication skills:
- *"How to communicate with people through social media, how to convey information to people through a single message, how to attract them to your page, how to turn something mundane into something beautiful, fun and enjoyable."*

Another significant achievement was that students learnt how to boost their intrinsic motivation and became aware of their impact on community life:

- *"I have learned how to communicate more effectively, and perhaps most importantly, I have learned about myself, that I don't have to wait for someone to motivate me to change something, but I have to look inside myself for that desire to get involved and bring more value to the community and in my own life."*

As students reported, the service-learning projects greatly impacted the perception and improvement of practical and interpersonal skills. This is most important for our Communication, Public Relations and Advertising students as they will eventually work in event planning, public relations, or marketing. Therefore, they need to improve their communication skills by working with others, in teams, or practical skills. The answers to the open-ended questions reinforced the conclusions of the two measurement scales included in the evaluation questionnaires. A significant relationship can be seen between students' community service self-efficacy and civic attitudes and skills (Culic & Pavelea, 2021), with increased civic involvement, leadership skills, and problem-solving skills felt by students at the end of the service-learning projects.

2) What did students learn about the community?

One interesting finding is emphasized by the second dimension of the open-ended questions: what students have learned about the community and how they perceived its needs and connected with its members. Not all the service-learning experiences were positive. Some students identified several negative aspects: often, the community is perceived as reluctant or uninterested in its problems, being civically or politically uninvolved:

- *"I have learned that it is difficult to convince and change the mentality and behaviours of this group in the community. We realised that in order to give continuity to the project and to achieve its objectives, the community must be analysed in depth. I have learned that the State does not provide the necessary support to this community."*

Students had a hard time communicating with the community representatives due to their reluctance to strangers or distrust:

- *"There are people who want to be helped, but there are few of them because not everyone trusts outsiders because they have had certain difficult situations and have been fooled in the past."*

Nonetheless, direct interaction with the community members and people of different backgrounds, ages and positions challenged students to be more empathetic tolerant, open to experiences, and more aware of their power to fight inequalities:

- *"We need to pay more attention to the needs of those around us because we never know how they feel."*
- *"The differences between generations and their mentalities are not so deep."*
- *"They want a change, they want a healthy environment, but the lack of information leads to the stagnation of this desire. Thus, if the community has the necessary support and knowledge, change will take place."*
- *"I can say that I have learned that at the moment, people in the community do not help each other and that those who need help the most are neglected because the world does not know how to get involved and do good, even if they are not necessarily part of large organisations."*

3) What was the most fulfilling project experience?

An essential part of the service-learning project's completion is the celebration phase, where positive and fulfilling experiences are highlighted and shared. Thus, when asked what they feel about their project, students emphasise that the most fulfilling experiences are seeing their communication skills improved, the ability to persuade, and change behaviours and mindsets, seen through the beneficiaries' participation and openness to project activities:

- *"I am grateful for the fact that I managed to find solutions, to find collaborators, and to maintain a relationship with them, and that I have met beautiful people who want a change, but especially, the most gratifying thing was that I managed to make a contribution to the community."*

Although only 30% of the students had previous experiences with volunteering during high school, and although in other courses they worked in freely chosen teams, the requirement of the service-learning project seemed challenging and new. This was because the students had to carry out (to deadlines) actual campaigns and activities actioned in the communities with colleagues they had never worked with before. So, one of the most fulfilling experiences perceived by the students at the end of the project was that they met the project requirement and restrictive conditions such as:

- *"That we managed to complete the project, although we had impediments in organising and changing the theme very near to the deadline."*

Moreover, the enthusiasm of the beneficiaries, their reactions, and their positive feedback made students more aware of the significant impact they have on others' lives:

- *"I was able to go to work with children, listen to them, give them gifts and see the joy on their faces."*
- *"Personally, what I enjoy the most is peoples' altruism. Thus, seeing people together in order to help each other gave me a feeling of well-being."*

4) What was the most negative experience?

Any new experience comes with a set of challenges; in this case, the negative feedback delivered by students highlights several aspects that can be improved in the future. Because students were assigned to project teams according to their alphabetical name order, they worked with new people and in unstructured teams. Some students perceived a lack of collaboration with colleagues as: *"the most unfulfilling experience ever"*. Others found a lack of communication and initiative from teammates: *"I'm sorry to say, but I didn't feel in an environment of (future) communication graduates"*. This happened even though we had intentionally assigned students to project teams and communicated it accordingly. We had also emphasised how they have to work with diverse types of people in their professional capacity and that this is a valuable opportunity for them to prepare for their future careers. Also, procrastination, the lack of community involvement and commitment, seen by a large number of refusals to participate in the project activities and poor communication with institutions and NGOs were also demotivating:

- *"The most negative experience refers to the impossibility of performing in-person activities (due to COVID), but also to the multiple refusals (or non-responses) from some people to whom I have asked for help."*

Negative experiences and challenges represent important feedback for future service-learning projects. There were delays in creating and implementing the projects, as the project's complexity was perceived to be high for a first-year student with no practical experience of implementing campaigns in the community and new to project management topics and service-learning. Future collaborations across different courses with faculty teaching PR campaigns, Corporate Social Responsibility and Event Planning are considered. A collaboration with a learning designer could be extremely useful in the future as it allows us to rethink active learning and teaching strategies (see also Forasacco & Freire, 2022, Chapter 4 in this book). Moreover, future service-learning projects should continue to emphasise the importance of team building activities, conflict resolution strategies, and time- and project-management discussions to reduce students' stress levels.

The course evaluation on the university's official platform offered another way to discover the students' perspective about the active learning process acquired through the service-learning projects. Out of five points, the course was evaluated with an overall grade of 4.64, summing up items such as the interest in the discipline, encouraging active class participation, assessing the context of acquiring new knowledge and skills, using real-life examples, and teacher performance.

From the students' feedback, we know that they have improved their interpersonal and leadership skills due to their active learning process. As previous experiences have shown, although students have reported improved leadership skills and confidence in their ability to improve the community's life, it is yet to be demonstrated that such improved skills will translate into their success in participating in future service-learning projects (Culic & Pavelea, 2021).

Teacher perspective – our reflections

Among the most valuable lessons learned from the service-learning project is that students have immense untapped potential. They graduate high school with valuable digital skills, entrepreneurial expertise, networking potential and social capital to help them build their service-learning experience. Service-learning projects provide students with the opportunity to experience real-life community contexts, to explore their own opinions and attitudes, to reflect upon societal differences, and as Godfrey et al. (2005) highlight, they open students' appetite for civic engagement, to help instil their moral responsibility for change in society.

At the same time, the collaboration between the University and other institutions is essential. The partnership with the New Horizons Foundation has been crucial for the success of our endeavour. With an expertise of over 18 years in service-learning projects in Romania, they have provided us with the necessary materials, links and social support to carry out a large project like this one involving 235 students. Their connection with the CLAYSS and Impact clubs all over Romania is also significant as excellent community relationships are needed. A service-learning centre is usually a valuable resource, as they have dedicated staff and expertise to build upon. Unfortunately, our university does not yet have one such centre, but examples from other countries have been beneficial.

Teacher expertise is essential, and during the first round of projects, we learned side by side with our students. Still, as we have learned, service-learning is a time-costly methodology, and it is extremely difficult to work with large groups of students. Also, when trying to connect the service-learning experience with research on this topic, several aspects need to be taken into consideration, like the ones listed by Conway et al. (2009) and Brandes and Randall (2011): 1) the duration and intensity of the service-learning programs, 2) the methodological designs which are not rigorous enough, 3) lacking control groups, 4) pre- and post-tests, 5) small sample size, 6) control for confounding variables, and, thus, 7) minor effects or mixed results. Connecting class topics with service-learning methodology, in some instances, can be challenging. Therefore, to support students in grasping abstract concepts and applying them in real-life settings while helping others, teachers need to encourage students to make them personally meaningful and constantly reflect on the experience (Chapman & Ferrari, 1999). Moreover, service-learning can become a significant source of accomplishment for teachers due to the large numbers of beneficiaries, the high student satisfaction rate, increased self-efficacy, improved skills, increased civic awareness, and change in beliefs and stereotypes.

What would we do differently?

Attention needs to be driven upon teamwork and team conflicts, as this was one of the most stringent aspects for our students. Not being able to choose the team members proved to be a difficult task for them, and combined with poor project-management skills, this was one of the most significant shortcomings.

Through working with Communication students, we have learned that there is a strong need to make all requirements explicit by communicating with them from the beginning of the project and explaining the importance of meeting strict deadlines. Any useful materials are a plus, such as previous projects developed by students, NGO examples and lists of potential partners. Smaller groups are not necessarily a plus, as, given the fair rate of dropouts, teams of 2 students are simply not viable for such a large group of students. Teachers can begin with larger groups of students as approximately one third of them will not make it to the 'finish line'. After assessing the number of individuals actively involved in the projects, reorganising groups could be an alternative after the first two weeks. Student-teacher and student-student communication are extremely important, yet personal interest and the freedom to choose the topic is also relevant. Setting major themes and allowing students to choose between the frames means facilitating their decision-making process. Monitoring projects with the provision of appropriate, timely scaffolding and feedback is imperative to facilitating student engagement for active learning. This year, we intend to encourage students to be bolder, address diverse communities, choose extreme users, out of their comfort zone, and challenge their limits to fulfil their unmet potential within their zone of proximal development (Vygotsky, 1978).

Section 4: Moving forward

Looking forward, we have selected several projects and would like to connect them with other organisations' agendas. Some have the potential to become national campaigns, and we want to encourage students' voices to reach -as far as possible- a wider audience. The sooner students can identify service-learning projects as thesis topics at an early stage of their career and follow their research interest throughout the university, the better. Also, service-learning experiences could represent a potential career path to follow after graduation in areas such as NGOs, social media, youth workers and training, human resources, event planning, social entrepreneurship, and public institutions.

Students have expressed the desire to continue their service-learning projects, and some of them have the potential to become business opportunities. Therefore, we have offered students' feedback to Career Centre management, and it has been taken into consideration for future events, like Career Days and Internship and Volunteering Fair. Furthermore, during their second year of study, students can identify business ideas and develop business plans, to find funding opportunities supported by national and international institutions (such as innovation funds dedicated to financing young people's entrepreneurial initiatives or funds for strengthening civil society), or to transform their service-learning ideas into community campaigns supported at a local level through the funding opportunities offered by public institutions (one example is the participatory budgeting project organised by Cluj City Hall, 2021).

Service-learning projects are also great opportunities to discover personal or community resources. They can identify similar interests, including relevant events, networks; projects; map community initiatives; identify internships and job openings. Moreover, service-learning projects could be a good start for research material. It is difficult to work with large numbers of students, but this could be a plus when thinking about sample sizes. Yet, it is essential to follow the guidelines offered by other researchers who have travelled this path and bear in mind the previously mentioned service-learning research shortcomings.

Conclusion

Teaching staff satisfaction at the end of the semester is highly influenced by the students' learning outcomes and engagement. Luckily, the service-learning projects, seen as an active learning experience, offer students the possibility to pinpoint the connection between theoretical and practical information and contexts and can and indeed should be included in the university curriculum. At the same time, service-learning projects are a good opportunity for universities to meet their triple mission: didactic, research and community involvement, and to increase their visibility, students being agents of universities multiplying image, and key figures in creating a more involved community and society.

We perceive the context of integrating a service-learning project into a university course as an extension of active learning, with many benefits for students' skills development and their civic involvement. These benefits include communication skills, team-building and management, sense-making skills, social intelligence, adaptability and flexibility, interdisciplinarity and many more - measured by the community service self-efficacy scale and civic attitudes and skills scale. We consider education to be not just knowledge but a winning combination of knowledge, skills, attitudes, and values.

In our relatively short history of implementing this active learning methodology, we have learned so far that our service-learning project can be time-consuming and, thus, can be more challenging to implement with a larger student cohort. However, we encourage other educators to integrate service-learning into their course requirements, firstly with a relatively small cohort. This active learning methodology has proven to be a very rewarding experience for teachers and students, community stakeholders, and the general public.

Acknowledgements

This work was supported by CORE - Communication and Social Innovation Research Centre, Babes-Bolyai University, Romania and by the 2021 Babes-Bolyai Development Fund.

About the Authors

Lorina Culic is a research assistant in the Faculty of Political, Administrative and Communication Science at Babes-Bolyai University, Romania. She can be contacted at this email: culic@fspac.ro.

Anisoara Pavelea is a Lecturer in the Department of Communication, Public Relations and Advertising at Babes-Bolyai University, Romania. She can be contacted at this email: pavelea@fspac.ro.

Bibliography

Allport, G. W. (1961). *Pattern and growth in personality*. New York: Holt, Rinehart and Winston.

Astin, A. W., & Sax, L. J. (1998). How undergraduates are affected by service participation. *Service Participation*, 39(3), 251-263.

Barrows, H. S., & Wee, K. N. L. (2007). *Principles and practice of a PBL*. Singapore: Pearson Prentice Hall.

Berson, J. S., & Younkin, W. F. (1998). Doing well by doing good: A study of the effects of a service-learning experience on student success. *Higher Education*, paper 184.

Bonwell, C. C., & Eison, J. A. (1991). Active learning: Creating excitement in the classroom. *ASHE ERIC Higher Education Report No. 1*, Washington, DC: George Washington University.

Brand, B. D., Brascia, K., & Sass, M. (2019). The community outreach model of service-learning: A case study of active learning and service-learning in a natural hazards, vulnerability, and risk class. *Higher Learning Research Communications*, 9(2), 1-18.

Brandes, K., & Randall, K. (2011). Service learning and civic responsibility: Assessing aggregate and individual level change. *International Journal of Teaching and Learning in Higher Education*, 23(1), 20-29.

Celio, C. I., Durlak, J., & Dymnicki, A. (2011). A meta-analysis of the impact of service-learning on students. *Journal of Experiential Education*, 34(2), 164-181.

Chapman, J. G., & Ferrari, J. R. (1999). An introduction to community-based service learning (CBSL). *Journal of Prevention & Intervention in the Community*, 18(1-2), 1-3.

Chi, M. T. H. (2009). Active-Constructive-Interactive: A conceptual framework for differentiating learning activities. Topics in Cognitive Science, 1, 73–105.

CLAYSS. (2022). Centro Latinoamericano de Aprendizaje y Servicio Solidario.

Conway, J. M., Amel, E. L., & Gerwien, D. P. (2009). Teaching and learning in the social context: A meta-analysis of service learning's effects on academic, personal, social, and citizenship outcomes. *Teaching of Psychology*, 36(4), 233-245.

Culic, L., & Pavelea, A. (2021). *Self-efficacy, attitudes and skills in service-learning projects of Romanian students* [Conference session]. UNISERVITATE II Global Symposium Service-Learning, Integral Education and Transformative Spirituality, Buenos Aires, Argentina, October 28-29, 2021.

Dilworth, R. L. (1996). Action learning: Bridging academic and workplace domains. *Journal of Workplace Learning*, 8(6), 45-53.

European University Association (2019). *Promoting active learning in universities*. Learning & Teaching Paper 5. Retrieved from https://www.eua.eu/resources/publications/814:promoting-active-learning-in-universities-thematic-peer-group-report.html .

Forasacco, E., & Freire, J. (2022). Using co-designed technology-enhanced learning to develop postgraduate STEMM students' research communication competencies. In K. Enomoto, R. Warner & C. Nygaard (Eds.), *Active learning in higher education* (pp. 83-106). Oxfordshire, U.K.: Libri Publishing Ltd.

Freeman, S., Eddy, S. L., McDonough, M., Smith, M. K., Okoroafor, N., Jordt, H., & Wenderoth, M. P. (2014). Active learning increases student performance in science, engineering, and mathematics. *Proceedings of the National Academy of Sciences of the United States of America*, 111(23), 8410–8415.

Gerholz, K. H., Liszt, V., & Klingsieck, K. B. (2018). Effects of learning design patterns in service learning courses. *Active Learning in Higher Education*, 19(1), 47-59.

Godfrey, P. C, Illes, L. M., & Berry, G. R. (2005). Creating breadth in business education through service-learning. *Academy of Management Learning & Education*, 4(3): 309–23.

Han, S. J., Lim, D. H., & Jung, E. (2021). A collaborative active learning model as a vehicle for online team learning in higher education. *Research Anthology on Developing Effective Online Learning Courses*, IGI Global, 217-236.

Heffernan, K. (2001). Service-learning in higher education. *Journal of Contemporary Water Research and Education*, 119(1), 2.

Hoeppner, A., & Reid, A. (2022). How voice students become professionals through active learning experiences. In K. Enomoto, R. Warner & C. Nygaard (Eds.), *Active learning in higher education* (pp. 35-62). Oxfordshire, U.K.: Libri Publishing Ltd.

Hollingsworth, P., & Lewis, G. (2006). *Active learning: increasing flow in the classroom*. Carmarthen, Wales: Crown House Publishing.

Hyun, J., Ediger, R., & Lee, D. (2017). Students' satisfaction on their learning process in active learning and traditional classrooms. *International Journal of Teaching and Learning in Higher Education*, 29(1), 108-118.

Isaías, P., Miranda, P., & Pifano, S. (2021). Learning with the practitioners: Defining and implementing active learning in higher education. In T. Bastiaens (Ed.), *Proceedings of EdMedia + Innovate Learning* (pp. 519-528).

United States: Association for the Advancement of Computing in Education (AACE).

Kolb, D. A. (1984). *Experiential learning: Experience as the source of learning and development*. Englewood Cliffs, NJ: Prentice-Hall.

Mezirow, J. (2009). An overview on transformative learning. In K. Illeris (Ed.), *Contemporary theories of learning: learning theorists...in their own words* (pp. 90-105). New York: Routledge.

Moely, B. E., Furco, A., & Reed, J. (2008). Charity and social change: The impact of individual preferences on service-learning outcomes. *Michigan Journal of Community Service Learning*, Fall 2008, 37-48.

Moely, B. E., Mercer, S. H., Ilustre, V., Miron, D., & McFarland, M. (2002). Psychometric properties and correlates of the civic attitudes and skills questionnaire (CASQ): A measure of students' attitudes related to service-learning. *Michigan Journal of Community Service Learning*, 8, 15–26.

New Horizons Foundation (2022). Retrieved from https://newhorizonsfoundation.com/about

Parker, K., & Igielnik, R. (2020). *On the cusp of adulthood and facing an uncertain future: What we know about Gen Z so far*. Pew Research Center.

Piaget, J. (1936). *Origins of intelligence in the child*. London: Routledge & Kegan Paul.

Prince, M. (2004). Does active learning work? A review of the research. *Journal of engineering education*, 93(3), 223-231.

Prober, C. G., & Khan, S. (2013). Medical education reimagined: a call to action. *Academic Medicine: Journal of the Association of American Medical Colleges*, 88(10), 1407–1410.

Reeb, R. N., Katsuyama, R. M., Sammon, J. A., & Yoder, D. S. (1998). The community self-efficacy scale: Evidence of reliability, construct validity, and pragmatic utility. *Michigan Journal of Community Service Learning*, 5, 48-57.

Regina, C., & Ferrara, C. (2017). *Service-learning in Central and Eastern Europe. Handbook for engaged teachers and students*. CLAYSS, México: Archivo Digital. Retrieved from https://www.clayss.org.ar/04_publicaciones/SL-EE_nov17.pdf

Rodríguez-Izquierdo, R. M. (2021). Does service learning affect the development of intercultural sensitivity? A study comparing students' progress in two different methodologies. *International Journal of Intercultural Relations*, 82, 99-108.

Rusu, A. (2020). *Education based on compassion and learning towards the community (Service-Learning)*. Cluj, Romania: Cluj University Press.

Rusu, A., Copaci, I. A., & Soos, A. (2015). The impact of service-learning on improving students' teacher training: Testing the efficiency of a tutoring program in increasing future teachers' civic attitudes, skills and self-efficacy. *Procedia - Social and Behavioural Sciences, 203*, 75–83.

Sosa Rolon, J. A. (2020). *Resourcebook for the development of service-learning projects.* CLAYSS, México: Archivo Digital. Retrieved from https://www.clayss.org.ar/04_publicaciones/ SLEasternEuropeResourcebook.pdf

United Nations Development Group. (2015). *Mainstreaming the 2030 Agenda for Sustainable Development. Interim Reference Guide to UN Country Teams.* Retrieved from https://www.undp.org/content/dam/undp/library/MDG/Post2015-SDG/UNDP-SDG-UNDG-Reference-Guide-UNCTs-2015.pdf.

Vygotsky, L. S. (1978). *Mind in society: The development of higher psychological processes.* Massachusetts: Harvard University Press.

Chapter 8
Fostering Active Learning Online Using Interactive Video Lectures

Luis da Vinha

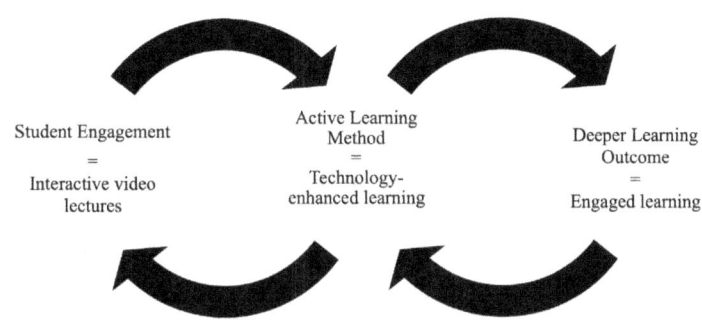

Introduction

My chapter contributes to this book, *Active Learning in Higher Education*, by detailing and discussing how I have developed and implemented Interactive Video Lectures (IVLs) in a broad array of undergraduate and graduate political science courses to transform passive educational materials into technology-enhanced active learning resources and increase student engagement with online content.

Over the past few decades, Australian universities have significantly increased their online presence (Norton et al., 2018). However, the COVID-19 pandemic forced universities to migrate all their teaching activities online quickly. This unexpected turn of events provided an opportunity to usher in and consolidate a new 'digital normalcy' in higher education (Williamson & Hogan, 2021). For instance, in Australia, most university lectures are already delivered online (synchronously or asynchronously), and it is expected that content delivery will be increasingly provided through this medium. While most Australian universities already employ lecture capture technology, which records classroom activities and makes that recording available electronically, the emerging paradigm in higher education compels us to rethink our online content (Halloran & Friday, 2018).

Besides using video recording studios and green screen rooms to provide higher quality educational media and videos, higher education staff, including teaching academics, are also increasingly producing more video and media content following the best pedagogical practices (see also Carloni (2022), Chapter 11 in this book). These include signalling key messages by incorporating cues, segmenting or chunking content into smaller parts, weeding unnecessary information, and providing information to target the different sensory modalities involved in learning.

However, merely producing quality educational media is not sufficient to keep students engaged in their learning process. It is argued that while traditional lecture videos have several benefits, they also risk providing a linear and passive, television-like experience – a.k.a., the 'couch-potato' effect – which can undermine the learning process by only contributing to superficial learning (Dror, 2008; Lord, 2002). More importantly, researchers such as Bawa (2016) also illustrate that student retention decreases in courses based solely on online delivery. Therefore, the main challenge for teachers is how to integrate active learning strategies that promote student engagement and learning when developing and producing online video content. In recent years there has been a growing emphasis on integrating interactive features in educational videos and media. Notably, university teaching academics are increasingly turning to IVLs – hyper-videos – to transform online videos from passive to active learning materials (Baker, 2016).

In this chapter, active learning is understood to be constituted by strategies where students assume centre stage in the (online) classroom and are encouraged to actively engage with each other, their instructors, and the content to enhance their learning experience. The chapter details how IVLs were used to address the institutional and educational challenges posed by the COVID-19 pandemic and increase the level of student engagement with the online video lectures.

When reading this chapter, you will gain the following insights:

1. what IVLs are and how they can be employed in university courses;

2. how to develop IVLs and use their multiple components to engage students; and

3. how IVLs can foster active learning.

Overview of main sections

This chapter has four main sections. In Section 1, I briefly discuss the concept of active learning, particularly in the context of online learning environments. Section 2 provides an overview of IVLs, highlighting their main characteristics and components. In particular, I explain how IVLs were employed as an innovative way of fostering active learning using video lectures. In Section 3, I reflect on how the use of IVLs contributed to fostering student engagement with course content and the broader institutional embrace of these tools. This is followed by Section 4 where I outline ways for improving my IVL-based active learning method to navigate future challenges. Finally, in the conclusion, I discuss the potential of further developing IVLs, increasing their integration with other active learning strategies, as well as challenges that require further reflection and consideration.

Section 1: The need for active learning in online environments

Considering the growing challenge in maintaining students' attention on political issues (see, for example, Majstorovic, 2001), teachers have increasingly tried to employ active learning strategies in their classrooms to foster greater student engagement with the specific course content and enhance learning outcomes (see Enomoto & Warner (2022), Chapter 5 in this book). Active learning is a very broad concept associated with a multitude of different learning strategies and, therefore, defies a single straightforward definition. However, common threads can be seen in the sense that active learning refers to any instructional methods that actively engage students in meaningful activities that enhance their learning of specific content (Carr et al., 2015:174). Despite some criticism (see Børte et al., 2020; Rochester, 2003), research has consistently demonstrated that active learning strategies promote student engagement and learning more effectively than traditional passive approaches (Wieman, 2017). While some differences in cultural contexts have been emphasised in the scholarly literature (see Fendos, 2018), on the whole, pedagogical studies tend to highlight that students in active learning classrooms:

- tend to outperform peers in traditional classrooms,
- exceed standardised grade expectations;
- learn more than in traditional lecture-based formats; and
- also have the opportunity to compensate for the loss of face-to-face time in the physical classroom (Baepler et al., 2016; Freeman et al., 2014).

In the particular context of surveying university political science programs, Archer and Miller (2011) found that most courses do not devote a significant proportion of their activities to active learning. While international relations courses score higher than the other subfields of political science, the overall percentage is relatively low, scoring less than 15 percent. Therefore, rather than allocating the bulk of their time to preparing and delivering lectures, emphasis has been placed on instructors to increasingly devote their resources to developing curriculums, lesson plans, and activities that maximise student learning through the inclusion of activities that foster greater student engagement with the content, and encourage critical and analytical thinking (Boyer, 2003). In fact, in recent years, there has been a growing number of studies highlighting a plethora of different activities and innovations used in political science classrooms to foster greater interactivity and engagement, ranging from board games (Hoy, 2018), to policy writing such as policy briefs and memos (Pennock, 2011), to real-world political simulations (Frank & Genauer, 2019).

In addition, this type of interactivity has been particularly difficult to emulate in virtual and remote educational environments. Some of these activities have been upscaled to online platforms using new educational technologies (see Biro, 2021; da Vinha, 2021). Nevertheless, video lectures continue to thwart instructors' best intentions in creating active and engaging content. Video-based learning is defined as *"the learning process of acquiring defined knowledge, competence, and skills with the systematic use of video resources"* (Giannakos et al., 2016: 1260). Video lectures are one form of video-based learning and have multiple advantages for students. More precisely, the following benefits have been identified in using video lectures (Giannakos et al., 2016; Kinash et al., 2015; Ozan & Ozarslan, 2016; Scagnoli et al., 2019) by way of:

- providing students with greater convenience and flexibility in their learning;
- assisting students in taking better notes of class content;
- assisting students in studying and reviewing for tests and exams;
- helping improve students' learning experience and outcomes;
- helping students obtain higher scores on final tests and exams.

Despite these advantages, research has also identified several challenges in engaging students with online videos. For instance, while Massive Open Online Courses (MOOCs) have considerably altered the educational environment by greatly increasing the dissemination of educational materials and connecting students, their ability to motivate students and keep them engaged is relatively low. Even when active learning strategies have been introduced in MOOCs, studies demonstrate that problems regarding communication and collaboration were pervasive (Topali et al., 2019). Research conducted by Guo et al., (2014) also found that the average student did not watch the entirety of their video lectures, with students watching under two-thirds of 9-12 minute lecture videos and less than half for 12-40 minute videos. Moreover, studies indicate that there is a correlation between online video lectures and retention. According to Geri et al. (2017a:101) *"the availability of online video lectures increases student dropout, even by students that are enrolled in face-to-face classes"* since the access to the content online contributes to procrastination and lack of participation with the other coursework.

To address some of these challenges, there has been an increasing emphasis on developing and implementing IVLs as a way of transforming online videos from passive to active learning materials in recent years. Palaigeorgiou and Papadopoulou (2019:86) argue that IVLs offer students a more participatory experience by allowing them to *"interact with sensitive regions of the video, answer questions, select how they would like the video story to develop, click on external links and access additional information"*. The authors emphasise that while instructors are still responsible for video design and development, *"students are able to actively engage with it [each video] and, therefore, their interest in exploring, thinking about, and discussing the presented ideas increases"* (Palaigeorgiou & Papadopoulou, 2019:86).

Research attests to the success of IVLs in fostering greater student engagement and learning by providing more opportunities for learner-content interaction and greater flexibility and non-linearity for students (Smithwick et al., 2018). Learner-content interaction is the process by which students engage directly with the course content in ways that transform their comprehension of the learning material (Moore, 1989). IVLs facilitate this process by providing multiple points of direct interaction with the content by allowing students to answer and place questions, access auxiliary sources and materials, and give them the opportunity to tailor their learning experience in accordance with their specific needs and requirements. Equally important, by involving students and giving them options in how they partake in their learning process, IVLs also foster reflection, which further contributes to higher-order thinking and learning (Harvey et al., 2016). As a result, students shift from passive recipients of content to active participants in developing their knowledge and understanding. IVLs also contribute to learning by reducing cognitive overload, guiding viewers' attention, and triggering students' reflection of the content (Palaigeorgiou & Papadopoulou, 2019). Finally, student enthusiasm also increases when using ILVs, since having choices on how to interact with the content provides an additional source of motivation for students to engage with the videos (Wachtler et al., 2016). Smithwick et al. (2018:41) have compared learning using IVLs to that of more traditional approaches, arguing that: *"the ability to conduct nonlinear searches, control the pace (and even content), and greater opportunities for repetition and self-pacing may be more similar to learning through reading in which microlevel (stopping, browsing) and macrolevel (seeking) activities can be pursued simultaneously."*

Section 2: Interactive video lectures and active learning

To address the challenges posed by COVID-19 and prepare for the new digital normalcy in Flinders University's International Relations and

Political Science program, I adopted the use of IVLs across a wide range of courses. More specifically, to stimulate greater student engagement and learning, I implemented IVLs in the following courses:

Academic level	Course code and title	Mode of delivery
Undergraduate	GOVT2003: The International Political System	Face-to-face (S1 2021)
Undergraduate	Research Methods in Political Science	Face-to-face (S2 2021) Online (S2 2021)
Undergraduate	INTR 7017: From Topic to Thesis: Honours Workshop	Face-to-face (S2 2021) Online (S2 2021)
Graduate	POAD 9045: Qualitative and Quantitative Research Methods	Face-to-face (S2 2021) Online (S2 2021)

Table 1: Courses with IVLs.

The courses were delivered during the 2021 academic year, both online and face-to-face, as detailed in Table 1. In the face-to-face courses, the tutorials and seminars were held in person, while all the lectures were delivered asynchronously online, using the IVLs. The IVLs were created using the Camtasia software for the production and post-production of the videos. The interactive features were embedded in the lecture videos, which were saved as Sharable Content Object Reference Models (SCORM) packages that allow for the "plug-and-play" functionality. Subsequently, videos were uploaded to the university's learning management system (LMS) – Flinders University Online (FLO). Following best technological and pedagogical practice, the IVLs offered a combination of the following methods of interaction:

- Embedded Questions & Quizzes;
- Embedded Hyperlinks;
- Embedded Content Hotspots.

Chapter 8

Embedded questions and quizzes

One of the most common interactive strategies in IVLs is to embed questions and/or quizzes in the video in order to cultivate more active or deeper lecture processing (van der Meij & Böckmann, 2021). Accordingly, the IVLs incorporated, on average, between 3-5 multiple-choice, true/false, and short answer questions. The results of the questions and quizzes did not count towards students' final evaluation, rather their use serves five distinct pedagogical objectives. The first objective is to foster engagement with the videos. As explained above, traditional video lectures are passive learning tools, and students often do not watch them completely or multitask their viewing with other activities. Embedding questions and quizzes compel the student to interact with the IVL as the video pauses automatically and will only recommence once the student answers the question. Accordingly, students are forced to engage with the content to proceed with the video. Secondly, the use of questions and quizzes fosters greater student reflection on the issue under consideration. It prompts them to articulate their understanding of the content, further enhancing their learning experience. As van der Meij and Böckmann (2021:236) argue *"Such questions can stimulate students' retrieval practice and can help them realise that they did not comprehend a message, or cannot remember key facts."* Thirdly, the use of questions and quizzes allows the instructor to assess whether students completed the assigned readings (Figure 1).

At the beginning of the semester, students are instructed to watch the video lectures only *after* completing the readings for each individual module. By embedding questions from the reading materials, instructors can gauge which students have completed the readings and assess whether students understood the content. This is particularly important for hybrid courses that blend online and face-to-face classes. Before each face-to-face tutorial, I reviewed the results for each week's video lecture questions. When specific questions received lower overall scores, I would reinforce the specific content in further detail in the subsequent tutorial to clarify any lingering misconceptions or misunderstandings. Finally, each question or quiz in the IVLs has a feedback mechanism that provides additional comments to students in accordance with their responses. When students answered incorrectly, the IVL provided the correct answer and directed them to the specific section(s) of the readings where they could find more details on this specific issue. This is particularly important considering that empirical research has shown that the presence of feedback in IVLs enhances learning (van der Meij & Böckmann, 2021).

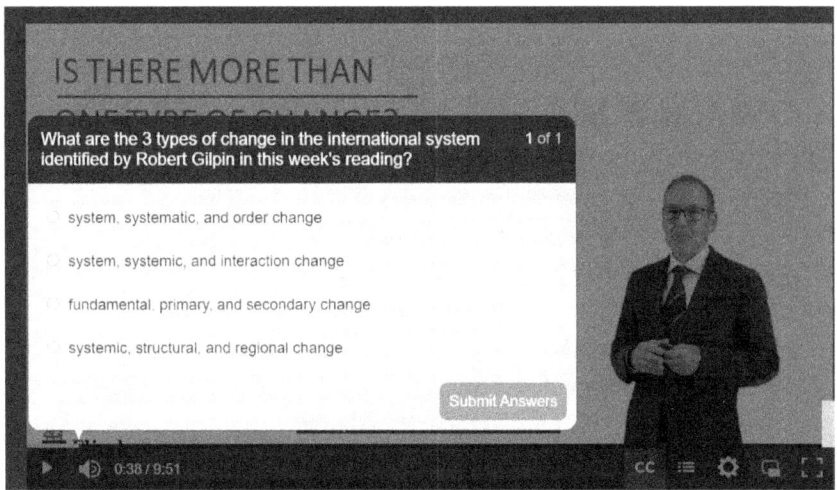

Figure 1: Example of an embedded question or quiz in IVL.

Embedded hyperlinks

The IVLs contained hyperlinks that allowed students to view and download (via pop-up windows) supplementary material used for the class, including additional readings, access to institutional websites (such as the United Nations, the International Monetary Fund and the World Trade Organisation), and other related digital media (interviews, documentaries, news sources, and other videos). By employing hyperlinks within the IVLs, not only do students have a greater opportunity to engage with the video, but they also multiply their resource accessibility by providing access to a plethora of additional information without exiting the video. Besides providing access to complementary sources, the use of hyperlinks further enabled students to actively tailor their learning experience by having the choice to access only the sources they chose.

In our videos, hyperlinks were added when I discussed new information or sources not listed in the assigned readings. For instance, as illustrated in Figure 2, when discussing economic development in the post-war era, we introduced a graphic to explain variation in income growth rates over a twenty-year period. We explained the graphic and its underlying rationale whilst also embedding a hyperlink to the original source. In this case, students could access the full article if they so desired, enhancing the resources available to them. To ensure all complementary resources were openly available to students, I only used publicly available sources (including institutional websites, news sources, and YouTube videos) or that can be accessed digitally through the Flinders University Library website (for example, e-books, articles and documentaries). When embedding the hyperlinks in the video lecture, the settings were configured to pause the video when students clicked on a link, only resuming when students returned to the video lecture.

Hyperlinks were also used to provide feedback on questions and quizzes in the lecture video. For instance, when providing students with feedback on the history of an international institution, I added a link that would encourage students to visit that organisation's institutional website. Moreover, by embedding hyperlinks with complementary readings, I was able to provide students with a more concise course syllabus that does not overwhelm students with 'unrealistic' expectations regarding the number of readings they are expected to complete – usually under the heading of 'suggested', 'secondary', or 'complementary' readings (Davidson, 2020).

Figure 2: Example of an embedded hyperlink in IVL.

Embedded content hotspots

Another strategy employed consisted of embedding content hotspots in the IVLs, allowing students to jump to specific parts of the video, typically divided into subsections according to the week's content. By employing greater interactivity with the subsections, students can have more proactive and unfettered access to video content based on thematic sections or search queries. This element is essential considering that *"browsing a non-interactive video is more difficult and time-consuming than browsing a textbook, because people have to view and listen to the video sequentially and thus searching for a specific portion remains a linear process"* (Zhang et al., 2005:17).

Moreover, the availability of searchable content hotspots also contributes to reducing students' cognitive load. Research demonstrates that with lengthier videos, students tend to use "frame-seeking" strategies to locate specific content, placing an additional cognitive burden on students that does not contribute to their learning (Costley et al., 2020). By providing tools that facilitate the identification of specific content using an interactive, searchable table of contents, students can easily find and access the information they are looking for without spending needless time and effort. For example, as we can verify in Figure 3, when discussing the institutions of global economic governance in the GOVT2003: The International Political System course, the IVL content is organised into the different international intuitions (e.g., International Monetary Fund, World Bank, World Trade Organization) and indicators on economic development. This allows students who want to view or review the material on, for instance, the International Monetary Fund, to open the content hotspot menu and click on the reference to that institution.

Chapter 8

Figure 3: Example of embedded searchable content hotspots in IVL.

Additionally, if a student wants to search for or review a particular topic associated with the institution, for instance, the "Washington Consensus", the student can type keywords into the search tab in the interactive table of contents. Then they click on any reference to the keyword term to be directed to that specific issue in the video. This last feature is only possible, however, if the IVL is closed captioned. Accordingly, all the IVLs referenced are closed captioned to maximise their interactivity and effectiveness. The students have the option of activating and deactivating the closed captions on all the videos. Equally important, by creating internal hotspots linked to different content sections in the videos, feedback on the embedded questions and quizzes can direct students to specific sections of the lecture for further review.

Moreover, considering the multiple interactive features included in the IVLs, the traditional "six-minute rule" can be supplanted by videos of more extended duration. As Lagerstrom et al. (2015:15) have concluded, IVLs provide the opportunity for employing a: *"however-many-minute rule"*. Accordingly, our video lectures were on average 15-20 minutes each, providing sufficient time to cover the content with a great degree of depth and detail. This is in line with recent research that demonstrates that adding interactive features in video lectures increased engagement.

More specifically, Geri et al. (2017b:42) found that *"the interactive layer, which was added to video lectures, allowed learners to significantly extend their attention span"* when analysing and comparing completion percentages in over 100,000 episodes of online video lectures before and after implementing interactive features.

The IVLs also generate analytic content, which allows the instructor to assess how the class is engaging with the videos and its multiple components, providing the opportunity for implementing real-time interventions and changes to improve student learning. These analytic features are integrated into the LMS, namely into the student gradebook. For example, the IVLs produce a record of the students that viewed each one of the lecture videos, identifying the number of times the students accessed the lecture video, the logon and logoff times, and the number of attempts answering the questions/quizzes and the scores.

Section 3: The outcome

As can be seen in Sections 1 and 2, the research has emphasised the tripartite value of IVLs for students, instructors, and educational institutions. An evaluation of the IVLs implemented in Flinders University's International Relations and Political Science program supports the aforementioned research findings. I will briefly discuss the outcomes regarding the student and teacher perspectives.

Student perspectives

While IVLs foster greater student engagement and contribute to student learning, their development is resource-intensive. However, their successful development and implementation have a significant return on investment. In our case, overall, the majority of the students completing the course viewed the IVLs and engaged with their functions, particularly the questions/quizzes. As we can verify in Figure 4, in the largest course where IVLs were employed – i.e., with over 70 students – almost half the students (47%) that completed the course viewed over 70% of the IVLs provided throughout the semester. This means that over two thirds of the students who completed the course viewed at least 10 of the 14 video lectures. This value is significant considering that research demonstrates that, traditionally, students watching video lectures is low (Costley et al., 2017). Moreover, even knowing the scores of the quizzes in the lecture videos did not affect their final evaluation, several students made several attempts to answer these questions/quizzes demonstrating their interest and involvement with the topic.

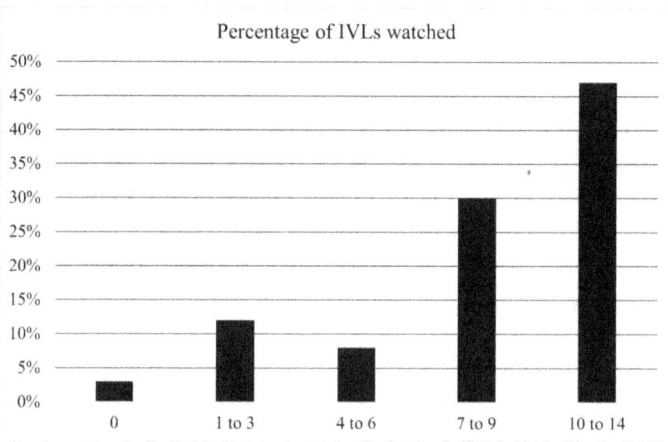

Figure 4: Student viewership of IVLs over the semester.

While student engagement with the IVLs was positive, when reviewing the level of engagement in the different courses over the semester, two aspects do merit consideration. The first is that student engagement with the lecture videos tended to decrease towards the end of the semester. This is consistent with research confirming that this decrease is a condition permeating all forms and levels of higher education, as students increasingly experience burnout over the semester and tend to be less motivated to engage (Maricuțoiu & Sulea, 2019). Secondly, with one exception, the levels of engagement with the IVLs were higher in the fully online courses. In other words, in courses where students had a face-to-face component, the level of engagement was lower. This was expected, as many students do not tend to review material after discussing it in class and address issues regarding any misunderstanding of the content in the classroom while the instructor is present. Nevertheless, in the course evaluations, students emphasised the quality and the utility of the IVLs in contributing to their engagement and learning of the content.

Teacher perspectives

The success of the development and implementation of IVLs in the courses identified above spurred Flinders University's College of Business, Government, and Law to organise several hands-on training workshops to further disseminate their use in other courses and programs. Accordingly, an initial session was organised in June 2021 to sensitise faculty to using the College's new recording studio and upgrade their videos with interactive features. During the month of September 2021, three subsequent workshops were structured as hands-on training sessions and organised for all interested College faculty staff. In these faculty-targeted workshops, I demonstrated how to use the Camtasia software to embed questions and quizzes, hyperlinks, and table of content hotspots in lecture videos and close caption the videos (even in other languages).

The importance of IVLs in fostering greater student engagement and learning was also acknowledged when the author was awarded the 2021 College of Business, Governments and Law's Vice-President and Executive Dean's Award for Excellence in Teaching and the 2021 Vice-Chancellor's Award for Teaching Innovation. New initiatives to continue to promote the use of IVLs are planned for the 2022 academic year. In particular, due to faculty demand, the College of Business, Government, and Law's online learning team has rolled out a host of interactive video and editing tools on the Kaltura online video platform already available at Flinders University. This is accompanied by other dissemination and promotional events, as well as technical support in using this platform to develop and create IVLs across several university colleges.

Section 4: Moving forward

The results of these initiatives are already visible across Flinders University, as several programs have embraced the use of IVLs or many of their components. For example, in the recently issued Teachers Guide 2021-22 for the Master of Arts in International Relations in Economy and Trade (MAIRET) program, many of the elements discussed in the training workshops are now recommended when producing video content, and the demo video available for consultation is an IVL developed and used in one of the courses referred to above. More specifically, the document states *"Advanced objectives: videos can be embedded with a table of contents, clickable URLs, quizzes and other feedback mechanisms (these can be automatically linked to a participation grade)"* (College of Business, Government and Law, 2021:6). Also, a new Master of International Relations was developed in which all core courses are structured around the use of IVLs. Similar recommendations are currently being discussed for upgrading the College's online Law program. Other faculties have also sought to implement IVLs in their courses. For instance, in early 2022, the College of Humanities, Arts and Social Sciences organised a session dedicated to interactive videos in their Teaching Preparation Week program. The author had the opportunity to showcase the benefits of IVLs, demonstrating their main components and operationalisation.

Initiatives such as these are critical since their use will be limited without adequate training on how to produce and employ IVLs. As mentioned above, the development – i.e., planning, production, and post-production – and implementation of IVLs is resource-intensive. As Hung et al. (2018:117) highlight *"creating an interactive video lecture is not just about recording a lecturing process; it involves a lot of effort from instructors and can be very time-consuming and challenging"*. Creating an IVL requires planning and organising the content (a.k.a., "storyboarding") in accordance with solid pedagogical methods, scripting the lecture, filming the video, editing the content, embedding the interactive features, generating the final interactive video, uploading to the LMS, and testing the IVL before release. Therefore, the initial development of each IVL discussed in this chapter took, on average, 6-8 hours to develop a 15-20 minute video lecture.

Also, the development of IVLs using Camtasia has additional challenges. To begin with, instructors need technical proficiency that goes beyond mere introductory editing knowledge (see Figure 5). The platform is complex and, for beginners, might impose a significant learning curve that can take time to master. In addition, Camtasia is only available by subscription and, therefore, instructors or institutions must purchase a license, incurring additional costs.

Figure 5: Example of Camtasia editing environment (with interactive features included).

However, as universities adopt strategies that focus on augmenting online learning options (OECD, 2021), resources are increasingly being attributed to help promote the successful employment of technologies. Also, an increasing number of software solutions and technologies – such as H5P – allow users to add interactive features to digital media (see Baker, 2016). IVLs are not a panacea for addressing the challenges that students, instructors, and institutions face with the increase of online delivery of content. IVLs need to be complemented with other forms of engagement, particularly strategies that foster greater learner-to-learner interactions. Several examples exist already – such as Perusall, Hypothes. Is – and provide options to enhance students' active involvement in their learning (Aturban et al., 2015; Clarke, 2021). In the immediate future, we seek to complement IVLs with these resources to further enhance student engagement and learning in the Flinders University's Government programs.

Conclusion

As discussed in Section 1, past research demonstrates that there are several advantages to employing IVLs in university topics (Harvey et al., 2016; Smithwick et al., 2018). More precisely, a growing body of evidence attests to their effectiveness in generating greater levels of student interactivity, self-control, personalisation, and engagement with learning (Najmi, 2021). While there as several challenges to successfully implementing IVLs in university courses, they are effective tools for transforming online videos from passive to active learning materials. The examples illustrated in this chapter attest that their benefits outweigh the costs of not using them. Ultimately, we should keep in mind Catherine Middlecamp's (2005:17) claim that *"If students do not engage, they are unlikely to learn."* Student engagement, particularly through active learning strategies, has long been understood as essential for learning. However, we must also consider Middlecamp's (2005:17) subsequent assertion that *"if we [instructors] do not engage, we are unlikely to engage our students"*. Therefore, it is incumbent on us as educators to also take advantage of the current challenges in higher education and embrace the opportunity to experiment and try to make students' educational experiences in the 21st century as engaging as possible.

About the Author

Luis da Vinha is a Lecturer and coordinator of the Master of International Relations at Flinders University in Australia. He can be contacted at this email: luis.davinha@flinders.edu.au

Bibliography

Archer, C., & Miller, M. (2011). Prioritizing active learning: An exploration of gateway courses in political science. *PS: Political Science & Politics*, 44(2), 429-434.

Aturban, M., Nelson, M., & Weigle, M. (2015). Quantifying orphaned annotations in hypothes.is. In Kapidakis S., Mazurek C., and Werla, M. (Eds.), *Research and advanced technology for digital libraries* (pp. 15-27). Cham: Springer.

Baepler, P., Walker, J., Brooks, C., Saichaie, K., & Petersen, C. (2016). *A guide to teaching in the active learning classroom: History, research, and practice*. Sterling: Stylus Publishing

Baker, A. (2016). Active learning with interactive videos: Creating student-guided learning materials. *Journal of Library & Information Services in Distance Learning*, 10(3-4), 79-87

Bawa, P. (2016). Retention in online courses: Exploring issues and solutions – A literature review. *SAGE Open, 6*(1), 1-11.

Biro, S. (2021). Reading in a time of crisis: Using Perusall to facilitate close reading and active discussion in the remote philosophy classroom. *Teaching Philosophy, 44*(3), 241-254.

Børte, K., Nesje, K., & Lillejord, S. (2020). Barriers to student active learning in higher education. *Teaching in Higher Education*, 1-19.

Boyer, M. (2003). The potential perils of slack (not pack) pedagogy: A response to J. Martin Rochester's remarks about active learning strategies. *International Studies Perspectives, 4*(4), 432-435.

Carloni, G. (2022). Pre-service second language teachers' co-design of virtual exchanges as a form of active learning in higher education. In K. Enomoto, R. Warner, & C. Nygaard, C. (Eds.), *Active learning in higher education* (pp. 263-288). Oxfordshire, U.K.: Libri Publishing Ltd.

Carr, R., Palmer, S., & Hagel, P. (2015). Active learning: The importance of developing a comprehensive measure. *Active Learning in Higher Education, 16*(3), 173-186.

Clarke, A. (2021). Perusall: Social learning platform for reading and annotating. *Journal of Political Science Education, 17*(1), 149-154.

College of Business, Government and Law (2021). *MAIRET Teachers Guide 2021-22*. Adelaide, SA: Flinders University.

Costley, J., Fanguy, M., Lange, C., & Baldwin, M. (2020). The effects of video lecture viewing strategies on cognitive load. *Journal of Computing in Higher Education, 33*, 19-38.

Costley, J., Hughes, C., & Lange, C. (2017). The effects of instructional design on student engagement with video lectures at cyber universities. *Journal of Information Technology Education: Research, 16*, 189-207.

da Vinha, L. (2021). Using hybrid simulations to enhance student learning of international relations theories. *Issues in Educational Research, 31*(3), 739-759.

Davidson, C. (2020). Quantity is not rigor. *Inside Higher Education*. Retrieved March 1, 2022, from https://www.insidehighered.com/advice/2020/05/13/academics-should-rethink-way-they-assign-homework-opinion

Dror, I. (2008). Technology enhanced learning: The good, the bad, and the ugly. *Pragmatics & Cognition, 16*(2), 215-223.

Enomoto, K., & Warner, R. (2022). Partnering with student leaders: active learning through integration of Peer Assisted Study Sessions into an undergraduate language course. In K. Enomoto, R. Warner, & C. Nygaard (Eds.), *Active learning in higher education* (pp. 107-134). Oxfordshire, U.K.: Libri Publishing Ltd.

Fendos, J. (2018). US experiences with STEM education reform and implications for Asia. *International Journal of Comparative Education and Development, 20*(1), 51-66.

Frank, R., & Genauer, J. (2019). A classroom simulation of the Syrian conflict. *PS: Political Science & Politics, 52*(4), 737-742.

Freeman, S., Eddy, S., McDonough, M., Smith, M., Okoroafor, N., Jordt, H., & Wenderoth, M. (2014). Active learning increases student performance in science, engineering, and mathematics. *Proceedings of the National Academy of Sciences, 111* (23), 8410-8415.

Geri, N., Winer, A., & Zaks, B. (2017a). Challenging the six-minute myth of online video lectures: Can interactivity expand the attention span of learners? *Online Journal of Applied Knowledge Management, 5*(1), 101-111.

Geri, N., Winer, A., & Zaks, B. (2017b). Probing the effect of interactivity in online video lectures on the attention span of students: A learning analytics approach. In Y. Eshet-Alkalai, I. Blau, A. Caspi, N. Geri, Y. Kalman, & V. Silber-Varod (Eds.), *Proceedings of the 12th Chais Conference for the study of innovation and learning technologies: Learning in the technological era* (pp. 39–44). Raanana: The Open University of Israel.

Giannakos, M., Jaccheri, L., & Krogstie, J. (2016). Exploring the relationship between video lecture usage patterns and students' attitudes. *British Journal of Educational Technology, 47*(6), 1259-1275.

Guo, P., Kim, J., & Rubin, R. (2014). How video production affects student engagement: An empirical study of MOOC videos. In *Proceedings of the first ACM conference on Learning@ Scale conference*, Atlanta, GA, 41-50.

Halloran, L., & Friday, C. (2018). *Can the universities of today lead learning for tomorrow? The university of the future.* Australia: Ernst & Young Global Limited.

Harvey, M., Coulson, D., & McMaugh, A. (2016). Towards a theory of the ecology of reflection: reflective practice for experiential learning in higher education. *Journal of University Teaching & Learning Practice, 13*(2), 3-21.

Hoy, B. (2018). Teaching history with custom-built board games. *Simulation & Gaming, 49*(2), 115-133.

Hung, I., Kinshuk, & Chen, N. (2018). Embodied interactive video lectures for improving learning comprehension and retention. *Computers & Education, 117*, 116-131.

Kinash, S., Knight, D., & McLean, M. (2015). Does digital scholarship through online lectures affect student learning? *Journal of Educational Technology & Society, 18*(2), 129-139.

Lagerstrom, L., Johanes, P., & Ponsukcharoen, U. (2015). *The myth of the six minute rule: Student engagement with online videos*. 122nd American Society for Engineering Education Annual Conference & Exposition, Seattle, WA.

Lord, T. (2002). Are we cultivating 'couch potatoes' in our college science lectures. In National Science Teachers Association (Eds.), *Innovative techniques for large-group instruction* (pp. 5-8). Arlington, VA: NSTA Press.

Majstorovic, S. (2001). Short attention spans and glazed eyes: Teaching world politics in the university trenches. *International Studies Perspectives*, 2(4), 1.

Maricuțoiu, L., & Sulea, C. (2019). Evolution of self-efficacy, student engagement and student burnout during a semester. A multilevel structural equation modeling approach. *Learning and Individual Differences*, 76, 1-7.

Middlecamp, C. (2005). The art of engagement. *Peer Review*, 7(2), 17–20.

Moore, M. (1989). Editorial: Three types of interaction. *American Journal of Distance Education*, 3(2), 1-7.

Najmi, A. (2021). A framework for formative assessment within interactive video lectures and its relation to reading comprehension skills. *Life Science Journal*, 18(3), 32-41.

Norton, A., Cherastidtham, I., & Mackey, W. (2018). *Mapping Australian higher education 2018*. Carlton, VIC: Grattan Institute.

OECD (2021). *The state of higher education: One year into the COVID-19 pandemic*. Organisation for Economic Co-operation and Development.

Ozan, O., & Ozarslan, Y. (2016). Video lecture watching behaviors of learners in online courses. *Educational Media International*, 53(1), 27-41.

Palaigeorgiou, G., & Papadopoulou, A. (2019). Promoting self-paced learning in the elementary classroom with interactive video, an online course platform and tablets. *Education and Information Technologies*, 24(1), 805-823.

Pennock, A. (2011). The case for using policy writing in undergraduate political science courses. *PS: Political Science & Politics*, 44(1), 141-146.

Rochester, J. (2003). The potential perils of pack pedagogy, or why international studies educators should be gun-shy of adopting active and cooperative learning strategies. *International Studies Perspectives*, 4(1).

Scagnoli, N., Choo, J., & Tian, J. (2019). Students' insights on the use of video lectures in online classes. *British Journal of Educational Technology*, 50(1), 399-414.

Smithwick, E., Baxter, E., Kim, K., Edel-Malizia, S., Rocco, S., & Blackstock, D. (2018). Interactive videos enhance learning about social-ecological systems. *Journal of Geography*, 117(1), 40-49.

Topali, P., Ortega-Arranz, A., Er. E., Martinez-Monés, A., Villagrá-Sobrino, S., & Dimitriadis, Y. (2019). Exploring the problems experienced by learners in a MOOC implementing active learning pedagogies. In M. Calise, C. Kloos,

J. Reich, J. Ruiperez-Valiente & M. Wirsing (Eds.), *Digital education: At the MOOC crossroads where the interests of academia and business converge* (pp. 81-90). Switzerland: Springer.

van der Meij, H., & Böckmann, L. (2021). Effects of embedded questions in recorded lectures. *Journal of Computing in Higher Education, 33*(1), 235-254.

Wachtler, J., Hubmann, M., Zöhrer, H., & Ebner, M. (2016). An analysis of the use and effect of questions in interactive learning-videos. *Smart Learning Environments, 3*(1), 1-16.

Wieman, C. (2017). *Improving how universities teach science: Lessons from the science education initiative.* Cambridge, MA: Harvard University Press.

Williamson, B., & Hogan, A. (2021). *Pandemic privatisation in higher education: Edtech and university reform (summary of research findings).* Brussels, Belgium: Education International Research.

Zhang, D., Zhou, L., Briggs, R., & Nunamaker Jr, J. (2005). Instructional video in e-learning: Assessing the impact of interactive video on learning effectiveness. *Information & Management, 43*(1), 15-27.

Chapter 9

Using Active Learning to Help Retention Rates for Women in Engineering through a Virtual Undergraduate Mentorship Program

Kristina Rigden

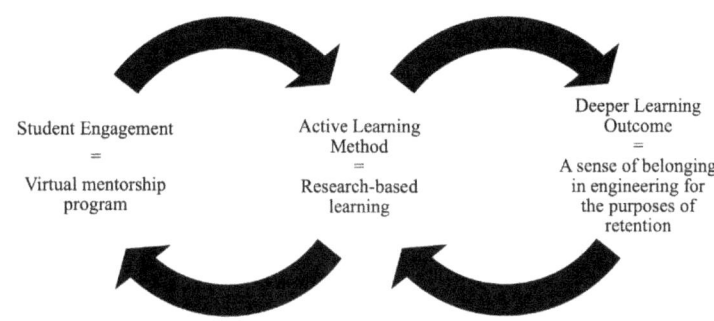

Introduction

With my chapter, I contribute to this book, *Active Learning in Higher Education,* by showing how I have used a virtual mentorship program to engage undergraduate engineering students who identify as female in research-based learning to develop their sense of belonging and improve their retention effectively. The mentorship program utilised active learning in the form of research-based learning within Maslow's (1943) Hierarchy of Needs framework, with a focus on belonging and social relationships. Using research-based learning helped students develop competencies, analysis, and reflection, allowing them to construct their knowledge (Vazquez Parra, 2021). In this case, I define active learning as a process that engages students in their learning process by taking part in an academic and social support network. This perspective enables students to establish a network to create and develop a sense of belonging by involving students in all aspects of a university community (Beck & Malley, 2003) to assist undergraduate student retention.

When reading this chapter, you will gain an understanding of:

1. research-based learning as it pertains to retention of women in engineering;

2. the implementation of a virtual multi-mode mentorship program;

3. implications for cohort two of the program.

In this chapter, I address the issue of whether the mentorship program assisted peer mentors and mentees in developing an engineering identity. The findings will discuss how the mentees, peer mentors, industry mentors and teacher mentors interacted through the sessions provided. Then, the findings of programmatic activities will discuss the different components of the mentorship program and suggestions that the participants offered to the program for the launch of cohort two.

Overview of main sections

The chapter has four main sections. In Section 1, I explain research-based learning related to Maslow's (1943) Hierarchy of Needs framework. Research-based learning was chosen as the foundation for this project within the framework of Maslow's (1943) Hierarchy of Needs to assist the students in developing their sense of belonging in engineering for retention. In Section 2, I then describe the virtual multi-mode mentorship program and the different stakeholders involved in the program. Section 3 describes the program's outcome with the mentees, peer mentors and industry and teacher mentors. In Section 4, I outline implications for practice before I conclude this chapter.

Section 1: The background for active learning

Active learning has students involved in their learning process. An essential part of active learning is student activity and engagement (Prince, 2004), as when students participate and engage with the content, they become self-directed learners. For this chapter, students use research-based learning, a form of active learning in the multi-mode mentoring program, to create an academic and social support network for female undergraduate students in engineering. Research-based learning was selected for this project within Maslow's (1943) Hierarchy of Needs framework to assist the students to enhance their professional actions through participation in this mentorship program (Behrmann, 2019). Students' professional actions refer to undergraduate student retention of program participants. A humanistic pedagogical orientation of Maslow's (1943) Hierarchy of Needs was also used by Jaunzems-Fernuk (2022, Chapter 12 in this book) for pre-service teachers within their health methods courses.

Why we use active learning

The daunting American statistics of women in engineering are evidence of the disadvantages that society is encountering with the shortage that occurs as talented women are lost through the engineering higher education pipeline. According to the American Society for Engineering Education, 21.9% of engineering bachelor's degrees were awarded to females in 2018, increasing from 17.8% in 2009 (Roy, 2018; Gibbons, 2009). This shows that there has been a 4.1 percentage point increase in the last nine years, indicating that some progress is being made in engineering for female students.

This multi-mode mentoring program was developed and implemented in the 2020-2021 academic year at California State Polytechnic University, Pomona (Cal Poly Pomona), to further increase female engineering enrolment and persistence. The purpose is to provide students with an increased sense of belonging and awareness of how the engineering profession is valuable and positively impacts society. Based on the preliminary work by Rigden (2021), this chapter presents how research-based learning guided this virtual mentorship program. Program implementation was funded by a United States Engineering Information Foundation grant.

Active learning theory and methodology

The pilot of this undergraduate mentorship program had a single research focus. This was to establish how peer mentors and mentees, through involvement in this program, develop a sense of belonging through an enhanced engineering identity; with the goal of greater retention in the profession. The sense of belonging refers to the peer mentors and mentees belonging within the Cal Poly Pomona community. The research question is: How are peer mentors and mentees developing a sense of belonging with engineering identity for retention through participation in this female-serving mentorship and undergraduate research program? The research question is grounded in the pedagogy of belonging with Maslow's (1943) Hierarchy of Needs framework.

A sense of belonging is crucial in university settings for students to succeed. As Sibley (2006) articulates, belonging is a state of social inclusion, and a pedagogy of belonging takes the method and practice of teaching and applies it to a sense of belonging. A pedagogy of belonging shapes a person's self-identity, norms and values (Matheson & Sutcliffe, 2017). These *"social and academic interactions shape how students experience belonging in college"* (Fry & Schell, 2019:174). If students feel they do not fit in at a higher education institution, they may be more inclined to withdraw from the institution (Meeuwisse et al., 2009). Therefore, higher education institutions need to increase a sense of belonging by involving students in all aspects of a university community (Beck & Malley, 2003). The university community comprises both the classes that students are taking and students' involvement in academic or social clubs, volunteering, and student success programs.

A pedagogy of belonging is within Maslow's (1943) Hierarchy of Needs framework. Abraham Maslow (1943:372) first developed his basic needs framework as an attempt to formulate a positive theory of motivation in his paper "A Theory of Human Motivation". His basic needs had five stages:

1. The physiological needs: homeostasis meaning breathing, eating and drinking

2. The safety needs: orderly, predictable and organised world with personal, mental and physical safety

3. The love needs: love, affection and belongingness explained as *"He*

will hunger for affectionate relations with people in general, namely, for a place in his group, and he will strive with great intensity to achieve this goal." (Maslow, 1943:381).

4. The esteem needs: desire for a stable and high evaluation of themselves, self-respect, self-esteem and for the esteem of others

5. The need for self-actualization: for an individual to reach full potential in their life. Examples include making music, writing poetry, being an athlete, or the desire to be an ideal mother.

People can move from one stage to the next if their needs are met. If the needs are unmet, people would remain at that stage and not be able to move up the hierarchy of needs. From the five stages presented above, belonging is stage three and is a basic human need dependent on social relationships (Floyd Smith et al., 2012). If stage three is unmet, *"…it may become the bottleneck in the goal to improve learning outcomes and achieve educational objectives"* (Floyd Smith et al., 2012:2). This shows the importance of the sense of belonging among students in an academic setting.

Within this academic setting, mentoring needs to take place. Mentoring partnerships with cross-age peer mentoring and industry-based mentors can provide solid foundations for a diverse engineering pipeline, including women and underrepresented minorities (Ilumoka et al., 2017). Üst and Kepez (2022, Chapter 6 in this book) acknowledge a thriving learning community should offer mentorship from experts. Additionally, cross-cultural differences and similarities can strengthen the mentorship relationship since the mentors and mentees discuss their different experiences and perspectives (Fry & Schell, 2019). To promote this demographic, *"no amount of technological gadgetry, pedagogical innovation, or financial intervention can replace the person-to-person bond of encouragement forged in a structured and intentional mentoring relationship"* (Ilumoka et al., 2017:15). This reiterates the importance of mentoring, especially with the female population.

Section 2: The case of active learning

The multi-mode mentoring program implemented activities to increase female engineering students' recruitment, retention, and graduation through a mentoring network that includes undergraduate research engagement plus social, academic, and professional support. A *"woman's engineering identification may be increased by helping students understand how engineering is useful and increasing their sense of belonging in engineering"* (Bossart & Bharti, 2017:128). It is not necessarily that female engineering students who leave the major lack the academic capability of succeeding. Instead, they may leave because of their perception of the engineering profession and lack a sense of belonging. This program intervened by exposing students to female role models who positively contribute to society and a sense of belonging. The mentoring model incorporated the following stakeholders and is also illustrated in Figure 1:

1. Mentee: Female lowerclassman defined as first and second-year students majoring in engineering;

2. Peer Mentor: Female upperclassman majoring in engineering, acting as mentors for the mentees;

3. Industry Mentor: Female engineering professionals and/or alumnae of Cal Poly Pomona acting as mentors for mentees and peer mentors during group mentoring sessions;

4. Teacher Mentor: Female engineering teachers at Cal Poly Pomona acting as mentors for mentees and peer mentors during group mentoring sessions.

Mentees participated in group mentoring (11 mentees: 1 peer mentor) and one-on-one mentoring with their peer mentors, and group mentoring with industry and teacher mentors. Peer mentoring can draw on relatable experiences, and *"…peers can provide emotional and psychological support that facilitates individual learning and career success"* (Parker et al., 2008:490). Industry mentors and teacher mentors provided mentoring to mentees and peer mentors electronically utilising email, social media and video conferencing, known as "E-Mentoring". E-Mentoring provides an accessible and cost-effective method for mentors to communicate with mentees. When subject-based mentoring (engineering) is utilised, interventions that seek to recruit and retain females in engineering are more likely to be successful (Ilumoka et al., 2017). The above interactions included a resumé review, interview preparation, and examples of engineering's positive impact on society.

The purpose of the program was to identify factors of engineering identity for retention through participation in this mentorship and undergraduate research program. This mixed-method study had the following participants: 34 mentees, three peer mentors, nine industry mentors, and two teacher mentors. The basis of analysis was developed from the literature of pedagogy of belonging by involving students in all aspects of a university community (Beck & Malley, 2003), Maslow's (1943) Hierarchy of Needs framework and mentoring partnerships (Ilumoka et al., 2017).

The mentees and the mentors were grouped by major or field of study and profession. The Group 1 peer mentor majored in mechanical engineering, with the mentees majoring in mechanical engineering, aerospace engineering and electrical engineering. The three industry mentors worked in the field of electrical engineering. The Group 2 peer mentor majored in electronic systems engineering, with the mentees majoring in electromechanical engineering, chemical engineering, industrial engineering and manufacturing engineering. The three industry mentors worked in the field of chemical engineering and industrial engineering. The Group 3 peer mentor majored in computer engineering, with the mentees majoring in computer engineering and civil engineering. The three industry mentors worked in the field of civil engineering and systems engineering. The incentive for the peer mentors participating in the program was to add this experience to their curriculum vitae and network with the industry mentors to secure an internship during university or employment after graduation. Since the mentees were first or second-year students at the university, they were encouraged to participate to get to know their classmates and the university environment. The teacher mentors volunteered their time as part of their personal commitment to broaden and diversify the pipeline of future engineers. The industry mentors volunteered since they had previously been involved with the women in the engineering program. The peer mentors met with their mentees a cumulative two hours a month. The mentees and peer mentors met with their industry mentors and teacher mentors two hours a month, every other month.

An overview of how students work with active learning

Research-based learning, a form of active learning, aims to improve students' motivation for learning to improve interactivity and collaboration

(Dafik et al., 2019). This collaboration was used in the peer mentoring groups to enhance student attitudes and retention (Prince, 2004). This collaboration and learning environment is essential for women in engineering to retain, persist and graduate. The multi-mode mentoring program assisted with this objective to build a sense of belonging among the women in the program through the program goals listed below. The following were the program goals and objectives:

1. Create an academic and social support network for female engineering students.

2. Increase awareness of how engineers make a positive impact on society.

3. Increase career and internship opportunities for female engineering students.

4. Increase female engineering student participation in undergraduate research.

5. Increase recruitment, retention and graduation of female engineering students by fostering a supportive community and enriching their experiences within the College of Engineering.

The mentees and peer mentors achieved these goals and objectives through their participation in the program. Mentees and peer mentors attended welcome events, an engineering club fair and regularly met with their industry and teacher mentors. They also attended sessions with an engineering career counsellor and the university Office of Undergraduate Research about getting involved in research. The sessions covered the topics: resume and cover letter writing, interviewing skills, time management and study skills. These activities of the mentorship program are described further below.

How I prepare and organise active learning

The multi-mode mentorship program ran from August 2020 to April 2021. The program consisted of virtual sessions and meetings between the mentees, peer mentors, industry mentors and teacher mentors. The mentorship program model is illustrated in Figure 1, and Table 1 shows the dates, events, and number of attendees for the program duration.

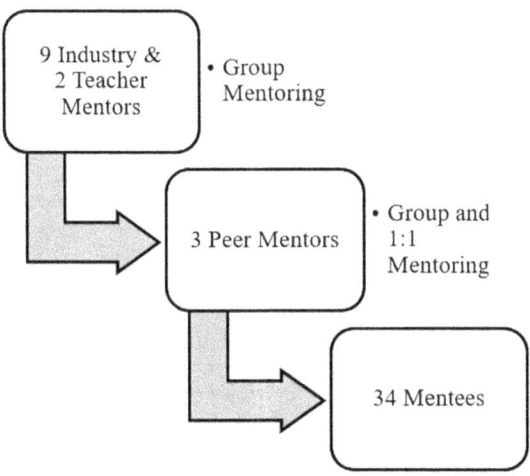

Figure 1: Mentorship model.

Date	Event	Attendees
August 27, 2020	Welcome Event for new engineering female students. Announcement of a new mentorship program with mentee and peer mentor link to enrol.	40 undergraduate engineering students, 1 industry guest speaker, 3 student guest speakers and 2 staff members
September 1, 2020	Welcome Back Event for female engineering teachers. Announcement of new mentorship program with teacher mentor link to enrol.	7 engineering teachers, 1 industry guest speaker and 2 staff members
September 3, 2020	Engineering Club Fair on Discord (a free voice, video and text app) for new engineering students. Announcement of new mentorship program with mentee and peer mentor link to enrol.	33 undergraduate engineering students and 2 student guest speakers

Date	Event	Attendees
September 24, 2020	Women in Engineering meeting for engineering female students. Announcement of new mentorship program with mentee and peer mentor link to enrol.	51 undergraduate engineering students, 2 industry guest speakers and 2 staff members
October 1, 2020	Applications due for mentees, peer mentors, industry mentors and teacher mentors.	
October 5, 2020	Written communication sent to all participants with list of events, Institutional Review Board (IRB) consent forms, and expectations of participating in the program.	34 mentees, 3 peer mentors, 9 industry mentors and 2 teacher mentors
October 8, 2020	Mentee and peer mentor 2 hour session with an engineering career counsellor. Topic: Resume and Cover Letter Review, and Interviewing Skills	17 undergraduate engineering students, 1 guest speaker and 2 staff members
October 20, 2020	First session with mentees and peer mentors. Topic: Orientation, ice-breaker activity, mentees meet peer mentors	21 mentees, 3 peer mentors and 2 staff members
October 22, 2020	Session. Topic: How to get hired in the industry	23 undergraduate engineering students, 6 industry guest speakers and 2 staff members
November 5, 2020	Mentee and peer mentor session. Topic: Time management, studying, SMART goals: Specific, Measurable, Achievable, Realistic and within a Time Frame	9 mentees, 3 peer mentors and 2 staff members
November 10, 2020	Mentee, peer mentor and industry mentor first session. Topic: Industry mentor orientation, mentees and peer mentors meet industry mentors END OF FALL SEMESTER	6 industry mentors, 2 peer mentors, 13 mentees and 2 staff members

Date	Event	Attendees
January 26, 2021	BEGINNING OF SPRING SEMESTER Mentee, peer mentor and industry session. Topic: Working in the engineering industry	9 industry mentors, 3 peer mentors, 22 mentees and 1 staff member
February 2, 2021	Mentee, peer mentor and teacher mentor first session. Topic: Teacher mentor orientation	2 teacher mentors, 3 peer mentors, 11 mentees and 2 staff members
February 5, 2021	Women in Engineering meeting for engineering female students. Topic: Alumnae Talk	35 undergraduate engineering students, 1 industry guest speaker and 2 staff members
February 9, 2021	Women in Engineering meeting for engineering female students. Topic: Alumnae Talk	35 undergraduate engineering students, 1 industry guest speaker and 2 staff members
February 18, 2021	Mentee, peer mentor and industry mentor session. Topic: Getting internships/jobs in the engineering industry	4 industry mentors, 3 peer mentors, 11 mentees and 2 staff members
February 23, 2021	Mentee and peer mentor session. Topic: Cal Poly Pomona Office of Undergraduate Research guest speaker, how to get involved in research	3 peer mentors, 9 mentees, 1 guest speaker and 2 staff members
March 5, 2021	Women in Engineering meeting for engineering female students. Topic: Alumnae Guest Speaker	13 undergraduate engineering students, 1 guest speaker and 2 staff members
March 16, 2021	Mentee and peer mentor session. Topic: Guest Speaker from Cal Poly Pomona Career Centre Resume and Cover Letter Writing	3 peer mentors, 9 mentees, 1 guest speaker and 2 staff members

Date	Event	Attendees
April 8, 2021	Mentee, peer mentor and industry mentor session. Topic: Writing a resume and cover letter to get hired in the engineering industry	6 industry mentors, 3 peer mentors, 8 mentees and 2 staff members
April 16, 2021	Mentee, peer mentor and teacher mentor session. Topic: Graduate university and getting involved in undergraduate research	2 teacher mentors, 3 peer mentors, 5 mentees and 2 staff members
April 20, 2021	Mentee and peer mentor session. Topic: Building relations and connections, networking	3 peer mentors, 3 mentees and 2 staff members
April 22, 2021	Women in Engineering meeting for engineering female students. Topic: Resume and interviewing tips from the engineering industry	15 undergraduate engineering students, 2 guest speakers and 2 staff members

Table 1: Academic-year calendar with virtual events and number of attendees.

Regarding Table 1, many industry guest speakers and student guest speakers were industry mentors and peer mentors, respectively. The two staff members were employees of the university that manage the mentorship program in addition to their other duties for the College of Engineering. The staff members regularly attended every session, and it should be disclosed that the author was a staff member in attendance. Additional guest speakers were brought into the virtual sessions to discuss resume and cover letter reviews, interviewing, engineering industry work, and undergraduate research.

Section 3: The outcome

For the purpose of collecting data, the researcher conducted six one-hour virtual observations, four interviews with the industry mentors and teacher mentors and two focus groups with the mentees and peer mentors. Twenty-one out of 34 mentees took the pre-test survey, and seven out of 34 mentees took the post-test survey. The post-test response rate was low because the survey had to be conducted at the end of the academic year. Although there was multiple follow-up for the mentees to complete the electronic survey, they did not. Therefore, to obtain further qualitative data, the researcher also engaged in document collection consisting of curricula and mentee assignments. The data collected addressed the following research question: '*How are peer mentors and mentees developing a sense of belonging with engineering identity for retention through participation in this female-serving mentorship and undergraduate research program?*'

In this section, based on the collected data, viewpoints of the mentees, peer mentors and industry and teacher mentors will be discussed from their standpoints through interviews and focus groups, including results from the pre-test and post-test survey taken. The participant perspectives, including the program activities, attendance, and sessions, will be discussed as part of the outcome of the multi-mode mentoring program. Lastly, my perspective will be detailed regarding the program sessions offered.

Mentees and Peer Mentors

There were several participants in this program: mentees, peer mentors, industry mentors, and teacher mentors interacting with each other and through the sessions provided. Starting with the mentees and peer mentors, the peer mentors thought the mentees were engaged when they did attend the sessions. A peer mentor reported the sessions gave the mentees:

- "*...a sense of purpose, a community that cared about them; especially in an online environment where [mentees] might not see anyone their age for literal months at a time.*"

This comment was attributed to the COVID-19 pandemic when the State of California, United States, was shut down and all classes were 100% remote. This response is exhibited in the pre-test, and post-test mentee survey with an increase of 56% agree/strongly agree who feel part of the engineering community and a 51% agree/strongly agree increase in personal growth through participation in the program, as seen in Figure 2. One peer mentor remarked:

- *"When the mentees were in the meetings, they were always really engaged, always asking questions, answering questions well, not just like 1 or 2 words, but actually engaging in the conversation."*

This related to peer mentoring support (Parker et al., 2008) and the mentees having peer mentors, industry mentors and teacher mentors. All peer mentors said they would have liked more mentees in their group (originally 11) since there was declining attendance throughout the program, evidenced in Table 1. But besides this fact, the mentees mentioned that the mentorship program's presence was always there throughout the year, and they liked having scheduled time to meet with their peer mentor. It made organising such interactions easier since this was already on their calendar for the academic year.

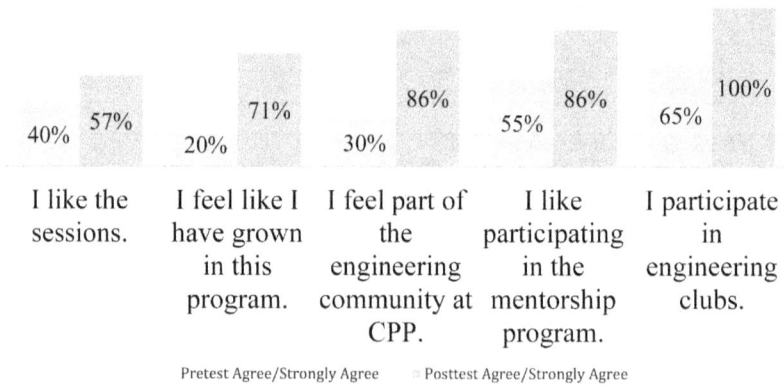

Figure 2: Mentee's participation in the program.

Regarding the mentees and their retention through the program, one industry mentor remarked:

- "It's interesting to see that a lot of the experiences I had many, many years ago are still relevant and persistent today. And just being able to give them confidence that you can persevere and get through these, and things will work out."

Mentees speaking with the industry mentors was helpful for them to see how the industry mentors made it through university, graduated and are now working in the industry as successful engineers. One mentee remarked:

- "I have really enjoyed this program and am really thankful for the opportunity to have this program because otherwise I honestly don't think I'd ever...have the opportunity to actually see the women in STEM (Science, Technology, Engineering and Mathematics) fields that are currently taking hands-on to their career and just being an example for us and what we can do, and how far we can go, and what our ideas are right now, how our careers can change and not necessarily be the same thing, but we end up where we need to be."

The mentees indicated a growth of 46% agree/strongly agree from the pre-test and post-test survey that they like the industry mentors, as shown in Figure 3. The industry mentors conveyed the real-life implications of being an engineer and their daily life in the profession.

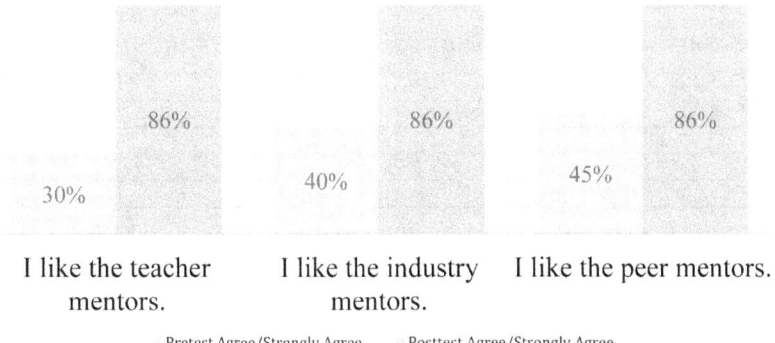

Figure 3: Mentee's interaction with mentors.

While the mentees demonstrated growth on several pre-test and post-test survey indicators, there was a decline on two survey questions. The survey question *"I have a lot of friends who are NOT engineering majors"* decreased from 55% agree/strongly agree pre-test to 29% agree/strongly agree post-test. This can be attributed to the mentees (70% first-year) making friends outside their major during the virtual academic year, which assists their social inclusion (Sibley, 2006). In addition, there was a nine-percentage point decline from 80% agree/strongly agree pre-test to 71% agree/strongly agree post-test on the survey question *"I like my engineering major"*. This can be connected to the mentors in the program and the mentees learning more about their engineering major and the possibility of switching majors due to learning more about the other eight undergraduate engineering and engineering technology majors in the College of Engineering.

Industry Mentors

One peer mentor described the mentees' interaction with the industry mentors as highly engaged and:

+ *"...a very nice way to get comfortable, to talk to industry people, and see them more as like, you know, people who have also gone through that, our experiences."*

One industry mentor remarked that:

+ *"if you can create a connection with the students between the mentors and the mentees, you know that's the first step, is establishing that connection. But then really to cement it and bond, you have to get their engagement, if you will. It's their investment in terms of the relationship. And I think when you've got that combination, you begin to establish a sense of belonging between the students and the engineering program. It's a bit of an investment, if you will, of their time and commitment, and with that comes that sense of belonging."*

These shared experiences provided a strong foundation for the mentorship program (Ilumoka et al., 2017). Two peer mentors remarked that the industry mentor sessions were their favourite sessions. One mentee said the small breakout groups (within the virtual meeting room) with the industry mentors:

- *"felt more personal, and it was really nice building relationships."*

Throughout the sessions, the industry mentors were able to share more in-depth and ask mentees questions at the end of the sessions. One industry mentor said it is vital for those younger women participating in the program to see that there were women out in the industry that had successful careers in varying fields, and that there was a path for them in engineering. The industry mentors also liked the structured mentorship program, with all sessions being scheduled and the content managed by the program. Since all of the sessions were conducted virtually through Zoom (a teleconferencing software program), the peer mentors commented that they would prefer the industry mentoring in-person the following academic year if possible.

Teacher Mentors

For the duration of the mentorship program, there were only two teacher mentors. One was from the Aerospace Engineering department, and the other teacher was from the Industrial and Manufacturing department. During the teacher mentoring sessions, the teachers discussed their experiences and opportunities available to students. The teacher mentors enjoyed their time with the mentees and sharing advice. One of the teacher mentors mentioned:

- *"I think it's really interesting when we talk about certain things and everyone is just like "Ah yeah, I feel like I know how it feels," and you know there are some students that often time, they already know how to handle that better and actually share it with others. So, it's really, I really enjoy it. The time that I had with them."*

Programmatic Activities

There were different components of the mentorship program and suggestions that the participants offered to the program for the launch of cohort two. The first meeting of the mentorship program introduced all of the program participants to the program's goals and objectives (shown above). The peer mentors conducted a *get to know you* game virtually with the mentees using Kahoot, a free game-based learning platform. The second meeting had a second *get to know you* game with the peer mentors and mentees in small breakout rooms (breakout rooms allow one to split the Zoom meeting into up to 50 separate sessions) on Zoom. These ice-breaker activities helped all the participants to get to know each other as the program commenced.

Declining Attendance

Continuous communication created a sense of belonging (Sibley, 2006) in the mentorship program. The peer mentors were instructed to connect with their mentees between the scheduled sessions. One peer mentor communicated by group text messaging and email. Two peer mentors communicated by group text messaging and the platform Discord. While the additional communication was utilised, it may not have been effective at retaining mentees to attend sessions, and attendance declined throughout the program with only three mentees at the last session. Part of this declining attendance could be attributed to Zoom fatigue, which is tiredness or burnout associated with overusing Zoom (Lee, 2020).

Additionally, while mentees knew about the time commitment involved when they signed up for the program, mentees may not have fully engaged with their mentors due to poor matching, building a relationship with their peer mentor or engagement (Art of Mentoring, 2019). One teacher mentor also encouraged her students to attend the sessions and participate in the program. While the students verbally confirmed that they would attend the sessions, none showed up to the virtual sessions. All sessions were held during lunchtime, 12:00 pm to 1:00 pm, when student clubs have meetings, and other events are happening during this time, which could have been attributed to the low attendance rate of the mentees.

Since the peer mentors followed up individually with their mentees, several mentees acknowledged missing the meetings and sessions. One mentee said:

- *"I've been a bit inactive with mentee sessions because I had some stuff going on, and I wanted to apologise for that, but I also can't make it to today's meeting because I have class. I'm sorry for not letting you know sooner, and I hope you're doing okay."*

Another mentee said:
- *"I'm sorry I have not been attending because of a busy schedule and some family issues. I would like to attend in the future, but this school year has been a bit of a struggle. I know I would like to rejoin once things get better for me."*

Lastly, a mentee said of her absence:
- *"I'm sorry I didn't show up the other day. I'm not sure why I thought the meeting was on Thursday. Sometimes I get a little overwhelmed with everything going on."*

These messages from the mentees put the program attendance into perspective when the mentees expressed difficulty with managing their schedule virtually. Furthermore, it was mentioned by a peer mentor that there should be:
- *more conversations about mentees' interests, what they enjoy, what they are passionate about. Like even as simple as what TV shows they enjoy."*

Having the mentees engage with each other, and their mentors build upon the program's cohort model. The cohort model can help sustain retention and have the mentees build friendships instead of just logging into the sessions and being in the same group every time. In the past, when the programming of the Women in Engineering (WE) events was in-person, there would be lots of social activities, such as a recreational paint class for the students. This mentorship program was academic and focused on creating a sense of belonging, as illustrated by Bossart and Bharti (2017), by involving all aspects of engineering mentorship, from peer mentors to industry mentors to teacher mentors. Involving a social component, even if it is done virtually or hybrid, can build upon retention in this program.

Sessions

A staff member who managed the mentorship program set up all the Zoom sessions for the participants and continuously emailed out reminders and calendar invitations. There were different facilitators for the different sessions, including the Cal Poly Pomona Office of Undergraduate Research, the engineering career counsellor, the mentorship program staff, and the peer mentors. The breakout groups were also kept small during the Zoom sessions, from three to ten people. One peer mentor remarked to keep the breakout groups small:

- "...because if we keep increasing the amount of mentees, some people might not be comfortable, and I feel it's easier to lose students because the larger the group, it's easier to disconnect. I mean, I felt that way with the many student clubs I've joined in the past because it's harder to connect with either your mentor or the other mentees. So I feel like keeping smaller groups to take our time to make that quality connection. I feel like that will retain more of our students."

An industry mentor felt that this mentorship program can be used as:

- "...a recruitment tool because students are looking, not just at what the university offers academically, but also what it offers from a support standpoint. And the diversity of the university, how it embraces that within the context of the overall culture."

The university can promote this mentorship program as a form of professional networking to recruit incoming female students majoring in engineering. This industry mentor also explained the value of diversity and creating an inclusive work environment:

- "So now people aren't told when they come in the door or even when they are at the university, here's how you need to act, here's how you need to speak and here's how you need to fit into a cultural norm. They're told to bring the diversity of their perspective, their experiences, and we recognize the value in not all being groupthink participants, but in fact having a diverse perspective, experience and point of view."

There were mixed opinions on what the favourite session was for the mentees. One peer mentor believed the time management session was the most helpful for the mentees because most mentees were first-year university students coming from high school and:

- "...it's very different from university, and I think that was really helpful for them."

Another peer mentor believed the resume workshop with the engineering career counsellor was the mentees' favourite session, and the mentees concurred with this information in the focus group.

Teacher Sessions

Because of scheduling conflicts, there were only two teacher mentoring sessions. One peer mentor thought there was only one teacher mentoring session because the session was forgetful, *"didn't have much impact"*, and didn't feel like the teacher mentors were trying to build a relationship with the mentees. Another peer mentor thought:

- *"...the teachers in general; they didn't connect with the mentees. I felt like the mentees related to [industry mentors] more than the teacher mentors. Whereas I felt like the teachers were kind of scary people from above. Um, but I mean, the conversation was so great in terms of the teacher."*

When this was further probed, the peer mentor did not think a teacher from each engineering department was needed. This was not the case with the industry mentors from different engineering fields because the peer mentor believed the mentees created a relationship with the industry mentors, unlike the teacher mentors. Student mentorship is not part of the teacher research, tenure and promotion requirement at Cal Poly Pomona; therefore, many teachers do not volunteer their time to mentor students. From this feedback, it seems that stage three of Maslow's (1943) Hierarchy of Needs, belonging and dependent on social relationships (Floyd Smith et al., 2012) was not achieved. This portion of the mentorship program will be revised for cohort two of the program.

Hybrid

An industry mentor believed that cohort two of the mentorship program should be:

- *"...in-person or opportunities to have some sort of additional networking events, but then also continue to do things virtually. It supports everyone. It kind of allows additional participation for those that it is too challenging to get to the university. And then I think, I would love to be able to have some sort of in-person connection as well. But I also understand that that might be a little bit before we get there too."*

The hybrid modality was brought up by all participants moving forward with cohort two. It was reminded that the mentees need to get comfortable face-to-face again because most workplaces require people to engage in interdisciplinary teams (Matheson & Sutcliffe, 2017).

Teacher Perspective – my reflections

Two peer mentors mentioned that the teacher mentors did not connect to the mentees as the industry mentors did. Even though the mentees expressed a 56% increase agree/strongly agree on the pre-test and post-test survey regarding the teacher mentors, as seen in Figure 3, there was no additional follow-up from the teacher mentors or encouragement to join their research project/laboratory. This specific program component will be revised to encourage more teachers to motivate the students in their journey as engineering students and get more involved in undergraduate research. The idea for revising this program is to have a WeChat with teachers, and students from different engineering majors will be invited. Teachers will present their current research projects, and students will be invited to participate. More teachers will present at the WeChat while also mentoring students throughout the academic year since teachers are already working on their research projects. This idea came from one of the teacher mentors who remarked that it is easier to mentor a group of students in her laboratory since she is already working on her research. The students can create a relationship with each other. This teacher mentor community will help students create a sense of belonging by involving them in undergraduate research, introducing them to other mentees organically and getting involved in the university community (Beck & Malley, 2003). Teacher mentors of all genders will participate in cohort two of this program to expose mentees to several different teachers and their current research projects.

During the interviews and focus groups, one teacher mentor, two peer mentors and three industry mentors mentioned how the questions during the sessions were repetitive. One peer mentor commented:

- *"There is one thing I disliked about the program actually; it was the questions. A lot of them were repeating. In our breakout rooms, especially with our industry mentors, they would be like, we already answered this, like let's just skip these questions and move on...then as the [sessions] progressed, it should be shorter questions, not a long list of questions. So, then we'll have the time to have discussions at the end."*

This component will be revised for cohort two to develop different questions by involving other stakeholders and participants. This will be discussed further in Section 4. One industry mentor had requested a list of her mentees and their attendance at the sessions because she was not sure if she was repeating herself to the mentees or if she had the same mentees or different mentees in her Zoom breakout group. In the future, a live, updated Google Doc will be provided to every industry and teacher mentor with this information. The staff of the program and the three peer mentors had access to this document, but it was never shared with the industry or teacher mentors. Mentors having access to the same document may help hold all participants accountable.

Section 4: Moving Forward

Retention throughout the program was difficult in regard to mentee participation. The peer mentors reached out to their mentees using email, group text messaging and Discord, but the attendance rate remained low at the sessions. This can be attributed to Zoom fatigue and mentees being overwhelmed with their virtual schedule. Moving forward for cohort two, a hybrid model with some sessions virtual and some sessions in-person (like teacher mentoring) may engage the mentees to attend. In addition, social activities like a paint class, whether in-person, hybrid or virtual, may help with retention. Restructuring the teacher mentoring component will assist in integrating undergraduate research into the program. This WeChat (described above) will enable teachers to present their research, and students will be invited to participate in their research projects. This would enable more teachers to participate as mentors and get students involved in undergraduate research.

Developing diverse questions that are short will help avoid repetition during the sessions. The staff of the program developed the questions for cohort one. For cohort two, having peer, industry, and teacher mentors help develop the questions will make it collaborative. For the industry and teacher mentors, a live and updated Google Doc will be provided that will have attendance and discussion question topics. Hence, there is no repetition, and the mentors will get to know their mentees better. This document can help hold all participants accountable throughout the program.

It would be interesting to see the dynamic of this mentorship program with mixed-gender mentees and mentors. More research would need to be conducted on a hybrid or entirely in-person mentorship program using the same population of undergraduate women in engineering to see if a sense of belonging is created. Moreover, it may be possible that individual interviews with mentees or peer mentors may yield different results of the questions based upon group consensus in a focus group.

Conclusion

When students participate in active learning, they engage in the learning process to create an academic and social support network. This mentorship program used research-based learning, a form of active learning, within the framework of Maslow's (1943) Hierarchy of Needs to assist the students in developing their sense of belonging in engineering for retention. Retention of the mentees attending the sessions was difficult, even though 56% of mentees agree/strongly agree they feel part of the engineering community at Cal Poly Pomona. The mentees enjoyed the mentors of the program, evidenced in Figure 2. The mentors enjoyed the sessions and interacting with the mentees. Retention, teacher sessions, questions during the sessions and organisation of the participants will be improved upon for cohort two of the program.

This research-based program determined if peer mentors and mentees developed a sense of belonging with engineering identity for retention through participation in this mentorship program. The program consisted of sessions and one-on-one and small group mentoring using humanism as Maslow's (1943) Hierarchy of Needs as the program's theoretical framework. The multiple forms of mentors were helpful. The results showed that peer mentors and mentees developed a sense of belonging through the program.

Acknowledgement

This work was supported by a United States Engineering Information Foundation 2020-2021 grant.

About the Author

Kristina Rigden is a Research Development Officer at California State University, Fullerton, USA. Previously, she was the Director, Outreach and Women in Engineering at California State Polytechnic University, Pomona, USA. She can be contacted at this email: krigden@fullerton.edu

Bibliography

Art of Mentoring (2019). The common pitfalls in mentoring programs. Retrieved from https://artofmentoring.net/the-common-pitfalls-in-mentoring-programs

Beck, M., & Malley, J. (2003). A pedagogy of belonging. *Reclaiming Children and Youth, 7*(3), 133-137.

Behrmann, L. (2019). The halo effect as a teaching tool for fostering research-based learning. *European Journal of Educational Research, 8*(2), 433-441.

Bossart, J., & Bharti, N. (2017). Women in engineering: Insight into why some engineering departments have more success in recruiting and graduating women. *American Journal of Engineering Education, 8*(2), 127-140.

Dafik, Sucianto, B., Irvan, M., & Rohim, M. A. (2019). The analysis of student metacognition skill in solving rainbow connection problem under the implementation of research-based learning model. *International Journal of Instruction, 12*(4), 593-610.

Floyd Smith, T., Wilson, D., Carlson Jones, D., Plett, M., Bates, R. A., & Veilleux, N. M. (2012). Investigation of belonging for engineering and science undergraduates by year in school. *American Society for Engineering Education Conference and Exposition*, San Antonio, Texas, 1-11.

Fry, J. J., & Schell, J. (2019). Through a pedagogy of belonging: Creating cross-cultural bridges in doctoral programs. *Texas Education Review, 8*(1), 169-179.

Gibbons, M. T. (2009). Engineering by the numbers – Samples from the profiles by year. *American Society for Engineering Education.* 11-47.

Ilumoka, A., Milanovic, I., & Grant, N. (2017). An effective industry-based mentoring approach for the recruitment of women and minorities in engineering. *Journal of STEM Education, 18*(3), 13-19.

Jaunzems-Fernuk, J. (2022). Tracking the mental well-being of pre-service teachers in post-secondary health methods courses. In K. Enomoto, R. Warner & C. Nygaard (Eds.), *Active learning in higher education* (pp. 289-318). Oxfordshire, UK: Libri Publishing Ltd.

Lee, J. (2020). A neuropsychological exploration of Zoom fatigue. *Psychiatric Times, 17*, 2-6.

Parker, P., Hall, D. T., & Kram, K. E. (2008). Peer coaching: A relational process for accelerating career learning. *Academy of Management Learning & Education, 7*(4), 487-503.

Prince, M. (2004). Does active learning work? A review of the research. *Journal of Engineering Education, 93*(3), 223- 231.

Maslow, A. H. (1943). A theory of human motivation. *Psychological Review, 50*, 370-396.

Matheson, R., & Sutcliffe, M. (2017). Creating belonging and transformation through the adoption of flexible pedagogies in master's level international business management students. *Teaching in Higher Education, 22*(1), 15-29.

Meeuwisse, M., Severiens, S. E., & Born, M. (2009). Learning environments, interaction, sense of belonging and study success in ethnically diverse student groups. *Research in Higher Education 51*(6), 528–545.

Rigden, K. (2021). Women in engineering multi-mode mentoring and undergraduate research (WEM3UR): Semester 1. *Collaborative Network for Engineering and Computing Diversity (CoNECD) Conference*, virtual, United States.

Roy, J. (2018). Engineering by the numbers – Samples from the profiles by year. *American Society for Engineering Education*. 1-40.

Sibley, D. (2006). Inclusions/exclusions in rural space. In P. Cloke, T. Marsden & P. Mooney (Eds.), *The handbook of rural studies* (pp. 402–410). London: Sage Publications Ltd.

Üst, S., & Kepez, O. (2022). Impact of learning space design on students' experiences in an active learning classroom. In K. Enomoto, R. Warner & C. Nygaard (Eds.), *Active learning in higher education* (pp. 135-152). Oxfordshire, UK: Libri Publishing Ltd.

Vazquez Parra, J. C. (2021). How to trigger research-based learning in the classroom? *Institute for the Future of Education*. Retrieved from https://observatory.tec.mx/edu-bits-2/research-based-learning

Chapter 10
Constructing the Employable Graduate through Active Learning Projects

Sarah Swann

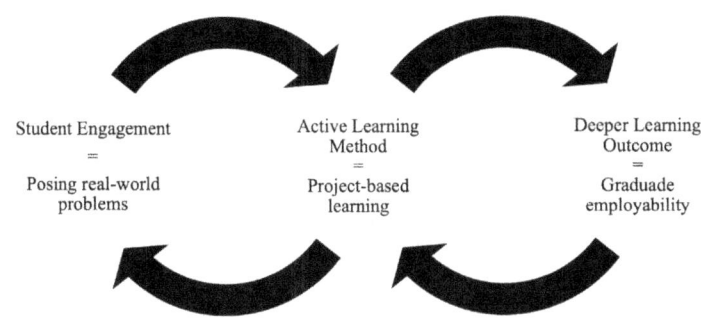

Introduction

My chapter contributes to this book, *Active Learning in Higher Education*, by showing how I have engaged students to pose real-world problems using project-based learning to enhance their graduate employability productively. Rather than being an 'add-on', employability is progressively embedded into a core spine of double-weighted modules on the BA (Hons) Childhood Studies degree at Leeds Beckett University. Our focus is on the third and final-year (L6) module, The Graduate Self, the design of which is underpinned by an adapted version of the Montessori trinity. The final year of any degree is significant since it marks the final transition from student to graduate and hopefully progression into postgraduate training or highly skilled employment. This module supports graduate employability through the Legacy Project assessment where students pose a real-world problem, issue, or challenge pertinent to children, young people, or families within a specific professional setting, which they then seek to solve.

We chose the word 'legacy' precisely because it delineates the quality of human potential and the possibility of passing something on. This altruistic goal is core to the whole landscape of working with and for children and families, but as an active learning assignment, what students choose to impart and how they accomplish this reveals a great deal about their volition. Crucially, the Legacy Project also facilitates students to gain a more focused sense of career trajectory. Through practical experiences, students reflect on the nature of their potential professional fit, or misfit, to specific career sectors: education, healthcare, social care, youth justice, creative arts and design, or counselling professions.

The definition of active learning that resonates with the learning and teaching philosophy on the BA (Hons) Childhood Studies degree is simple: students' deliberate efforts to construct knowledge from practical experience. Reflection or 'dialogue with self' is promoted both within our curriculum and the design of our summative assessments for The Graduate Self module because reflection is an essential skill for the workplace. To understand active learning, this chapter uses qualitative data from the summative assessment that formed part of The Graduate Self module. The rationale was that summative assessments were active learning activities that students engaged with most intensely.

When reading this chapter, you will gain the following three insights:
1. the main strengths of giving freedom and flexibility to students in how they choose to organise their work experiences to explore what they want;

2. the emotional dimensions of work experiences from the student perspective;

3. a demonstration of how the broad skill and knowledge base studying an undergraduate degree with work experience can provide and the breadth of career opportunities this could yield.

The chapter will primarily be of interest to readers looking to boost their employability metrics, but through these lenses, we anticipate the reader will reflect on broader epistemic questions regarding the role of the contemporary university in creating employable graduates; how teaching methods might support students to 'try on' different career identities;

as well as what 'counts' as graduate knowledge and skills for the future workforce.

Overview of main sections

This chapter has four main sections. Section 1 discusses the national policy context and the institutional objectives of active learning on the BA (Hons) Childhood Studies degree. Following this, the theoretical and methodology section describes how we integrated three key principles from the Montessori framework. Section 2 summarises our course design and details our case for active learning by introducing the Legacy Project as a mode of assessment across all our employability modules. To be helpful to the reader, we also provide descriptions of some of the material resources we used in practice. In Section 3, I review students' experiences within different work experience contexts and explore rewards and challenges from the teacher's perspective. The examples discussed here show students encountering an unpredictable situation, improvising, and deploying various coping tactics. Students' efforts to actively construct their knowledge varied, and students who were intrinsically motivated and had the emotional capacity to identify and act upon opportunities made the highest gains. Section 4 sets out key points about the lessons that have been learned to inspire and guide the journey forward.

Section 1: The background to active learning

The Legacy Project was the first step to reverse the underperformance of students entering highly skilled employment at the course level. The progression of graduates into 'highly skilled' jobs is one metric of success used in the Teaching Excellence Framework (TEF), by which universities in the UK are ranked. Rankings allow students to make an informed choice over which universities to apply for and where to accept when offers come in, although they are controversial in terms of what and how they measure (Frankham, 2017; Sayer, 2015). Since securing a graduate job with higher earnings is one important motivation to study in higher education, it is vital to design a curriculum allowing students to transition successfully into well-paid employment. With significant social change, and as advanced skills have become more important, nearly 50% of young people progress onto higher education in the UK (OECD, 2021).

However, while politicians often rationalise higher education in the UK as the engine of social mobility, the present reality is that the *"average mobility rate across all universities is 1.3%"* (Britton et al., 2021:2). Drawing on the Longitudinal Education Outcomes (LEO) dataset to document mobility rates for each university, subject and course in England, Britton et al.'s (2021) study operationalises mobility rates in terms of the share of students in each university, subject or course who were both eligible for free school meals (FSM) and reached the top 20% of the income distribution at age 30. This study shows that 5% of students who attended Leeds Beckett University in the mid-2000s were eligible for free school meals (FSM), and 15.1% of this cohort then reached the top 20% of the income distribution at age 30. This equates to a social mobility rate of just 0.8% compared to the benchmark of 4%. While the data is historical, it is one of the few studies to unravel disparities in mobility rates between different subjects at different universities and across different regions. This corroborates previous observations that higher education's neo-liberal 'deal' in exchange for social mobility and higher earnings does not pay off equitably (Belfield et al., 2018; De Vries, 2014). Whilst they are highly educated, students in the UK are likely to leave higher education heavily indebted in 2022, which arguably creates a double-bind for disadvantaged students.

This University has made progress by increasing applications from diverse groups and receives applications from all socioeconomic groups, but the largest number comes from the lowest socioeconomic group. While the TEF submission indicated that students achieved excellent outcomes for the University's full-time students in respect to retention and progression to employment and further study, the University was, in line with the national picture, below benchmark in progression to highly skilled employment or further study, teaching and assessment and feedback. This shortfall created the objectives and targets in the next access and participation plan (APP).

Highly skilled occupations are defined in the Office for National Statistics' (ONS, 2020) hierarchy as any within categories 1-3 of the nine Standard Occupational Classifications. This includes Managers, Directors, and Senior Officials; Professional Occupations; and Associate

Professional Occupations. A brief critique of this classification now follows as we examine how active learning on our degree connects to the reward of highly skilled graduate employment. In terms of students' employment destinations after the BA (Hons) Childhood Studies degree, the students who progress onto postgraduate training courses and qualify and work as teachers, social workers, and nurses will be classed as 'Professionals'. Conversely, a graduate who enters employment directly as a nursery nurse or assistant, playworker or teaching assistant will fall three rungs short of 'highly skilled' work into category 6: Caring, Leisure and Other Service Occupations.

While occupying a relatively lowly professional status in the graduate job hierarchy, these roles have traditionally been popular graduate destinations for our student cohorts and demand a high level of care and skill. For instance, a large portion of any nursery assistant's day involves extended periods of interacting with children aged 0-4. We later see some of the mastery this entails in the snapshots taken from the student caring for other critical workers' children on the frontline, in a nursery during the COVID-19 pandemic. Moreover, roles in category 6 were considered essential for keeping the rest of the country going through the pandemic. These were the people facing the biggest health risks, and making the biggest sacrifices (Bell et al., 2020). Despite being lowly-paid roles with limited scope for career progression, category 6 jobs are traditionally what some Childhood Studies students have consciously chosen to enter after graduation for a variety of reasons. Rather than maintaining a preoccupation with students entering 'highly skilled' employment, it might be more useful to look at category 6 jobs in terms of how they make use of graduates' skills and knowledge.

Active learning theory and methodology

Our case of active learning is founded upon a conception of choice and volition for the student and mirrored the core principles we were promoting in our undergraduate Childhood Studies curriculum: independent growth; freedom (albeit within time limits); hands-on learning; and creating knowledge through experience and discovery (Dewey, 1997; Montessori, 1964; Piaget, 1972). As an active learning activity, the Legacy Project allows students to negotiate their own work experiences, enabling them to play to their strengths and interests while still achieving learning outcomes and developing graduate attributes. While the Legacy Project assignment is designed to equip students with the work experiences needed to prosper in a competitive graduate job market, it also has a humanistic goal in ensuring students are *"equipped in their whole being for the adventure of life, accustomed to the free exercise of will and judgement, illuminated by imagination and enthusiasm"* (Montessori, 1989:1). Montessori's feminist pedagogy was best suited to this predominantly female course, with a predominantly female teaching team. Here we describe applying Montessori's theories in a new context while still adhering to the underlying philosophical principles.

Active learning was supported by an adapted version of the Montessori trinity *"a suitable environment, the humble teacher* [or, in our case, the academic advisor] *and, material objects adapted to children's* [or in our case, the students'] *needs"* (Montessori, 1972:137). In the context of our work experiences, a *"suitable environment"* (Montessori, 1972:137) is any work environment to which students orient themselves, in order to facilitate professional growth. On the BA (Hons) Childhood Studies degree, that environment might be a school, hospital, child contact centre, a family courtroom, a food bank or a baby bank, a virtual environment, or some other environment of the student's choosing which would provide them with a solid base of knowledge, skills, and experience for their intended employment destination.

Through a Montessori education, learners have contact with an immediate and developmentally responsive environment, which in the context of students' work experiences is interpreted as a living, breathing, ever-changing workplace. In this line of thinking, students listen, observe, and participate in all the creations of a living workplace, including its professional hierarchies and the organisation of the workplace. As a novice, and when learning from experts, students construct their own meanings of their work and what different job roles entail. As we see later, students' accounts emphasise the moral and emotional dimensions of care (Hochschild, 1989), which characterised their work with children and families.

Providing sufficient time to become absorbed in work is essential to a Montessori education. *"The mind takes some time to develop interest, to be set in motion, to get warmed up into a subject, to attain a state of profitable work"* (Montessori, 1989:135). Montessori education is based on a schedule with at least one uninterrupted 3-hour period a day. For our adult learners, we provide two full uninterrupted days every week across the year to achieve 180-hours of *"profitable"* (Montessori, 1989:135) work experience as well as the option of using block periods of university holidays. This enables flexible work experiences where students have full control over how they use and manage their time. This is not without commensurate responsibility, so the logbook of work experiences (Table 1, Task 2) allows students and academic advisors to keep track of events and activities on work experience and be accountable for them.

However, merely doing work experience does not produce active learning. While in our example, the responsibility for learning lies with the student's freedom to pursue a self-chosen work experience direction, they also need a dialogical learning space to create meaning and direction. Earlier, we defined active learning as being very much about deliberate action, energy and power, and the primary role of a *"humble"* (Montessori, 1972:137) Montessori teacher is rather wide They observe, guide, facilitate and oversee learning and understanding and stimulate new ways of thinking or new possibilities.

Dialogue thus plays a central role in furthering understanding, as this is a reflective process grounded in the student's everyday work experiences. Here, the student and academic advisor discuss the progress of the Legacy Project by unpacking the hows and whys of what the student has done and embracing the dead ends and false starts as part of the learning experience. These conversations represent a professional step back - an invitation for students to think objectively about their immediate work experiences - but are also preparing students for their *"life design"* (Guichard, 2016) after graduation. In the university context, advising is not the same as lecturing since the role of a lecturer involves organising and presenting 'knowledge'. In contrast, the academic advisor's role is to advise, guide, and support students responsively. This developmental relationship focuses on the students' needs, so skilful planning and differentiation and advising from the academic advisor is still very important. It would take a whole book to explore in detail the different approaches of the academic advising team to each of their student cohorts. Still, in these senses, we propose the academic advisor is *"humble"* (Montessori, 1972:137) because as Montessori (1995:283) says later *"The greatest sign of success for a teacher is to be able to say, 'The children are now working as if I do not exist'"*.

Active learning involves change and transformation, and material objects are intentional by design and part of Montessori's concrete learning. Montessori's planes of development from birth to adulthood highlights a linear progression from concrete to abstract learning. Since students on the degree are typically aged 18-24 years old and fall into Montessori's fourth plane of maturity, the two most crucial material objects adapted to our students' needs were *The Big Book of Work Experiences for Childhood Studies* and *The Big Book of Childhood Studies Careers*. Not only did these two material objects enable students to see something of the intent and expectations of the Legacy Project as a concept, but also to reveal new patterns and connections in their work that they had not seen before, which we explore in the following section. Although a Montessori education emphasises freedom, we found that students could be extremely critical if materials did not explicitly connect to the end assignments. We were mindful of this perceived disconnect, despite our misgivings, and connected seminar discussions to the specific learning outcomes.

Having outlined something of our approach and methodology, we turn now to the specific detail and discuss how the learning outcomes connected to active learning and how this learning is measured in The Graduate Self module before considering the end academic, emotional, and experiential outcomes of this work for this group of students.

Section 2: The case of active learning

The BA (Hons) Childhood Studies degree was revalidated in 2018, and the starting point was improving both the student experience and graduate outcomes. We enhanced course cohesion by clarifying how modules were interrelated, both horizontally and vertically. We later see some of the cohesive strands articulated as evidence of career-readiness in the example of the Children's Nurse. The goal was to open students' eyes to their degree's prospects. We wanted students to explore possible career opportunities as part of their learning experience, so we created a core spine of 40-credit double-weighted 'employability' modules: Y1 The Academic Self; Y2 The Professional Self; and Y3 The Graduate Self. Each module has four learning outcomes which considers the level of learning and the appropriate attributes of that level. Each module builds on the work of the previous - not only in the learning outcomes assessed and the way they are assessed - but also in the work experiences accrued. As an active learning experience, this works on the premise that learning is successive rather than linear, and new knowledge connects to and builds upon existing knowledge.

By progressing through this module spine, we want to see our students grow in academic independence and make a full transition from being taught to a deeper and more meaningful active learning experience. The inclusive design was central to both the curriculum and assessment. In all these modules, the premise for assessment is the same: students must pose a real-world problem, issue, or challenge relevant to children, young people, or families within a specific professional setting of their choosing, which their Legacy Project seeks to solve. To carry out a Legacy Project, our expectation was for all students to complete a total of 180 hours of work experience. Because of the uncertainty related to the COVID-19 pandemic, we did give flexibility both in the ways students managed this requirement across all year groups and in what would 'count' as a successful work experience in 2020-21. Flexibility by our rationale would allow students to focus on their end goal and how they would meet this rather than being fixated by time constraints, as often happens in summative assessments assignments.

An overview of how students work with active learning

Active learning is integral throughout the BA (Hons) Childhood Studies curriculum- we discuss the collaborative group work of the Y2 Legacy Projects elsewhere (Swann, 2021), but the third and final year of the degree represents a professional step-up. The Graduate Self is the very last university assignment students submit, so here we expect to see a deeper shift in both their academic and professional thinking, which increases their ability to be successful not only in this module but also as a beginning apprentice member of a disciplinary community (i.e. by the end of The Graduate Self module, they are now beginning to think like a nurse, or a counsellor, or a primary school teacher for instance). Of the 2019-20 cohort, our External Examiner commented of this module:

- *"It is evident from the work I have seen that students have developed a thorough knowledge and understanding of core module themes. The reflective approach facilitated opportunities for students to consider their own learning and link this to professional placement practices and future plans."*

I asked the previous student cohort to contribute sage-like guidance or any 'lessons learned' that they wished they had known at the start of their work experiences, which might benefit the next class of students who were just starting on the same journey. Their voices of experience were included in the module handbook.

Assessment Summary

The Graduate Self module is a 40-credit module with two key elements submitted as the summative assessment. The first assessment required students to deliver a presentation of a maximum of 20 minutes in which they should: critically reflect on their learning journey through this course; critically evaluate their placement experience; demonstrate knowledge of the changing landscape for working with children (including safeguarding); summarise their career and employment plans; and use appropriate digital tools to communicate their messages. Both components have a 50% weighting.

The second assessment is a Professional Portfolio that facilitated active reflection of work activities through directed tasks (Table 1). As a cumulative whole, these assignments are interpreted here as the product of active learning.

Directed task	Description
1. Engaging and utilising academic feedback to enhance my learning	The first Directed Task we set students was to collate feedback from their Y2 assignments and evaluate how they would make the best use of this feedback in their last round of University assignments. Students' final assessed presentations will draw on this task as part of their evidence base to document their meeting of learning outcome 4: *'critically reflect on your learning journey through this course'*

Directed task	Description
2. Work experience logbook	This document provides a log of all the activities students completed in their 180-hour placement or digital Legacy Project.
3. Emotional labour in the workplace	The following prompts were offered to students: • Consider the ways in which you are encouraged to manage your own and the emotions of others (i.e. children, colleagues) • Describe a real situation that was important to you on placement in which you experienced a deep emotion • Describe as fully and concretely as possible a real situation that was important to you in which you either changed the situation to fit your feelings or changed your feelings to fit the situation. Consider the ways in which you are encouraged to manage your own and the emotions of others (children, colleagues) • Consider your answers in relation to literature that discusses the concept of emotional labour
4. Reflection on a 'critical incident'	Here we look at the student's ability to connect academic learning to the 'real world'. In this task, they reflect on the theorists and thinkers they have studied throughout the degree programme. Which theory helps students to understand their work experience, and why? How will they use these theories to make sense of their 'critical incident'?
5. Safeguarding children and young people in professional contexts	The following prompts were offered to students: • What are your attitudes towards safeguarding and child protection? • If you are in a physical workplace, what are your organisation's safeguarding policies and procedures? What would you do if you had a safeguarding concern about a child? • What do you think makes your workplace setting safe and supportive? • What do you do to safeguard children in your workplace?

Directed task	Description
6. My Postgraduate Destination	This piece of work showcases how the knowledge, skills and experiences students have gained on this degree makes them a suitable candidate for their next steps after graduation. Students also include any offers and acceptances of employment or postgraduate training in this section of the portfolio
7. Placement Supervisor's Report	This is to be completed by the placement supervisor at the end of the 180- hour work experience and details areas such as punctuality/ timekeeping, reliability, standard of work, initiative, motivation, etc.

Table 1: Summary of professional portfolio tasks.

How we prepare and organise active learning

This active learning activity does need some preparation before it can be started and the five bullet points below serve as a quick reference for lecturers of resources needed. A more detailed description of each resource follows:

- Resource 1: The Module Handbook (Swann 2020a).

- Resource 2: Set the students a time-bound work experience with maximum flexibility.

- Resource 3: *The Big Book of Work Experiences for Childhood Studies* (Swann 2020b).

- Resource 4: *The Big Book of Childhood Studies Careers* (Swann 2020c).

- Resource 5: A team of specialist academic advisors to provide ongoing responsive support.

Resource 1: The Module Handbook

The module handbook is a key document since it outlines the responsibilities and expectations of students through a weekly schedule of pre-recorded lectures, fortnightly seminars and timetabled tutorials with their academic advisor, which span across the whole academic year. These provide students with a common base of activities for active learning to support the development of their Legacy Projects.

Resource 2: Set the students a time-bound work experience with maximum flexibility

We give students 180 hours to identify, implement and evaluate a Legacy Project, but they are free to organise their time in a way that suits them best. They can complete the 180 hours 'long and thin', 'short and fat' or a hybrid model somewhere in between. To support a long and thin model, we keep students 'off timetable' every Thursday and Friday throughout both semesters to complete 180 hours of work-based learning, which means no other educational activities, lectures or seminars are timetabled for these days. Where students want to focus intensively and exclusively on their Legacy Projects, there is also the option to complete block periods of work experiences in the holiday periods if desired. In the module handbook, I provide examples of how students might complete their 180-hour placement for illustration purposes.

The course director spent weeks creating two substantial new resources to support this module: *The Big Book of Work Experiences for Childhood Studies* (Swann, 2020b) and *The Big Book of Childhood Studies Careers* (Swann, 2020c). We now turn to these two resources in some detail since they form the heart of the Legacy Project across all year groups.

Resource 3: The Big Book of Work Experiences for Childhood Studies (Swann, 2020b)

The Big Book of Work Experiences is sent out to students before the break for summer, and as detailed below, we offer three options: paid work, voluntary work, or a digital Legacy Project. The onus is placed on the students to take charge of their own work experience by researching the opportunities given to them, with some guidance and encouragement.

Option 1: Paid work

This section of the book offers listings of where jobs are advertised. We emphasise two main opportunities which we know work particularly well for students due to the flexibility of work patterns compatible with full-time study. We first provide a list of the main Education Agencies. Paid work with an Education Agency is highly beneficial for any career involving children, since it enables students to gain practical skills of working with children throughout different age groups, in different work roles within a school (i.e. as a Cover Supervisor, SEN Teaching Assistant), and in different settings including nurseries, Primary Schools, Secondary Schools, Pupil Referral Units (PRUs) and schools for children with Special Educational Needs and Disabilities (SEND). This experience could equip students with useful skills and knowledge in communication and interaction; cognition and learning; social, emotional and mental health; and sensory and physical needs - all of which are very useful for careers supporting families and safeguarding as well as teaching. For any student struggling with the decision to apply for postgraduate teacher training, we strongly advise them to sign up for this since it would allow them to explore with an 'insider's eye' whether teacher training is for them.

Alternatively, students can choose to sign up for paid work within the Children's Care Sector which enables students to gain practical skills of working with children in specialist areas such as children with complex needs, children and young adults with complex medical care needs, children with complex disabilities and their families/carers, or children who have been placed in the care system. The work setting might be a secure children's home or supporting vulnerable children and young adults in their own homes to promote their independence and provide respite for the parents/guardians of the children and young people they support. Duties and responsibilities are diverse and will be specified in the job specifications and might include challenging areas like supporting vulnerable children and young people separated from family members. We advise students to search for current vacancies such as a Children's Support Worker, Children's Residential Support Worker, Complex

Needs Support Worker, Health Care Assistant, Family Support Worker, Youth Support Worker, Family Support Worker, Children's Health and Education Support Worker and Family Centre Outreach Worker. We provide a list of contacts who regularly advertise for these roles.

Option 2: Voluntary work

Voluntary work too opens countless possibilities for rewarding, varied and challenging work experiences. Here we work hard to include something that would appeal to everyone. Our entries include everything from applying to be a magistrate to training a guide dog for visually impaired children. I include shortened versions of three entries below to give the reader an idea of the variety of voluntary work experiences promoted:

1) *"Family Court magistrates"* undertake difficult and sensitive work, which might include resolving disputes between separated parents, making arrangements for surrogacy or adoption, and making different types of court orders for children to prevent domestic abuse molestation or abduction. Training and working as a magistrate will give you insight into a range of child welfare issues which is useful grounding for a career in Social Work or Family Mediation as well as Family Law.

2) *"Raising a Buddy Dog for a child with sight loss"*. Raising a Buddy Dog is a time-consuming commitment as you will live with your puppy to develop her into a happy, relaxed, obedient companion for a child with sight loss. Buddy dogs can positively affect a child's well-being by helping to develop their self-confidence, alter social interactions with other people, and build a greater sense of trust.

3) *"Volunteering for Childline"* is a valuable opportunity for anybody considering a career in counselling or psychotherapy. As a volunteer counsellor, you will receive training to enable you to listen and respond to children and young people who have got in touch via phone, online chat or email. Volunteer counsellors support young people whatever worries them, whether it's bullying, abuse, self-harm or family relationships. You will need to commit to a regular shift of 4 hours each week.

Option 3: Online Legacy Projects

Due to the uncertainty surrounding COVID-19 in 2020-21, the course director built an alternative to the traditional 'real world' work experience placement, which was for students to design and work on a virtual Legacy Project. Students choosing this option work remotely, rather than in a work setting, but still need to document the activities they completed within the 180 hours in their work experiences logbook (Table 1, Task 2). Students are constrained only by imagination; some of the examples in 2020-21 include:

1) a Rainbow Treasure Hunt for families to complete in local neighbourhoods to spread hope and optimism during the pandemic;

2) discussion guides and creative activities for Patrick Ness' *A Monster Calls* (film and book) aimed at helping families understand and cope with grief; and,

3) devising, creating and evaluating the success of new YouTube resources which parents could use at home with their children during lockdown.

Resource 4: The Big Book of Childhood Studies Careers (Swann, 2020c)

This resource documents the journeys of previous BA (Hons) Childhood Studies students who have successfully transitioned into a wide range of career paths. By reading individual entries, students could note how their predecessors have drawn on specialist knowledge, skills, and experiences from their three years on the degree to reach their career goals. After reading through this booklet, students' long-term task is to write their vision statement (see Table 1, Task 6). To reach the highest marks, we expect students to make authentic connections to the occupational standards, which marks the profession they aim to join. The following is a shortened extract linking degree-specific knowledge, skills and work experience to the standards of proficiency for nurses (NMC 2018):

- "Completing a 'Legacy Project' supports 'Platform 1: Being an accountable professional' because I sought out my own work experiences, identified and took responsibility for what I was going to work on. I was *also willing to stand back and measure the work that I did, reviewing whether it was effective or not. To support 'Platform 4: providing and evaluating care', I achieved an accredited Emergency Paediatric First Aid qualification in The Professional Self module, which taught me how to help a baby or child who is unresponsive and not breathing normally, having a seizure, choking, suffering from shock, or bleeding. In the Perspectives on Play module, I researched how therapeutic play helped hospitalised children and also helped nurses to assess and communicate with young patients. I gained a better understanding of 'Platform 7: Coordinating care' when I volunteered at an 'Outstanding' SEND school in my final year. My Legacy Project focused on creating a positive school experience for children with complex and high-level needs, including cerebral palsy, multiple sclerosis, autism, and sensory-processing disorders. The children attending this school received professional support from Speech and Language Therapists, Occupational Therapists, Physiotherapists, and a Play Therapist which provided insight into how coordinated care brings together people with different expertise and roles."*

Resource 5: A team of Academic Advisors to provide ongoing and responsive support

The fifth step is to allocate each student an academic advisor as their first point of contact. These academic advisors are drawn from the real world of work and provide students with specialist knowledge and expertise with contemporary professional experience. Each student has an allowance of 30 timetabled hours to meet with their academic advisor to share progress, talk through ideas, talk through problems as they occur, and gain feedback. To enable the module leader to sort and sift students into smaller, more specialised groups, students were asked to fill in an online sheet that captured basic information (Table 2). We used this information to group together students who shared the same career goals (i.e., grouping our future teachers, future social workers, future nurses together), and the data from this also helped each academic advisor understand each of their students' positions at the start of the year and what support they might require. We set a strict deadline for this to be completed for effective staff provision– if this was not met, students are told they will be allocated an academic advisor based on availability rather than by specialism.

Name	Career goal	Entry requirements	Plan for Y3 Legacy Project	How can your Academic Advisor best support you?
Anne Example	Speech Therapist	Need a 2:1 to undertake MA in Speech and Language Therapy at University X	Paid work at Special School- Legacy Project will focus on my work with children with speech and language needs. Need contingency plan if we have another lockdown	Not sure how I can show evidence of NHS values in my MA application

Table 2: Data collection for the 'sort and sift'.

Section 3: The outcome

Students were sorted and sifted into seven specialised academic groups in 2020-21. Once collated, the professional portfolios submitted for The Graduate Self module resulted in a total of 412,813 words which provide some of the rich textual data analysed in this section. Marks ranged from 10-78%. The relative performance of students can be seen as a tool to gauge the effects of the Legacy Project as an active learning experience, and the students who secured the highest marks were doing active learning when they:

- were intrinsically motivated and had the emotional capacity to identify and act upon opportunities.
- posed a problem, issue or challenge within this specific setting which their Legacy Project seeks to solve;
- adaptively responded to challenges and persevered to bring about meaningful learning and an end 'legacy';
- fulfilled the learning outcomes of the module in authentic ways.

Student perspective

Compiling the student portfolios into a large Word Cloud (Figure 2) represented word frequency. As a simple visual reflection of students' collective learning, it was reassuring that 'child', 'children' and 'work' were central to students' focus, indicating some alignment between what the students had learned and the intended learning outcomes for this module.

As a mode of active learning, the Legacy Project focused on the action; the process of identifying, implementing, and evaluating a Legacy Project of their own choosing aimed to solve some of the kind of practical problems that workplaces already face. Students with a clear sense of career goals strategically sought out work experiences which would give them the experiential knowledge valued by employers or postgraduate training providers. Some students based their Legacy Project around a paid work role they already did while others chose to complete a digital Legacy Project which otherwise meant a lot to them. Some students actively sought out challenge and a Legacy Project that would take them beyond their normal range of activities. A minority of students struggled either to secure work experience in a 'real world' setting or to commit to a single idea which made the developing phases of active learning very difficult for them, but we view this as a natural part of the active learning cycle for some students as they move from dependence to autonomy.

Figure 2: Visual representation of word frequency.

Over the pandemic, securing a placement became notably more difficult, but in 2020-21, students' work experiences were diverse and included:
- enhancing patients' well-being through paid work as a ward hostess in a large hospital;
- volunteering at a food bank or a baby bank to support hard-pressed families;
- delivering fun educational activities to critical workers' children through paid work in schools and nurseries;
- promoting a fun and relaxed space for families via paid waitressing work at a cat café;
- setting up the 'Season of Giving' scheme for a local child poverty charity, which resulted in gifts being given to 200 children;
- solving a short-term supply and demand problem for a neonatal unit by knitting baby bonnets, blankets and socks.

Active engagement with the learning environments and materials- or lack of- explained a student's ability to understand and manage their own learning and performance. On the one hand, using active learning strategies and setting goals affected the depth of student engagement with both the learning resources and each professional portfolio task, which was reflected in high levels of self-efficacy. On the other hand, where students had, for example, not read emails, nor followed the schedule in the Module Handbook, nor watched the lecture, or attended the seminar, there was an expectation of a customer service experience from academics to fill in the gaps (Nixon & Scullion, 2021). For instance, early on, two students had not filled in the sifting and sorting sheet and who then complained that they were allocated an academic advisor, not of their choosing. A lack of focus resulted in student reflections that were naïve, vague, or generic in quality:
- *"I have a strong passion to change the world."*
- *"I aspire to positively influence these children from similar backgrounds and let them know that they are capable of anything they want to do."*
- *"My sole aim for this project is to make a difference to the lives of the young people."*

However, most were rich with the experience, knowledge, and insight they gained, and we share a few examples in the following sections.

Workplace Socialisation

As students navigated different professional fields, they became socialised into the rhythm of work schedules. Most of the work settings involved direct contact with children, young people or families and students became acclimatised to working within specific frameworks of legislation, protocols and procedures, and understanding the need for them. Ward hostesses had an important role in maintaining hygiene standards to patients, and practical experience brought about greater insight and understanding of the different medical care roles and day-to-day procedures associated with patient care. To ensure health and safety for the neonatal unit, one student had to place the items she had knitted in a dated, clear, sealed bag, so they could be isolated for 72 hours before being used on the wards during the pandemic. In educational settings, students took part in various forms of record-keeping, including taking the register, recording observations on a child's records in early years settings, or filling out an accident form.

Data security and maintaining client confidentiality in the context of working with vulnerable families was an important area of responsibility. While we had provided lectures on safeguarding, following data protection procedures, and keeping personal data anonymous, it was outside of students' normal range of activities until practical experience guided its application. Caitlyn's Legacy Project aimed to relieve the strains and suffering of local families living in poverty. She volunteered at a charity that provided baby essentials to families facing an acute, immediate financial crisis. To ensure it served the right people, the charity only accepted referrals from professionals in contact with vulnerable families such as a midwife, health visitor or social worker. Deciding to accept help from a charity- even as a short-term emergency measure, as was the case with these families- was often difficult as families felt embarrassment, guilt or shame associated with poverty (Jones et al., 2020). Caitlin's reflection discusses the procedure she followed with an accompanying rationale:

- *"Labelling up bundles [of resources] the Health Professional's initials are used, then the postcode of the family in need so if labels were to go*

> *missing, seen by visitors or posted on social media there is no way of relating it back to the direct person in need. All data on families and the situation related to them are kept on a password-protected tablet to ensure data will not be leaked."*

Navigating Brave New Worlds

Through their work experiences, some students saw how professionals keep pace and cope with continual change, churn, and flux. This was sometimes in the context of constant policy reform, so the students working in Early Years settings were part of planning the transition to the new Early Years Foundation Stage (EYFS) statutory framework, which applied from 1st September 2021. Other students gained experience in managing change amidst the rapidly evolving situation of COVID-19. One student who continued to volunteer in a Child Contact Centre worked within a team of paid professionals who switched from facilitating in-person contact between a child and one or both non-resident parents in a safe, neutral physical environment to using virtual platforms such as Zoom. Other students were working in the aftermath of sudden disruptive change, so students in secondary schools experienced the backwash of the UK government cancelling all of the examinations due to being held in the summer of 2020 with grades being replaced by teacher predictions in 2020 and 2021, which predictably caused turbulence (Noden et al., 2021).

In short, active learning for students meant negotiating the intricacies of different scenarios and workplaces and becoming exposed to ambiguity, uncertainty, and vulnerability. Student reflections tell us how through practical experiences, they learnt to adapt their knowledge and skills to the given task. In large institutions like schools, some students' Legacy Projects were developed against a background of managerialism within a shifting neo-liberal agenda. In this situation, students were sometimes taking their first steps into what can be essentially hard and unforgiving workplaces.

Hannah described bearing witness to an Office for Standards in Education (Ofsted) inspection, resulting in the primary school teacher she shadowed taking stress leave. Hannah held this teacher in high esteem as she was a seasoned professional with over two decades of experience, ran a well-organised classroom and importantly for Hannah, had also taken the time to prepare and support her for everyday classroom demands *"...with lesson plans and who and where we needed to be and who to support at all times"*. Through this mentor, Hannah had found a safe space for learning some of the tools of the teaching trade.

Beyond the immediacy of the classroom, extended Ofsted as the state's apparatus for judging and evaluating teachers. Experiencing a live inspection exposed in brutal terms *"the management prerogative"* (Noon & Blyton, 2007:67), which aimed to *"...improve the effectiveness and efficiency of the outcomes of learning"* (Jeffrey, 2002:531). Hannah was intimidated by the unfriendly inspection process, and observing the real human impact of a negative Ofsted judgement, was a challenging experience:

- *"I was nervous being in the environment where Ofsted were judging and evaluating the school to start off with and then for a teacher to leave due to the blame they received. I was shocked and upset."*

It was an experience that threw her former understandings of the teaching profession into question, resulting in disorienting dilemmas: *"...I was going into this profession, and it just shows how quickly things can change"*. An important part of active learning for Hannah was how she adapted her role. She chooses to:*"...step up and help the new teacher"* since she *"was the only other adult in the class that knew the children well."*

Moving forward meant creating a stable and purposeful learning environment that minimised change for the children. This was a positive, ethically responsible, proactive choice that bodes well for Hannah's close future as a postgraduate teacher-training candidate.

Healthcare is also a complex adaptive system marked by shifting demographics, change and unpredictability. For the students who completed work experiences in a hospital, this was a workplace containing illness, pain and death, as well as care and cure. Many important skills and attributes such as teamwork, communication skills, and openness and friendly were fostered. Driven by a desire to do the best for the patients they served, these students emphasised the role of emotional connections in shaping interactions. Working on the frontline in hospitals did, on occasion, expose students to overwhelming situations. One particularly humbling reflection came from Mariana, who describes witnessing the death of a patient:

> *"One real situation that changed me forever is when I spoke to a patient, made him a cup of tea and joked with him. He was laughing and looked healthy, ready to go home the day after. Sadly, as I was walking him and the nurse to the lifts, he put his head down and died suddenly. [The nurse] had to run back to the room, and an alarm started ringing. All of the staff from the ward, as well as from the other side, had to run into the room and try to help him …I could not believe it as I was just talking and laughing with him."*

This exerted a considerable emotional impact on Mariana, as we see in her next reflection when she describes her immediate feelings and response and tries to find the best way to cope:

> *"I decided to remain quiet and not say anything to the nurses. I went downstairs into the main kitchen, and all of a sudden, I began crying. I felt like I could let my emotions go as long as I was not around the people and the place where it happened. I could not sleep that night and was in shock for another 2 days."*

Learning to deal with difficult situations was part of active learning. This honest and vulnerable account shows something valuable about the generative potential of emotion in constructing students' professional identities. Complex and messy, Mariana's account matches the emotional experiences reported of nursing students responding to distressing situations at the beginning of their own careers (Heise et al., 2018). The following example also points to some of the tacit skills and knowledge Mariana was harnessing in her role. She describes the natural connections she was able to forge during patient interactions: *"I spoke to a patient, made him a cup of tea and joked with him. He was laughing"*. Humour is a valuable asset because it helps put people at ease, as studies of caring behaviours within healthcare settings have documented. For instance, Broom and Cavenagh's (2011:109) described how care relations in hospices were marked by *"cheer and life"*. Mariana was fully present for the patient and has fit comfortably into working alongside nurses, but concerning professional boundaries, as we can discern when she retreats to let the nurses work on the patient.

Learning to manage diverse needs

The demands of coming face-to-face with people with complex mental, physical, cognitive and behavioural care needs helped students better understand the inclusive practice and built students' capacities to meet diverse needs in different ways. Although lectures covered the main definitions and concepts of inclusion and diverse needs, they soon became apparent that they did not help them apply what they had learned. Sometimes learning came through odd, unusual, or unexpected workplace experiences as they spontaneously occur, which we see in the following example:

- *"… we had a patient with schizophrenia [who] asked me to make him tea. He told me to make it really strong, add a lot of sugar in, not much milk and spin the spoon left 13 times and then right 13 times. At first, I thought that he was joking …but he did not find anything funny. Instead, he started calling me bad names and saying that we are useless and don't know anything. Another patient told me [this patient had schizophrenia] so immediately I started acting accordingly. I asked him to please repeat what he wanted and that I would make his tea exactly like that. He calmed down and told me again. I did what he asked of me and put on a smile even though he had just called me names. He said, "that will do", but did not look too satisfied. I decided to just smile anyway and walk away. The next day when I saw the same patient, I acted like the day before had not happened."*

At one level, we can read this as a demonstration of coping skills, resilience and adapting to the challenging behaviour of a patient. However, active learning lies in the disjuncture between the norms held by the student and the norms held by the patient with schizophrenia. As an occasion for sensemaking, this experience let the student into the uniqueness of this patient's subjectivity and everyday way of seeing – as reflected through the patient's need to have the spoon stirred 13 times left and then right. Understanding the needs of this patient and behaving in a way that supports and connects to him brings to life some of the philosophy of mind concepts covered a year earlier in the Philosophy of Childhood module. This 'knowability' is all part of learning to care. In this case,

Chapter 10

managing diverse needs through assimilation and adapting through accommodation brought about meaningful learning.

Understanding the experience of poverty through the eyes of local families was a powerful means to understand issues of inclusion, equity, and access. Through their contributions, students working within food banks and baby banks often expressed a genuine and deep-rooted sense of pride and self-esteem which came from feeling valued and appreciated. We return to Caitlyn, who describes her emotional reaction after giving an 'essentials' bundle to a hard-pressed family:

- *"The expression of gratitude and sense of relief the mother gave me was unbelievable and touched my heart. The idea that a heavily pregnant mother can relax and settle knowing the upcoming children have all the necessary items gave me a huge sense of pride and relief. The overwhelming response has stuck with me as the level of appreciation shown was lovely to hear and helped me to evaluate my worth and importance."*

In the examples described, we see students encountering an unpredictable situation, improvising, and deploying various coping tactics. The next section focuses on the specific context of active learning through work experiences during the COVID-19 pandemic.

Active Learning through Work Experiences during the COVID-19 Pandemic

The COVID-19 pandemic began in December 2019, and by March 2020, the UK Prime Minister announced the first lockdown in the UK, ordering people to 'stay at home'. Hence, University students in the UK abruptly transitioned from in-person classes to remote learning. References to the COVID-19 pandemic was relatively small in the word count of the completed professional portfolios at 249. Still, where it was mentioned, students expressed prevalent feelings of anxiety, fear, insecurity, and apprehensiveness:

- *"...the overwhelming emotion was uncertainty, not only regarding the pandemic as a whole but also uncertainty about university, placements and society [returning] to normal. Other emotions also accompanied feelings of uncertainty; not being able to complete my placement in*

2020 or finding a volunteering position for Level Six [which] resulted in a great amount of frustration as I had no control over the situation."

A sense of powerlessness and lack of control stand out here, highlighting the importance of building coping strategies as a higher-order skill to cope with uncontrollable events and change. Although unprecedented in the context of a global pandemic, change is an inevitable feature of a modern workplace during periods of organisational change or restructuring, for instance (Smollan, 2017). The COVID-19 pandemic saw a rapid pace of change in all workplaces, and against this flux and churn, students like the professionals, of course, had to adapt and learn constantly. While some students did not adapt easily to active learning in the context of COVID-19, most students did accept the situation, adapted their role to it on work experience and sometimes even confronted it directly, as we see with the students who worked on the frontline.

Early years settings remained open during later national lockdowns, and some of our students worked in the nurseries and took care of the young children of keyworkers for prolonged periods. This constituted a valuable Legacy Project- since solving childcare challenges was a national priority during the pandemic. In their respective settings, students noted how the children would often ask questions about 'the bad virus' or 'the nasty virus'. Listening to the talk of children to understand and meet their needs was a core skill. Ella explained some of how the staff within her room adapted the activities, materials, and games in concrete and meaningful ways to support children emotionally, but also develop healthy patterns of understanding of what the pandemic meant and what illness was:

- "We set up an activity to take care of our poorly babies [dolls]… with doctor and nurse equipment set up. We also did lots of singing, 'Miss Polly had a Dolly who was sick, sick, sick' and tied in the story of Ness the Nurse."

It was encouraging to hear of the strategies students had taken to respond to children's needs in light of children's advancing (but not yet fully developed) abilities. The strategies Ella employed rested on a secure base of knowledge of child development. For instance, in a core module, Developmental Psychology, students had learned about the different stages of children's cognitive, social, and emotional development. Ella's Legacy

Project depended on good communication skills, especially communicating appropriately with very young children, to help them develop confidence. In Ella's example, she needed to connect to the developmental level of these pre-school children who might not yet hold abstract concepts of why, when, or how, for instance. The hospital role-play area was equipped with doctors' and nurses' uniforms, thermometer, stethoscope, masks, gloves and blankets and a reception desk which children incorporate into their play to make sense of each doll's illness. The scaffolding from the adult provides support and direction, so Ella, for instance, holds up a stethoscope and says to the 'nurse', *"can you hear any funny noises from your patient's body? What do you think we could do to help her feel better?"* Instrumentally, we can also see how Ella's work supports the aim of the new EYFS framework to improve outcomes at age 5 in early language and literacy (Department for Education, 2021).

Teacher perspective – my reflections

Through the Legacy Projects, I wanted to open students' eyes to the diverse landscape of work– both in terms of the types of work experiences they might obtain and the employment prospects they might later yield. I sought to present the newly revalidated BA (Hons) Childhood Studies degree as an ambitious space of possibilities. To a large extent, this worked because work experience- where it worked well- did succeed in making students feel optimistic and purposeful about their future job prospects:

- *"I feel like I would do well at helping care for other people. …until I had my placement experience, I did not know what my passion was. However, working here has opened up my eyes to a lot of things."*

In many cases, this was meaningful work which brought students up close to different professional worlds. Rather than students taking a critical look at salary potential or the potential for career progression, we saw emotional experiences as a consistent strand of students' active learning and career planning, which indicated vocation:

- *"…holding patients' hands, working together with other members of staff and offering patients kind words, is what has made me realise that I would love to work within a hospital environment."*

The confidence that came from the overall experience of active learning on the Legacy Projects did in many cases prepare students for specific occupational domains and supported them as they applied for their first steps towards a career path:

- *"I cannot even put into words how much I love working with lovely little children and the friendships we build …the staff have been so kind to me, they helped me with my interview, they guided and showed me everything I needed to know about every individual, they were patient and understanding with me, and they accepted me as a trustworthy member of staff and friend. I can't thank them all enough for the encouragement and confidence I've developed in the little 5 weeks I was there. I was constantly given positive feedback from all members of staff, and they pushed me when I doubted myself and my choices. … Bless them all! I would return there in a heartbeat."*

The overall enthusiasm of the students who have reached their end career goal has made me more confident that we are focusing our efforts in the right place. Frequently, true understanding only came once they had experienced the competitive application and interview process as graduates. A student from the first cohort reflected three years after graduation: *"I understand the purpose of the Legacy Projects a lot better now I'm working. When I tell employers that I've done a Legacy Project at [names setting] and what I've gained from it, they always seem intrigued"*. Another student from the same cohort depicts a need for perseverance which is a skill cultivated through experience and challenge. She describes adaptively learning from and responding to unsuccessful attempts in a competitive job market:

- *"Each year, I have progressed further and achieved a higher level of the selection process. This year I applied again for the third time, and I have made it to the final stage of the application process. I find out [in two days] whether I will be offered a place."*

Promoting employability in real-time

During the pandemic, the course director made greater use of social media platforms and inputted information onto the module homepage to communicate postgraduate opportunities to university students as soon as advertised. This included the paid Unlocked two-year social work graduate programme, the highly prestigious Mi5 graduate development programme, and links to miscellaneous graduate opportunities such as Aldi's Area Manager programme. When the graduate employment field is competitive, complex, and volatile, up-to-date information is vital for students to stay one step ahead. This meant keeping them informed of various deadlines and closing dates for applications, quickly responding to changing requirements or conditions, and building new processes.

Section 4: Moving forward

When viewed as a collective whole, the work experiences accrued in 2020-21 demonstrate the broad skill and knowledge base studying an undergraduate degree can provide. At the individual level, practical work experiences enabled most students to build a refined skill and knowledge base, which enabled them to test out occupational areas, build confidence and increase their chance of securing postgraduate training in those areas where appropriate. Therefore, our first goal is to continue to connect students to challenging and ambitious work experiences that are relevant to them.

In practice, our main difficulties arise not from a lack of, or exposure to, opportunity but a lack of uptake. Law and youth justice remained a largely unexplored base for work experience, which was surprising. For instance, a student has yet to apply to train and work as a magistrate in the courts or as an Appropriate Adult. Both roles have been widely promoted since our employability modules came into being, so it seems unlikely they have gone unnoticed. Neither is it likely that these settings would not pique students' interest. Children, Crime and Social Justice is a popular elective module in the final year, complemented by the practical experience of either hearing cases in the youth courts or being the principal safeguard for children and young people detained in police custody following arrest. Our next step is to ensure that students understand all the available opportunities and are confident to apply for and try out roles beyond their direct experiences. To elaborate this further, we need to understand more about the career motivations and aspirations of all our Childhood Studies students. An uncomfortable truth might be that when students do not invest, it might express a powerful disconnect between our course expectations, the dominant employability agenda in higher education and students' own commitment to their own employment trajectory.

Emotional learning represented an important part of students' work experiences which is not directly addressed in the formal learning outcomes of our module. It is impossible to predict what students will face during their work experiences yet coping with the effects of emotionally difficult work is a vital and quotidian part of many settings involving children and families. We want to adequately prepare our students for dealing with demanding situations when they arise. We shall retain the lectures and portfolio task on emotional labour. Still, we intend to include more intensive focused 'debriefings' over the academic year via the academic advisor groups. For example, in Chapter 12 in this book, Jaunzems-Fernuk (2022) shows how tracking student well-being through a daily in class check-in can impact students' personal and professional development. This would help our students to make sense of their experiences as they happen and add value to our debriefings, which long term, we hope will embed strategies for the resilient practitioner. In doing this, we need to be mindful of the additional emotional labour this would necessitate from academic advisors- which tends to be under-recognised. Tailoring learning to be meaningful and supportive for students is costly in terms of time, so additional work is needed to balance the economics of delivery with the type of personalised, bespoke academic advising role described here.

Conclusion

As an active learning strategy, practical work experience enables students to meaningfully engage with and be responsive to institutional norms and practices. Students' reflections were richer in experience and reflected a truer, more authentic sense of vocation than might otherwise have been expressed in a traditional university project. This is because they assess changing environments and adjust by using appropriate strategies to respond to the needs of those in their care whilst having the emotional capabilities to manage their own emotions. These examples mark out the key qualities of active learning on a Legacy Project: autonomy, meaningfulness, purposefulness, and belonging.

This chapter began by defining active learning as students' deliberate efforts to construct knowledge from practical experience; in the context of undertaking a Legacy Project, active learning is very much about deliberate action, energy, and power. As an action, active learning in our context of Legacy Projects means that students are proactive since they must ask their own questions, devise their own solutions, and identify, create, and act upon opportunities. As energy, action learning is about thinking and problem-solving and persevering. The power comes from imagining, designing, creating, and building. Yet, it is also about change: the ability to manage change or unpredictability through adapting, but also, as a deeper, more personal, developmental change.

An important goal for teaching staff is not to become disillusioned when students are resistant. As this chapter emphasises, active learning is about change and transformation, and resistance can be framed as a feature of students forming, building, challenging and sometimes, even losing, aspects of their own personal identities.

About the Author

Sarah Swann is Course Director and Employability Lead in the Carnegie School of Education at Leeds Beckett University. She can be contacted at this email: S.Swann@leedsbeckett.ac.uk.

Bibliography

Belfield, C., Britton, J., Buscha, F., Dearden, L., Dickson, M. van der Erve, L. Sibieta, L., Vignoles, A., Walker, I., & Zhu, Y. (2018). *The returns of different subjects and university choices in England*. Department for Education Report.

Bell, T., Cominetti, N., & Slaughter, H. (2020). *A new settlement for the low paid: Beyond the minimum wage to dignity and respect*. London: Resolution Foundation.

Britton, J., Drayton, E., & van der Erve, L. (2021). *Which university degrees are best for intergenerational mobility?* London: Sutton Trust.

Broom, A., & Cavenagh, J. (2011). On the meanings and experiences of living and dying in an Australian hospice. *Health (London), 15*(1), 96-111.

De Vries, R. (2014). *Earning by Degrees: Differences in the career outcomes of UK graduates*. London: The Sutton Trust.

Department for Education (2021). *Statutory framework for the early years' foundation stage: Setting the standards for learning, development and care for children from birth to five.* Nottingham: DfE publications.

Dewey, J. (1997). *Democracy and Education: An introduction to the philosophy of education.* New York: The Free Press (Original work published 1916).

Frankham, J. (2017). Employability and higher education: the follies of the 'productivity challenge' in the teaching excellence framework. *Journal of Education Policy, 32*(5), 628-641.

Guichard, J. (2016). Reflexivity in life design interventions: Comments on life and career design dialogues. *Journal of Vocational Behavior, 97,* 78-83.

Heise, B., Wing, D., & Hullinger, A. (2018). My patient died: A national study of nursing students' perceptions after experiencing a patient death. *Nursing Education Perspectives, 39*(6), 355-359.

Hochschild, A. (1983). *The managed heart: Commercialisation of human feeling.* Berkeley: University of California Press.

Jaunzems-Fernuk, J. (2022). Tracking the mental well-being of pre-service teachers in post-secondary health methods courses. In K. Enomoto, R. Warner & C. Nygaard (Eds.), *Active learning in higher education* (pp. 289-318). Oxfordshire, U.K.: Libri Publishing.

Jeffrey, B. (2002). Performativity and primary teacher relations, *Journal of Education Policy, 17*(5), 531-546.

Jones, D., Lowe, P., & West, K. (2020). Austerity in a disadvantaged West Midlands neighbourhood: Everyday experiences of families and family support professionals. *Critical Social Policy, 40*(3), 389-409.

Montessori, M. (1964). *The Montessori method* (A. E. George, Trans.). New York: Schocken Books (Original work published 1912).

Montessori, M. (1972). *The secret of childhood* (M. Joseph Costelloe, Trans.). New York: Ballantine Books (Original work published 1966).

Montessori, M. (1989). *Creative development in the child* (R. Ramachandran, Trans.). Madras, India: Kalakshetra Press.

Montessori, M. (1995). *The absorbent mind.* New York: Owl Books.

Nixon, E., & Scullion, R. (2021). Academic labour as professional service work? A psychosocial analysis of emotion in lecturer–student relations under marketization. *Human Relations, 74,* 1-26.

Noden, P., Rutherford, E., Zanini, N., Stratton, T., & Bowsher-Murray, J. (2021). *Grading gaps in summer 2020: who was affected by differences between centre assessment grades and calculated grades?* Coventry: Ofqual.

Noon, M., & Blyton, P. (2007). *The realities of work: Experiencing work and employment in contemporary society* (3rd ed.). New York: Palgrave.

Nursing and Midwifery Council (2018). Future nurse: Standards of proficiency for registered nurses. London: NMC.

OECD (2021). To what level have adults studied? In *Education at a Glance 2021: OECD Indicators*. Paris: OECD Publishing.

Office for National Statistics (2020). Standard occupational groups 2020 volume 1: Structure and descriptions of unit groups. Retrieved from https://www.ons.gov.uk/methodology/classificationsandstandards/standardoccupationalclassificationsoc/soc2020/soc2020volume1structureanddescriptionsofunitgroups

Piaget, J. (1972). Intellectual evolution from adolescence to adulthood. *Human Development, 15*(1), 1-12.

Sayer, D. (2015). *Rank Hypocrisies: The Insult of the REF*. London: Sage Swifts.

Smollan, R. (2017). Supporting staff through stressful organisational change. *Human Resource Development International, 20*(4), 22-304.

Swann, S. (2020a). *Module handbook: The graduate self*. Leeds: Leeds Beckett University.

Swann, S. (2020b). *The big book of work experiences for childhood studies*. Leeds: Leeds Beckett University.

Swann, S. (2020c). *The big book of childhood studies careers*. Leeds: Leeds Beckett University.

Swann, S. (2021). Building employability skills through collaborative group work. In K. Enomoto, R. Warner & C. Nygaard (Eds.), *Teaching and learning innovations in higher education* (pp. 475-506). Oxfordshire, U.K.: Libri Publishing.

Chapter 11
Pre-Service Second Language Teachers' Co-design of Virtual Exchanges as a Form of Active Learning in Higher Education

Giovanna Carloni

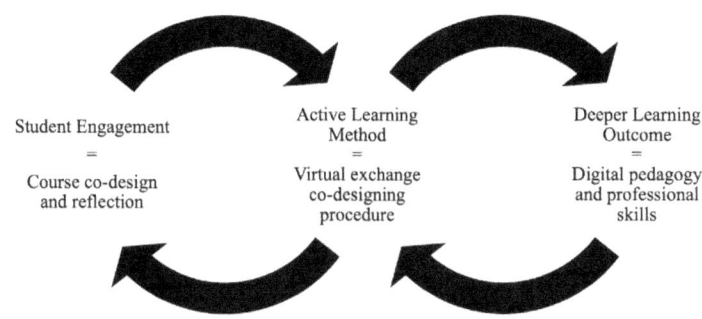

Introduction

My chapter contributes to this book, *Active Learning in Higher Education*, by showing how I have used a virtual exchange co-designing procedure to engage pre-service language teachers in course co-design and reflection-on-action. To develop their digital pedagogy and professional skills through active learning, the chapter describes a conceptual framework that was used to facilitate pre-service language teachers' virtual exchange co-design in the context of a master's program at the University of Urbino in Italy.

Virtual exchanges, in general, promote second language learning and cultivate intercultural awareness (Liddicoat & Scarino, 2013; O'Dowd, 2016b; Vinagre, 2016; Porto, 2017; Sykes, 2018) and have become increasingly important in higher education in the new normal. Virtual exchanges are a form of mobility whereby two groups of students or a

Chapter 11

group of pre-service teachers and students in different countries engage online. In this chapter, I refer to active learning as the processes in which pre-service language teachers co-design, implement, and analyse a virtual exchange as part of their practicum.

When reading this chapter, you will gain the following three insights:
1. how to facilitate pre-service language teachers' active learning by including them in the design of virtual exchanges from an intercultural perspective;
2. how to enhance pre-service language teachers' active learning by including them in the implementation of a co-designed virtual exchange;
3. how to promote pre-service language teachers' active learning through technology-enhanced reflection-on-action.

Overview of main sections

The chapter is divided into three main sections. In Section 1, I introduce the methodological construct underpinning the choice of promoting pre-service language teachers' active learning through virtual exchange co-design. Then, in Section 2, I describe how pre-service language teachers engaged in virtual exchange co-design and implementation as a practicum, the virtual exchange taking place in a graduate language teacher education course, namely a master's programme, delivered online at the University of Urbino in Italy. This is followed by Section 3, which outlines the outcome of my active learning case based on both quantitative and qualitative data, describing the main trends emerging from the findings. In Section 4, I discuss ways to further improve the current virtual exchange for the future before concluding this chapter.

Section 1: The background to active learning

In higher education, the COVID-19 disruption has led to intensive digitalisation; technology-enhanced learning has thus become an essential dimension of language teacher education. In this respect, to develop digital pedagogy skills, it is vital for pre-service language teachers:

- to be introduced to the theoretical framework underpinning digital learning;
- to design effective technology-enhanced language learning activities;
- to experience teaching a second language online; and
- to reflect upon the teaching practices adopted in online teaching.

Although there are myriad definitions of active learning, the core components of active learning may be traced back to Bonwell and Eison (1991:iii), who defined active learning as students' engagement in their learning process at cognitive and metacognitive levels: *"...[and] to be actively involved, students must engage in [...] higher-order thinking tasks as analysis, synthesis and evaluation. Within this context, it is proposed that strategies promoting active learning be defined as anything that involves students in doing things and thinking about the things they are doing".*

Students engage in individual and collaborative knowledge construction in active learning while carrying out tasks fostering critical thinking, skills development, and autonomy (Michael, 2006; Oros, 2007; Stefanou et al., 2013; Lee et al., 2018). Various methodologies can promote active learning, including problem-solving, inquiry-based learning, project-based learning, cooperative learning, collaborative learning, problem-based learning, role-playing, simulation, and peer learning (Bonwell & Eison, 1991; Walker, 2003; Prince, 2004; Ishiyama, 2013; Stefanou et al., 2013; Nelson & Crow, 2014). The active learning paradigm is engagement (Prince, 2004) and interactive engagement in particular (Børte *et al.*, 2020). Hake (1998:65) defines interactive engagement as follows: *"'Interactive Engagement' IE methods [are] [...] those designed at least in part to promote conceptual understanding through interactive engagement of students in heads-on (always) and hands-on (usually) activities which yield immediate feedback through discussion with peers and/or instructors."*

In a student-centred active learning environment, learners participate in their learning process by first engaging in meaningful tasks and thinking back about their learning practices afterwards, which is pivotal to developing autonomy (Prince, 2004). In this light, pre-service teachers' active learning may be envisioned through action and reflection-on-action (Argyris & Schön, 1974, 1978; Schön, 1983). In the context investigated here, pre-service teachers' active learning is conceptualised through i) the virtual exchange co-designing process in which they engage and ii) the analysis of the implementation of the collaboratively developed virtual exchange. As part of their technology-enhanced collaborative active learning process (Børte et al., 2020), our pre-service teachers actively engaged in digital course design, course implementation, and reflection-on-action. In virtual exchanges, at least two groups of students, or a group of learners and a group of pre-service teachers, from different areas around the world engage in curriculum-based activities in facilitated online learning environments (O'Dowd, 2015, 2016a, 2016b, 2020, 2021; O'Dowd & Dooly, 2020). Active learning is a paradigm of the virtual exchange pedagogical practise along with its intercultural dimension (Satar, 2021).

The development of language skills, digital literacy, online collaborative skills, critical thinking, and global intercultural awareness has emerged as a key pedagogical and professional affordance of virtual exchange. Such an affordance is also envisaged as a form of Internationalisation at Home (Helm & van der Velden, 2019; European Union and EACEA, 2020; Helm & O'Dowd, 2020). In this respect, virtual exchanges foster the development of professional global skills and literacies (Háhn, 2020). Furthermore, the development of digital competencies and innovative pedagogies represents the core of pre-service and in-service teacher training at the European Union policy level (European Commission, 2019). In this respect, in virtual exchanges, pre-service and in-service teachers can develop digital pedagogy and innovative pedagogies (European Commission, 2013, 2016, 2018) along with intercultural awareness-raising (Eren, 2021). In general, a virtual exchange is primarily instrumental in cultivating the development of active, innovative, digital pedagogies in keeping with the European Union policy (European Council and European Commission, 2015).

Section 2: The case of active learning

This subsection illustrates how pre-service language teachers engage in active learning through virtual exchange co-design, virtual exchange implementation, and reflection-on-action. Pre-service teachers took part in the virtual exchange as a practicum implemented in an online master's programme offered by the University of Urbino; the course trained teachers of Italian as a second language.

As a language teacher trainer, the instructor responsible for the virtual exchange project had already developed virtual exchanges where pre-service teachers of Italian as a second language at an Italian university had been partnered with language learners studying Italian as a second language at American, Australian, and South African universities (Carloni & Franzè, 2012, 2021; Carloni & Zuccala, 2018, 2020). In virtual exchanges, instructors usually provide pre-service teachers with a framework that they have to implement; as a result, pre-service teachers' creativity is limited to devising teaching activities since they are not involved in the development of the framework. However, after the pandemic, it is of paramount importance for pre-service teachers to learn how to co-design virtual exchanges themselves and test the effectiveness of the co-developed virtual exchanges while also reflecting on their teaching and learning practices through digital individual and collaborative metacognitive activities. Therefore, pre-service teachers' active learning and agency must take centre stage in the new normal, which expects language teachers to design digital learning environments and consistently adjust them to the ever-changing social and learning contexts.

Thus, a virtual exchange was developed as a practicum within a graduate language teacher training course, delivered online for the first time. Before engaging in their virtual exchange practicum, pre-service teachers had previously attended a language pedagogy workshop. In the workshop, they had been introduced to the tenets of digital pedagogy and had engaged in a virtual exchange project. In the virtual exchange, pre-service teachers had developed activities based on a framework provided by the workshop instructor. A month after completing the virtual exchange, a group of pre-service teachers participated in another virtual exchange as part of their practicum. Throughout this new learning context, pre-service teachers engaged in virtual exchange co-design.

Chapter 11

An overview of how pre-service teachers work with active learning

In the online language pedagogy workshop, pre-service teachers were introduced to virtual exchange first through a video tour of the South African city and university selected as the partner of the virtual exchange. Specifically, the pre-service teachers had experienced a 3D virtual tour where students of Italian as a second language studied. This approach highly motivated the pre-service teachers, who felt immersed in a new and engaging context. Afterwards, the pre-service teachers were provided with the syllabus of the Italian language course that the students were attending, the digital format of the textbook adopted in the course, and the topics that the instructor wanted the pre-service teachers to focus on during the virtual exchange project.

During the second virtual exchange, developed as a practicum, a group of pre-service teachers interacted with students of Italian of the same cohort. The pre-service teachers were provided with the more advanced Italian language course syllabus and the topics that the instructor wanted pre-service teachers to focus on during the virtual exchange. Thus, while co-designing the virtual exchange, the pre-service teachers could rely on similarities between the two projects, especially regarding students and requests from the Italian language instructor.

How to prepare and organise active learning

Under the guidance of their language pedagogy instructor, the pre-service teachers co-designed the virtual exchange in terms of synchronous and asynchronous activities; pre-service teachers also selected the open educational digital resources suitable for creating interactive technology-enhanced activities. The pre-service teachers developed the virtual exchange framework within a socio-constructivist view of language, where speakers socially co-construct knowledge and develop a language through dialogical interaction (Vygotsky, 1978; Lantolf, 2000; Lantolf & Thorne, 2006; Selwyn, 2016; Cope & Kalantzis, 2017; Lantolf et al., 2020). The framework scaffolded the development of university students' dialogical skills in an additional language and from an intercultural perspective. The pre-service teachers framed the virtual exchange co-design within the notion of investment: *"The notion of investment…conceives of the language learner as having a complex social history and multiple desires. The notion presupposes that when language learners speak, they are not only exchanging information with target language speakers, but they are constantly organizing and reorganizing a sense of who they are and how they relate to the social world. Thus, an investment in the target language is also an investment in a learner's own identity, an identity which is constantly changing across time and space"* (Norton, 2013:79-80).

In this light, while devising the virtual exchange experience, the pre-service teachers focused on activities suitable for enhancing students' investment in the language learning process (Norton, 2013). In this respect, the pre-service teachers were aware that the degree to which learners invest in the language learning practices is deeply affected by the way power is negotiated among the interactants in the class (Darvin & Norton, 2017). Furthermore, the pre-service teachers knew that learners' degree of investment in language learning affects how learners accept sharing their identities in the learning community (Darvin & Norton, 2015). As a result, the pre-service teachers devised activities and adopted teaching and conversational strategies, likely to make learners feel highly valued and listened to.

Together, the pre-service teachers co-designed the framework of the virtual exchange and the structure of each lesson. Then, in pairs, the pre-service teachers created the activities for each lesson and self-selected their peers. The pre-service teachers devised the framework and the lesson organization using the main tenets of digital pedagogy; as a result, they created highly chunked activities that promoted language skills and active learning (Bates, 2019; Hampel, 2020; Richmond et al., 2021; Russell & Murphy-Judy, 2021). Each lesson included two asynchronous digital pre-class activities and a 15-minute synchronous class. The asynchronous activities were aimed at fostering the students' review of targeted grammar and lexical sets, and the students completed the activities autonomously online.

In contrast, the students interacted in Italian during each synchronous class with the pre-service teachers. The pre-service teachers engaged with students in two tasks to foster meaningful dialogical interaction in the additional language. Each pair of pre-service teachers chose their topic, provided by the Italian language instructor teaching at the South

African university. Each pair developed the digital activities for one of the five one-on-one classes scheduled for the project and shared the activities, including the guidelines to implement them, on a Padlet-based noticeboard. The group self-selected a pre-service teacher responsible for supervising the co-designing process and the lesson schedule implementation; the pre-service teachers thus further engaged in active learning.

In the virtual exchange, nine pre-service language teachers were partnered with seven undergraduate students of Italian as a second language studying Italian at a university in South Africa. In the virtual exchange, each student engaged in five online one-on-one classes spread out over six weeks. Since there were fewer students than pre-service teachers, each student engaged in five lessons, while some pre-service teachers voluntarily taught more than one student. The lessons focused on the following topics:

- fashion;
- professions;
- food and friends;
- travelling;
- movies and shows;
- making requests politely;
- expressing one's desires;
- expressing one's opinions;
- giving orders;
- making predictions; and
- making hypotheses.

Since game-based learning may increase students' motivation, the pre-service teachers co-designed a game-based classroom to foster students' motivation and autonomy (Jones et al., 2022). At the same time, to foster equity, access, and inclusion in education, which are pivotal in the new normal, pre-service teachers opted for free-to-use digital resources (Rapanta et al., 2020; Van Allen & Katz, 2020). In particular, to create pre-class autonomous interactive activities, pre-service teachers used free-to-use digital tools. These included: Voki, suitable for creating speaking avatars either using text-to-speech software or recording one's own voice; Wordwall, suitable for devising fun interactive activities and games, such as random wheels, matching pairs, word searches, and game-show quizzes; Educaplay, suitable for devising interactive activities, such as crossword puzzles, word-search puzzles, memory games, matching games, and map quizzes. Interactive game-based learning was thus instrumental in fostering students' motivation and engagement in autonomous digital learning. For synchronous classes, pre-service teachers developed technology-enhanced role-plays and tasks, such as opinion exchange; the activities were screen-shared during the video calls.

Before each live class, pre-service teachers sent the students with whom they were partnered the links (via WhatsApp) to the asynchronous activities that they were expected to carry out before meeting on Google Meet, Zoom or WhatsApp. In this context, it is important to mention that before contacting the students for the first time, pre-service teachers recorded and shared a video with students on Padlet. In this video, they introduced themselves, talked about their interests, and mentioned what they hoped the students would gain from the virtual exchange and what they expected to learn as to-be teachers. Students could access the videos on the shared Padlet and thus get to know their teachers in advance, which is especially useful to lower students' and teachers' anxiety (Carloni & Zuccala, 2020). Furthermore, before meeting students online, pre-service teachers watched the self-introductions that students had video recorded for the previous virtual exchange. After each live class, pre-service teachers and learners filled in a semi-structured questionnaire to reflect on the experience. Furthermore, pre-service teachers shared a video with their peers. They reflected on the online lesson and commented on each other's videos; pre-service teachers also wrote an entry in their digital journals. Pre-service teachers' reflective practice was thus consistently fostered since they were instrumental to their practicum.

Finally, upon the conclusion of the virtual exchange, pre-service teachers shared their final reflections on the project in a visually-based collaborative noticeboard in Mural. Here, pre-service teachers pinned their ideas in a feedback template divided into four sections. In particular, they shared their final comprehensive comments on what worked well, what needed to be changed, unanswered questions, and new ideas to try out in future virtual exchanges. As a result of the whole process, pre-service teachers had the opportunity to co-design the project's macro-structure, devise activities in pairs, try out the activities designed by their peers, and reflect upon the teaching practices implemented.

Section 3: The outcome

A total of nine pre-service teachers of Italian enrolled in a master's programme (Teaching Italian as a Second Language) at the University of Urbino took part in the study. The study addressed the following research question: *How effective were the pre-service teachers' co-design active learning processes for developing their digital pedagogy and professional skills?* Both quantitative and qualitative data representing the pre-service teachers' perceptions of their experience were collected from the following three sources:

1) semi-structured questionnaires (quantitative and qualitative data): the pre-service teachers completed semi-structured questionnaires after each online live class;

2) digital journals (qualitative data): the pre-service teachers wrote their reflections in the digital journal entries after each online live class;

3) recorded videos (qualitative data): the pre-service teachers video-recorded their reflections after each online live class to share them with their peers.

As for the qualitative data obtained from the above three sources, thematic analyses, suitable for analysing qualitative data, were carried out (Braun & Clarke, 2021; Terry & Hayfield, 2021); the most recurring themes were thus codified. However, it should be noted here that the collected data represented the small sample (9) that was too small to yield conclusive results. However, the findings outlined below provide other language educators with useful ways to identify initial trends and indicators for successfully implementing pre-service teachers' virtual exchange co-designing procedures.

The findings

Most synchronous classes took place on Google Meet (83.1%), while the rest took place either on Zoom (12.3%) or WhatsApp (4.6%). Figure 1 shows that pre-service teachers mostly agreed (80%) that students found the dialogical interaction activities carried out during live classes to be most motivating. The rest of the pre-service teachers (20%) thought that students found pre-class asynchronous activities to be most motivating. Likewise, most pre-service teachers (83.1%) held that students found the dialogical interaction activities during live classes most useful. In comparison, the rest (16.9%) thought that students found pre-class asynchronous activities preferable. Overall, students' preference for activities fostering dialogical interaction with Italian native speakers seemed to emerge as a key paradigm of the virtual exchange.

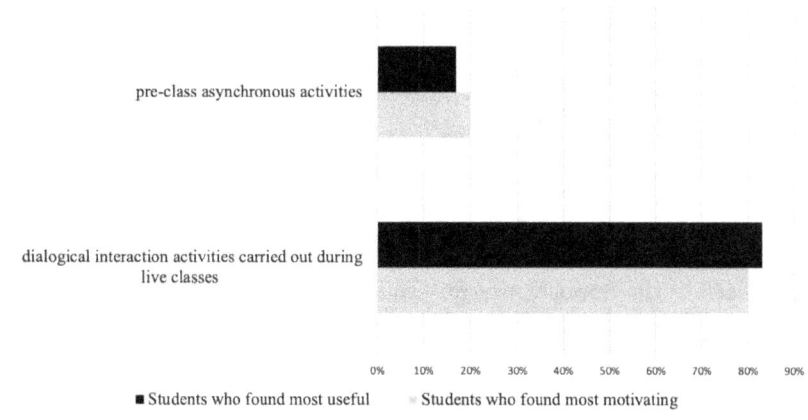

Figure 1: Pre-service teachers' answers to closed questions.

Thematic analyses, suitable for analysing qualitative data, were also carried out (Braun & Clarke, 2021; Terry & Hayfield, 2021) concerning the open-ended questions in the semi-structured questionnaires and the digital journal entries and the content of the videos; the most recurring themes were thus codified. Analysing qualitative data, a key topic emerged: the pre-service teachers' perceptions of students' preference for their activities during live classes and the reasons underpinning this preference. The pre-service teachers claimed that students preferred synchronous activities because the activities provided them all with the opportunity to talk about something they are proud of, such as their country and its history, and something about which they care deeply, such as specific cultural and socio-economic phenomena. As a result, the synchronous activities enabled learners to express their identity through the additional language. Furthermore, the pre-service teachers held that students especially appreciated synchronous activities because they felt that they helped them improve their speaking skills significantly, engage in intercultural awareness-raising dialogical interactions, experience self-correction, and connect with their teachers successfully. On the other hand, the pre-service teachers thought that students enjoyed pre-class asynchronous activities because they were highly interactive and suitable for autonomous, anxiety-free learning. Students especially enjoyed the Voki-based activities where, through avatars, they recorded a monologue or used text-to-speech software to generate a monologue on a given topic; this kind of activity fostered students' oral output production in a safe learning environment.

Using a 5-point Likert scale (with 5 corresponding to very useful and 1 to not-at-all useful), the majority of the pre-service teachers (72.3%) agreed that the live classes were 'very useful' to their students; 18.5% of the pre-service teachers agreed that the classes were 'useful' while the rest (9.2%) were 'neutral'. The usefulness of the live classes was mainly attributed to the opportunity for students:

- to review targeted grammar and language functions and to learn new vocabulary items in a contextualised and meaningful way;
- to engage in extensive dialogical interaction and negotiation of meaning in the target language;
- to increase their talking time, as well as improve their sense of self-efficacy;
- to keep their motivation high; and
- to become aware of Italian culture-specific practices.

Again, using a 5-point Likert scale (with 5 corresponding to very motivating and 1 to not-at-all motivating), the pre-service teachers agreed that the topics discussed during live classes were 'very motivating' (67.7%) or 'motivating' (23.1%) for the students. In contrast, the rest (9.2%) were 'neutral'. The pre-service teachers claimed that students found the topics motivating for various reasons: learners were deeply interested in Italian culture, including the Italian value system; the activities encouraged students to talk about their own culture and country from an intercultural perspective; and finally, the activities were highly engaging and enhanced high student talking time effectively.

The pre-service teachers designed activities aimed to foster intercultural awareness so that students could learn about Italian cultural practices and, at the same time, the pre-service teachers could learn about South African cultural practices. The findings show that both parties consistently analysed the two countries' value systems and social practices during synchronous classes. Students and pre-service teachers especially appreciated the intercultural awareness consistently emerging from the activities during live classes.

Most pre-service teachers (80%) thought they always made students feel welcome and comfortable during the project, while the rest (20%) claimed that they often succeeded. Figure 2 shows that, almost to the same degree, during live classes, pre-service teachers felt mostly comfortable (76.9%) and calm (20%) while they felt worried or nervous to a much lesser degree (3.1%). Likewise, during live classes, pre-service teachers claimed that students felt most comfortable (69.2%) and calm (27.7%) and only to a much lesser extent worried or nervous (3.1%).

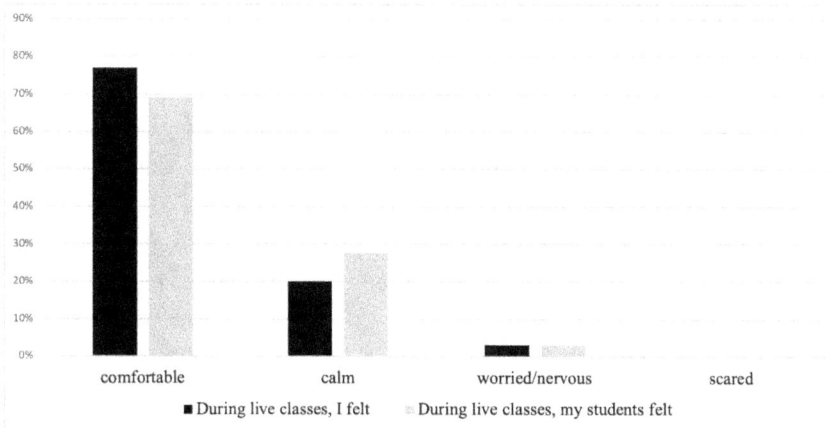

Figure 2: Pre-service teachers' perceptions.

A high degree of engagement seems to have occurred during live classes. About half of the pre-service teachers (52.3%) claimed that they spoke up to between 40-60% of the lesson time; 20% held that they talked less than 40% of the lesson time, while 20% thought that they talked up to between 60-80% of the time. The rest seemed to talk less than 10% of the time. As the project moved along, the pre-service teachers talked less and less while students' talking time increased. The co-devised activities seemed thus to foster students' dialogical skills significantly, especially if compared to the very limited student talking time language learners experienced during the Italian language classes at their university. During live classes, the pre-service teachers appreciated especially:

- the opinion exchange on topics discussed from an intercultural perspective where both interactants were deeply interested in learning about each other's cultural values and practices;
- the increasing emotional connection with students, also emerging from similar experiences as language learners;
- students' consistent motivation and positive feedback on asynchronous and synchronous activities;
- the possibility to experience students' study context thanks to technology (for example, one pre-service teacher enjoyed deeply being guided by the student to discover the campus of the South African university; the student used his/her camera phone to show and describe the various areas of university);
- their increased confidence as teachers.

When asked to indicate what they would change in the lesson structure, most pre-service teachers said 'nothing' (75.4%). At the same time, the rest wrote either the activities devised for live classes (26.2%) or, to a much lesser extent, the pre-class activity (3.1%). The pre-service teachers appeared highly satisfied with the lessons and the effectiveness of asynchronous and synchronous activities, although they seemed aware that something needed to be improved. In terms of synchronous activities, in particular, the pre-service teachers claimed the necessity to scaffold better the tasks provided.

When asked what they would change in the live classes, half of the pre-service teachers answered 'nothing', while the rest highlighted some key issues: adding an icebreaker at the beginning of each live class to increase teacher-student connection; being able to manage students' silence better during oral interactions; personalising the activities to cater to students' needs; and longer synchronous classes. Concerning the synchronous classes, it is noteworthy that although live classes were scheduled to last about 15 minutes, they mostly lasted much longer. 56.9% of live classes lasted about 30 minutes while the rest lasted even longer. These data suggest that the pre-service teachers and students were willing to engage for an extended period, probably because they both felt invested in the teaching/learning process.

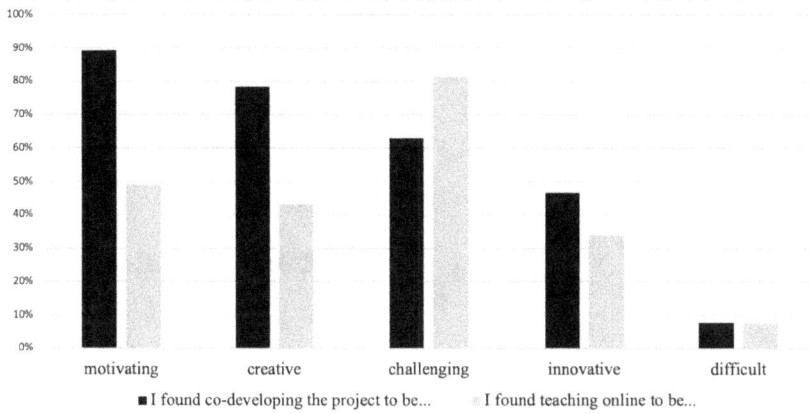

Figure 3: Pre-service teachers' perceptions.

When asked to evaluate the affordances and challenges of the co-designing process, the pre-service teachers, who were free to choose as many options as they wanted among those provided (the 'other' choice was also available), claimed that they found co-developing the project motivating (89.2%), creative (78.5%), challenging (63.1%), innovative (46.5%), and only to a very low extent difficult (7.7%) (Figure 3). Furthermore, one pre-service teacher added that they identified the opportunity to negotiate ideas with their peers as an affordance (1.5%). When asked to evaluate their online teaching experience, the pre-service teachers, who were free to pick as many options as they wanted among those provided (the 'other' choice was also available), claimed that they found teaching online challenging (81.5%), motivating (49.2%), creative (43.1%), innovative (33.8%), and to a much lesser extent difficult (7.7%) (Figure 3). Thus, the pre-service teachers found co-developing the project much more motivating and creative than teaching online, suggesting that virtual exchange co-design successfully fostered active learning. On the other hand, teaching online was experienced as marginally more challenging than co-designing, although both processes emerged as challenging to some extent.

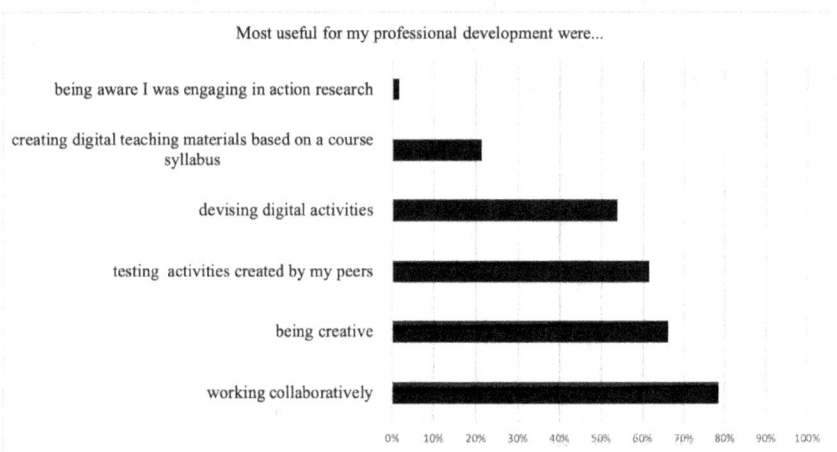

Figure 4: Pre-service teachers' perceptions.

The pre-service teachers were asked to highlight what they found most useful in the project for their professional development and were free to select as many options as they wanted among those provided (the 'other' choice was also available). They held that what they found most useful was working collaboratively (78.5%), being creative (66.2%), testing the activities created by their peers (61.5%), devising digital activities (53.8%), creating digital teaching materials based on a course syllabus (23.1%), and being aware, as one pre-service teacher added, that they were engaging in action research (1.5%) (Figure 4).

After each live class, the pre-service teachers reflected on their teaching practices in various ways. In particular, using a 5-point Likert scale (with 5 corresponding to very motivating and 1 to not-at-all motivating), the pre-service teachers found recording the videos after each live lesson, where they shared feelings and ideas about the teaching experience and commented on their peers' ideas, either very useful (66.2%) or useful (33.8%), which suggests the effectiveness of a reflective practice. The findings suggest that the pre-service teachers especially enjoyed watching their peers' reflections and commenting on each other's ideas. The pre-service teachers defined recording and watching the reflective videos as inspirational; they also described the video-based reflective practice as instrumental in learning about new techniques suitable for bonding with students and learning how to cater activities to students' needs more effectively. Furthermore, the pre-service teachers claimed that recording the videos helped them:

- to share their emotions about the live classes;
- to reflect more thoroughly on the lesson they had just taught;
- to share regrets and/or fears and receive encouraging feedback from their peers;
- to learn collaboratively;
- to remember and/or reorganise and analyse the various steps of the live lessons;
- to create a cohesive group; and
- to feel part of an engaging group.

The co-designing experience was thus likely to lead the pre-service teachers to perceive the added value of collaborative, reflective practices. After each class, the pre-service teachers were asked to mention a takeaway from the lesson. The pre-service teachers' takeaways can be classified into three categories:

1. the awareness of their increased sense of self-efficacy as language teachers;
2. the awareness of the pedagogical value of a welcoming learning environment where students feel safe to speak in the target language and make mistakes;
3. the awareness of the necessity to plan lessons in detail but at the same time to be flexible during lesson delivery.

Furthermore, the pre-service teachers pinpointed the ability to create a strong student-teacher connection and provide students with activities that enable them to express their identity through the medium of the additional language. The pre-service teachers also learnt that it is important to foster students' sense of self-efficacy and involve learners in activity design to increase their active learning and agency. The findings, in general, showed a very high level of satisfaction on the part of the pre-service teachers. In particular, the pre-service teachers pinpointed the affordances of the co-designing process in terms of digital pedagogy and professional development. They also valued creativity (a key dimension of online learning), self-empowerment (a form of self-efficacy), and reflective learning as dimensions of active learning.

Teacher perspective – my reflections

The findings indicate a high degree of satisfaction on the part of the language students. They highly valued their dialogical skills development (a key objective of the project) and intercultural awareness-raising, another key dimension of the virtual exchange. As suggested by the perceptions gathered through post-class semi-structured questionnaires, the language students involved in the virtual exchange were enthusiastic about the project. In this light, it is noteworthy that students' perceptions of the effectiveness of the virtual exchange in terms of dialogical skills and intercultural awareness development matched the virtual exchange objectives that the pre-service teachers had co-designed. Furthermore, students' perceptions consistently highlighted their appreciation for how the activities enhanced intercultural awareness in culture-specific practise analysis; in the virtual exchange, both pre-service teachers and students learnt something about each other's culture, which made the interactions more authentic and meaningful for them.

As part of the project and as a language teacher trainer, I learnt to decrease my control over the pre-service teachers' activity design, which was a challenge for me. Furthermore, I was pleasantly surprised by how well co-design worked for the pre-service teachers' professional development – although it was defined as challenging – and how satisfied they were with their digital pedagogy and digital materials design skills, which is pivotal for the development of pre-service teachers' sense of self-efficacy.

The co-designing process, meaning the involvement of learners in the course and curriculum design, thus seems to be a key paradigm of active learning (Enomoto & Warner, 2022, Chapter 5 in this book). I have also realised the increasing value of fostering active learning in teacher training courses, especially in the new normal, because teachers need to be more flexible and able to reframe their teaching practices at local and global levels. As part of the project, I also appreciated the high value that pre-service teachers recognised in reflective practices.

Section 4: Moving forward

The pre-service teachers illustrated their virtual exchange experience in their final papers, which they presented and discussed online in front of a committee as their final oral exam. In this context, it is worth mentioning that the pre-service teachers' analysis of the project was thorough and exciting, and the teacher education course director was deeply appreciative of the outcome of the virtual exchange-based practicum. As a result, the language pedagogy workshop instructor will have the opportunity to implement an expanded version of the virtual exchange as a practicum with the next cohort of pre-service teachers. The opportunity granted is representative of the effectiveness of the virtual exchange co-design framework developed in terms of pre-service teachers' active learning and professional development in the new normal.

The affordances of the virtual exchange co-design project are various. First of all, the framework collaboratively devised has proven to be effective in terms of pre-service teachers' digital pedagogy and professional development, which means that the newly developed collaborative procedures and processes succeeded in fostering pre-service teachers' active learning. Second, pre-service teachers realised the role of open educational resources to engage in course design targeted at equity and inclusion development. In this respect, the virtual exchange practicum developed emerges as a successful example of sustainable collaborative active learning in higher education, a field which still needs to expand: *"While policymakers and researchers assume a transforming potential of technology, a systematic review on the topic (Lillejord et al. 2018) find [sic] few examples of sustainable, innovative teaching practices and few examples of successful student active learning designs in higher education"* (Børte et al., 2020:4).

Some aspects of the project may be modified or improved in future reiterations. For example, language pedagogy instructors responsible for developing similar projects may use visually-based collaborative learning environments more extensively, such as Mural and Miro. Visual thinking might help pre-service teachers better brainstorm and organise ideas at macro and micro levels while engaging in divergent thinking during the co-designing process. The visual collaboration that pre-service teachers experienced only at the end of this virtual exchange project may thus become a more consistent aspect of the co-design project; the practice might also help pre-service teachers to convey complex ideas and thus communicate better. Furthermore, digital storytelling might be included in the project to contextualise further and personalise asynchronous and synchronous learning. In this light, language educators working in language teacher training programmes at national and international levels may adopt the framework devised to implement a virtual exchange co-designing process.

Conclusion

Working together with other pre-service teachers to co-develop, implement, and analyse digital learning experiences catering to language learners' needs has emerged as a key professional competence in the new normal. In this respect, this study shows that a pre-service teachers' virtual exchange co-designing process and a multimodal reflection-on-action successfully promoted the pre-service teachers' active learning. As a result, their digital pedagogy and professional skills improved. The findings also show the added value of using open educational resources to cater to students' needs and foster inclusion. Furthermore, the pre-service teachers succeeded in devising activities that enhanced students' dialogical skills and enabled learners to convey their own identity; the findings show that the pre-service teachers co-designed a learning environment where language learners felt they could invest in the target language.

The co-designed virtual exchange investigated in the study represents a cutting-edge practicum in which language teachers may engage successfully. This chapter may thus be beneficial to instructors planning to foster pre-service language teachers' active learning and digital pedagogy skills through virtual exchange co-design in teacher training courses.

About the Author

Giovanna Carloni is a Lecturer in Second Language Education in the School of Foreign Languages at the University of Urbino, Italy. She can be contacted at this email: giovanna.carloni@uniurb.it

Bibliography

Argyris, C., & Schön, D. (1974). *Theory in practice. Increasing professional effectiveness*. San Francisco: Jossey-Bass.

Argyris, C., & Schön, D. (1978). *Organizing learning. A theory of action perspective*. Boston: Addison-Wesley Publishing.

Bates, T. (2019). *Teaching in a digital age*. Vancouver, B.C.: Tony Bates Associates LTD.

Bonwell, C. C., & Eison, J. A. (1991). *Active learning: Creating excitement in the classroom* (ASHE–ERIC Higher Education Rep. No. 1). Washington, DC: The George Washington University, School of Education and Human Development.

Børte, K., Nesje, K., & Lillejord, S. (2020). Barriers to student active learning in higher education. *Teaching in Higher Education*, 1–19.

Braun, V., & Clarke, V. (2021). *Thematic analysis. A practical guide*. London: Sage Publishing.

Carloni, G., & Franzè, F. (2012). New York skypes Italy: let's get global! In Proceedings of *INTED 2012 – International Technology, Education and Development Conference* (pp. 6491–6500), 5-7 March, Valencia, Spain.

Carloni, G., & Franzè, F. (2021). A telecollaborative international exchange for foreign language learning and reflective teaching. In G. Carloni, C. Fotheringham, A. Virga & B. Zuccala (Eds.), *Blended learning and the global south. Virtual exchanges in higher education* (pp. 131–158). Venezia: Edizioni Ca' Foscari Digital Publishing.

Carloni, G., & Zuccala, B. (2018). Blending Italian 'down-under': Toward a theoretical framework and pragmatic guide for blending tertiary Italian language and culture courses through Skype-enhanced, pre-service teacher-centred telecollaboration. *LEA - Lingue e letterature d'Oriente e d'Occidente*, 7, 405–445.

Carloni, G., & Zuccala, B. (2020). Blending Italian through Skype: A diachronic and comparative account of a telecollaborative project. In J. Fornasiero, S. M. A. Reed, R. Amery, E. Bouvet, K. Enomoto & H. L. Xu

(Eds.), *Intersections in language planning and policy. Establishing connections in languages and cultures* (pp. 279–298). Cham, Switzerland: Springer Nature.

Cope, B., & Kalantzis, M. (2017). Conceptualizing e-learning. In B. Cope & M. Kalantzis (Eds.), *E-learning ecologies: Principles for new learning and assessment* (pp. 1–45). New York and Abingdon: Routledge.

Darvin, R., & Norton, B. (2015). Identity and a model of investment in applied linguistics. *Annual Review of Applied Linguistics, 35*, 36–56.

Darvin, R., & Norton, B. (2017). Identity, language learning, and critical pedagogies in digital times. In J. Cenoz, D. Gorter & S. May (Eds.), *Encyclopedia of language and education: Vol. 6, Language awareness and multilingualism* (3rd Edition) (pp. 43–54). Charm, Switzerland: Springer.

Enomoto, K., & Warner, R. (2022). Partnering with student leaders: Active learning through integration of Peer Assisted Study Sessions into an undergraduate language course. In K. Enomoto, R. Warner & C. Nygaard (Eds.), *Active learning in higher education* (pp. 107–134). Oxfordshire, U.K: Libri Publishing Ltd.

Eren, Ö. (2021). Raising critical cultural awareness through telecollaboration: insights for pre-service teacher education. *Computer Assisted Language Learning*, 1–24.

European Commission (2013). *Study on the policy measures to improve the attractiveness of the teaching profession in Europe*. Luxembourg: Publications Office of the European Union.

European Commission (2016). *Improving and modernising education*. Luxembourg: Publications Office of the European Union.

European Commission (2018). *Digital education action plan*. Luxembourg: Publications Office of the European Union.

European Commission (2019). *Education and training 2020: Highlights from the ET2020 Working Groups 2016-2017*. Luxembourg: Publications Office of the European Union.

European Council and European Commission (2015). *Joint Report of the Council and the Commission on the implementation of the strategic framework for European cooperation in education and training (ET 2020): New priorities for European cooperation in education and training*. Luxembourg: Publications Office of the European Union.

European Union and EACEA. (2020). *Erasmus+ Virtual Exchange – Handbook for international relations officers*. Luxembourg: Publications Office of the European Union.

Háhn, J. (2020). ICED 2020 proceedings: Virtual exchange: Future-ready teaching of multiliteracies across borders and cultures. *ETH Learning and Teaching Journal, 2*(2).

Hake, R. R. (1998). Interactive-engagement versus traditional methods: A six-thousand-student survey of mechanics test data for introductory physics courses. *American Journal of Physics, 66*(1), 64–74.

Hampel, R. (2020). *Disruptive technologies and the language classroom. A complex systems theory approach.* Cham, Switzerland: Palgrave MacMillan.

Helm, F., & O'Dowd, R. (2020). *Virtual exchange and its role in blended mobility initiatives.* UNICollaboration.org

Helm, F., & van der Velden, B. (2019). *Erasmus+ virtual exchange intercultural learning experiences: 2018 Impact Report.* European Union and EACEA.

Ishiyama, J. (2013). Frequently used active learning techniques and their impact: a critical review of existing journal literature in the United States. *European Political Science, 12,* 116–126.

Jones, M., Blanton, J. E., & Williams, R. E. (2022). Science to practice: Does gamification enhance intrinsic motivation? *Active Learning in Higher Education.*

Lantolf, J. (2000). Introducing sociocultural theory. In J. Lantolf (Ed.), *Sociocultural theory and second language learning* (pp. 1–26). Oxford: Oxford University Press.

Lantolf, J., Poehner, M., & Thorne, S. L. (2020). Sociocultural theory and second language development. In B. VanPatten, G. Keating & S. Wulff (Eds.), *Theories in second language acquisition* (3rd ed.) (pp. 223–247). New York: Routledge.

Lantolf, J. P., & Thorne, S. L. (2006). *Sociocultural theory and the genesis of second language development.* Oxford: Oxford University Press.

Lee, D., Morrone, A. S., & Siering, G. (2018). From swimming pool to collaborative learning studio: Pedagogy, space, and technology in a large active learning classroom. *Educational Technology Research and Development, 66*(1), 95–127.

Liddicoat, J. A., & Scarino, A. (2013). *Intercultural language teaching and learning.* Oxford: Wiley-Blackwell.

Michael, J. (2006). Where's the evidence that active learning works? *Advances in Physiology Education, 30,* 159–67.

Nelson, L. P., & Crow, M. L. (2014). Do active-learning strategies improve students' critical thinking? *Higher Education Studies, 4,* 77–90.

Norton, B. (2013). *Identity and language learning. Extending the conversation* (2nd Edition). Bristol, Buffalo, Toronto: Multilingual Matters.

O'Dowd, R. (2015). Supporting in-service language educators in learning to telecollaborate. *Language Learning & Technology, 19*(1), 64–83.

O'Dowd, R. (2016a). Emerging trends and new directions in telecollaborative learning. *CALICO Journal, 33*(3), 291–310.

O'Dowd, R. (2016b). Learning from the past and looking to the future of online intercultural exchange. In R. O'Dowd & T. Lewis (Eds.), *Online intercultural exchange: policy, pedagogy, practice* (pp. 273–298). New York: Longman.

O'Dowd, R. (2020). A transnational model of virtual exchange for global citizenship education. *Language Teaching, 53*(4), 477–490.

O'Dowd, R. (2021). What do students learn in virtual exchange? A qualitative content analysis of learning outcomes across multiple exchanges. *International Journal of Educational Research, 109*, 1-13.

O'Dowd, R., & Dooly, M. (2020). Intercultural communicative competence development through telecollaboration and virtual exchange. In J. Jackson (Ed.), *The Routledge handbook of language and intercultural communication* (pp. 361–375). New York: Routledge.

Oros, A. L. (2007). Let's debate: Active learning encourages student participation and critical thinking. *Journal of Political Science Education, 3*, 293–311.

Porto, M. (2017). Mural art and graffiti: Developing intercultural citizenship in higher education classes in English as a foreign language in Argentina and Italy. In M. Byram, I. Golubeva, H. Hui & M. Wagner (Eds.), *From principles to practice in education for intercultural citizenship* (pp. 226–239). Bristol, Buffalo and Toronto: Multilingual Matters.

Prince, M. (2004). Does active learning work? A review of the research. *Journal of Engineering Education, 93*(3), 223–231.

Rapanta, C., Botturi, L., Goodyear, P., Guàrdia, L., & Koole, M. (2020). Online university teaching during and after the Covid-19 crisis: Refocusing teacher presence and learning activity. *Postdigital Science and Education, 2*, 923–945.

Richmond, A. S., Gurung, R. A. R., & Boysen, G. A. (2021). *A pocket guide to online teaching. Translating the evidence-based model teaching criteria*. New York: Routledge.

Russell, V., & Murphy-Judy, K (2021). *Teaching language online. A guide for designing, developing and delivering online, blended, and flipped language courses*. New York: Routledge.

Satar, M. (2021). Introducing virtual exchange: towards digital equity in internationalisation. In M. Satar (Eds.), *Virtual exchange: Towards digital equity in internationalisation* (pp. 1–14). Research-publishing.net.

Schön, D. (1983). *The reflective practitioner. How professionals think in action*. London: Temple Smith.

Selwyn, N. (2016). *Education and technology. Key issues and debates*. London: Bloomsbury.

Stefanou, C., Stolk, J. D., Prince, M., Chen, J. C., & Lord, S. M. (2013). Self-regulation and autonomy in problem- and project-based learning environments. *Active Learning in Higher Education, 14*, 109–22.

Sykes, J. M. (2018). Interlanguage pragmatics, curricular innovation and digital technologies. *CALICO Journal*, 35(2), 120–124.
Terry, G., & Hayfield, N. (2021). *Essentials of thematic analysis*. Washington, DC: American Psychological Association.
Van Allen, L., & Katz, S. (2020). Teaching with OER during pandemics and beyond. *Journal for Multicultural Education*, 14(3/4), 209–218.
Vinagre, M. (2016). Promoting intercultural competence in culture and language studies: Outcomes of an international collaborative project. In E. Martìn-Monje, I. Elorza & B. Garcìa Riaza (Eds.), *Technological advances in specialized linguistic domains: Practical applications and mobility* (pp. 23–35). London: Routledge.
Vygotsky, L. S. (1978). *Mind in society: The development of higher psychological processes*. Cambridge, MA: Harvard University Press.
Walker, S. E. (2003). Active learning strategies to promote critical thinking. *Journal of Athletic Training*, 38, 263–7.

Sitography

Educaplay, https://www.educaplay.com
Google Meet, https://meet.google.com
Miro, https://miro.com
Mural, https://www.mural.co
Padlet, https://en.padlet.com
Voki, voky.com
WhatsApp, https://www.whatsapp.com
Wordwall, https://wordwall.net
Zoom, https://zoom.us

Chapter 12
Tracking the Mental Well-being of Pre-service Teachers in Post-secondary Health Methods Courses

Judy Jaunzems-Fernuk

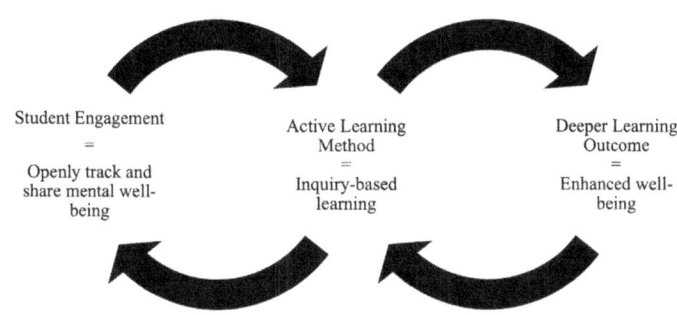

Introduction

With my chapter, I contribute to this book, *Active Learning in Higher Education*, by showing how I engaged students to openly track and share their mental well-being using inquiry-based learning, enhancing their overall well-being throughout the term. Students then used this process to implement wellness plans through a cumulative project focused on overall health. Well-being was tracked during weekly emotional and stress 'check-ins', and the process was aligned with an ongoing active learning assignment focused on personal and professional growth through applied health methods (self-study). The check-in process was the foundation of the active learning approach throughout, and it involved tracking 'temperature', i.e., emotional well-being or mood, as well as stress levels. Students then applied well-being strategies learned throughout the course to their own lives and assessed and shared the impact. At the end of the course, students were surveyed about their experiences, specifically about their mental well-being and the potential to bring well-being strategies into their lives and future classrooms to mitigate teacher burnout and support students.

This chapter presents the experiences of students who took part in health methods courses for pre-service teachers (PSTs) over three terms in the 2021-2022 academic year. Over 100 students, many of whom had just recently returned to in-person learning following the COVID-19 pandemic, completed the course in one or other terms. Valuable and anonymous survey data regarding the PSTs' experiences during these periods where they focused on mental well-being was collected, disseminated, and presented. How this active learning approach may apply to a larger group of students in various post-secondary contexts is explored.

In this chapter, I define the first portion of my active learning approach as an experience of ongoing attention to well-being through active reflection and connection to both self and others throughout the term. Bloom et al.'s (1956) three domains of learning underpinned this case of active learning (cognitive, affective, psychomotor) through a reflective process known as 'reflexive practice' (Coburn & Gormally, 2017). These learning domains aligned with student assignments (Table 1) and the active-reflective process of tracking and sharing daily mood and stress levels in classes (Figure 4). A cumulative active learning inquiry-based project, attending to an area of overall health, was presented and shared by students at the end of the course. The inquiry projects aimed to build well-being skills and strategies to support resilience to ongoing stress (i.e., coping). To be reflexive, the students engaged with a collective, active, and reflective awareness of their overall mental health while attending to and sharing their emotions and stress levels with fellow classmates (check-in) throughout. Enomoto and Warner (2022, Chapter 5 in this book) describe active learning as a metacognitive process requiring student engagement in authentic and relevant activities that promote understanding. The check-in process, combined with student action plans, supported this metacognitive process, also described by Schraw (1998) as an orientation aimed at 'improving' self versus 'proving' self in academic contexts. The process applied constructivist learning theories and methods, which encouraged personal and professional exploration, i.e., growth, and attention to care and coping strategies regarding stress and managing difficult emotions.

In this chapter, I discuss the implications of the daily check-in process used with the PSTs and review topics the PSTs engaged with as they planned and initiated health action to fulfil personal and professional goals. The check-in process is a main focus of this active learning approach. It could be used in any course and by any instructor who has a basic awareness or understanding of mental health literacy (Kutcher et al., 2016). In culmination of the learning, students completed action plans, shared experiences of personal and professional growth with one another, and completed anonymous surveys showing the benefits of this active learning approach and its contribution to overall student health. The data highlights how the check-in, specifically concerning mental well-being, was an essential component as a self-care and compassion tool. It alone brought needed attention to student mental health in this collegial environment.

Reading this chapter, you will gain the following insights:

1. how tracking student well-being with specific attention to mental health and stress through a daily in-class check-in can impact students personal and professional development in a health methods course;

2. what tensions can present when teaching about and tracking mental health, through a process of active learning known as Aware, Care, Cope (ACC); and

3. how health-enhancing strategies, attended to through personal inquiry (reflexive, therapeutic methods), are applied, supporting student well-being and mental health.

Overview of main sections

This chapter is divided into four main sections. Section 1 outlines the active learning model used as the foundation of a health methods course, designed around the principles of attending to 'self-care before care-give' (ACC). This model also brings active awareness to student mental well-being in K-12 environments. In this case, the model was used to decrease the potential for PST burnout in post-secondary programs by helping them mitigate and manage stress by attending to it actively in various domains of learning, i.e., through assignments (Bloom et al., 1956). Section 2 explains the rationale behind mental wellness check-ins in a classroom setting. Various strategies used to support calm management practices that work to highlight or enhance student well-being are also explored. In Section 3, the comments and experiences of student participants in the health methods courses are shared, with a special focus on the impact on their PST development. Lastly, Section 4 reviews the potential for this work in other disciplines or college programs as a means by which instructor and student health can be mitigated through attention, reflection, and action in a post-pandemic world.

Section 1: The background to active learning

Bonwell and Eison (1991) explicitly recognised that a process of *active learning* could include a range of activities, from the very simple, such as pausing a lecture so students may clarify ideas, to the more complex, such as engaging in the description and debriefing of complex case studies. They defined active learning as activities that involve an active over passive stance in the classroom experience (anything beyond simply listening); further defining it through the distinction that *true* active learning places a greater emphasis *"on the students' exploration of their own attitudes and values"* (Bonwell & Eison 1991:19). Olson (2022, Chapter 3 in this book) defines active learning as an experience whereby new knowledge and skills are developed, followed by reflective practice, further emphasising the routine nature of active learning as it can be used in everyday classroom practices.

The active learning environment described in this chapter is specifically built upon the following definition of reflexivity: which is an active, reflective process that works towards transformation and transference of learning through action. Coburn and Gormally (2017:111) extended such a definition when they expressed the belief that *"Being reflexive ensures a depth of understanding of who we are, our social context and our positionality in relation to ['other']. It argues that unless practitioners understand the impact that the 'self' can have on their practice, it is difficult to promote agency amongst people they work with, in seeking social transformation."*

This chapter views reflexion as a fluid active learning process. A fluid approach to practice integrates both theory and practice simultaneously to the benefit of one's self and others (Thompson & Pascal, 2012). The check-in process influences PSTs to focus on their own needs throughout the term to potentially continue the practice in their future classrooms to support student well-being; speaking to this practice's fluidity. This active learning approach is also described as 'constructo-interpretivist' (Coburn & Gormally, 2017). It works to actively construct knowledge through self-awareness and interpretations of well-being and growth. In sharing and listening to the resulting interpretations of others' collective states of well-being, compassion and empathy for others are also developed (Wei et al., 2011).

Specifically, this active learning approach provides a means by which educators can quickly assess and support students' mental health in school environments at both the K-12 and post-secondary levels (Daniel, 2020; Engelhardt, 2016). The check-in was an ongoing tool in this active learning approach that I have also successfully implemented in K-12 classrooms before teaching at the post-secondary level. The experience stimulated an emotionally safe and welcoming learning environment for K-12 learners and transferred effectively to a post-secondary classroom level. The foundational principle is that when students feel like their teachers care for and about them, they are more apt to do the same for themselves and others (Hargreaves, 2007).

After two decades of refining and utilising a check-in process as part of calm classroom management practices, the active process of ongoing check-ins was brought to my higher education learning environment. During several 2021-2022 health methods courses, the practice was aligned with inquiry projects focusing on health. As future teachers, the students experienced this active learning environment by acknowledging the mental health needs that arise in or disrupt learning. The goal of the experience was to inspire students to make use of this skill (checking in on others' well-being) in their future classrooms. Students shared vital information about how they were doing throughout the term by attending to personal well-being and completing reflections on self-care initiatives used throughout.

The in-class portion of the process was quick and simple; however, it was also a powerful tool for eliciting compassion and self-compassion for well-being as part of ongoing inquiry and self-study. As PSTs prepare for their role as educators and caregivers, this reflexive experience facilitates the discovery of important self-care strategies, like checking in with self, peers, and potential future students. Drawing attention to the needs of others in collective environments supports the development of compassion (Gilbert, 2014). Though the course content centred on health methods, my work's conclusions and future directions suggest that a check-in process could be used in any course, regardless of discipline or course focus. The impact may *"decrease stigma and enhance help-seeking behaviours for [students with] mental health concerns"* (Kutcher et al., 2016:690).

The orientation of this course prepared PSTs for their role in what can be a stressful profession (Skovholt & Trotter-Mathison, 2014). To support student and teacher well-being, the PSTs were taught to attend to and share their well-being in self-reflection daily and in conversation with peers through a therapeutic process (Jaunzems-Fernuk et al., 2021). Though preparing for the role of a teacher is not the same as preparing for the role of a therapist, I argue that the landscape of the twenty-first-century classroom, in addition to a post-pandemic environment, would benefit from educators who can exercise therapeutic elements as part of their everyday teaching roles and that doing so is 'human informed' practice (Jaunzems-Fernuk et al., 2021). The orientation of human informed practice was further emphasised in this course by the viewpoint that 'self-care is imperative to caregiving', seeing teaching as a caregiving profession.

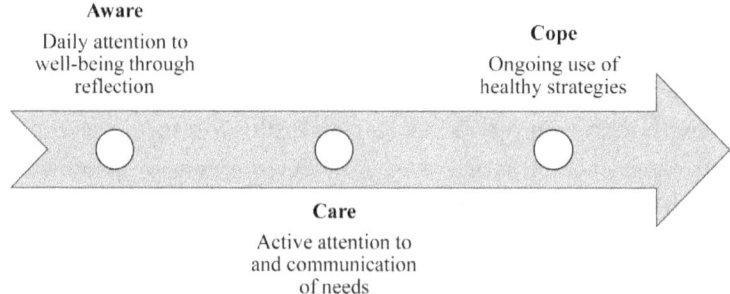

Figure 1: Process of Aware, Care, Cope (ACC).

The instructor designed the process at the root of this active learning approach (moving from a well-being check-in to an inquiry action plan), known as Aware, Care, Cope (ACC). ACC is an active reflexive learning process that stages students through 1) an awareness and attention to one's emotions and stress, 2) an understanding around care strategies that can be used to support well-being and manage stress, and 3) implementation of coping strategies found through inquiry and a process of self-study to support emotional regulation and management of overwhelming emotions (Figure 1). The first two stages of ACC can be attended to and applied through the daily check-in, which both instructor and student carry out. The action plan assignment for the students fulfils their obligation to self-care (cope) as they attend actively to personal and professional well-being and hopefully carry those skills throughout life.

Why we use active learning

The idea for this active learning approach came from my experience teaching in K-12 environments over the last twenty years, whereby I refined a process to attend to health through daily check-ins. Providing space for conversations related to mental health and overall well-being actively helped us develop care strategies and compassion for ourselves and others in real-time as needed. For the check-in process to be a success, students in K-12 learning environments, or, as is the case for this chapter, in pre-service health methods courses, were taught basic mental health literacy (Kutcher et al., 2016) and given instruction in The Human Curriculum (Jaunzems-Fernuk et al., 2021). The curriculum shares content, research, and experiences conducive to thriving in the profession of teaching and in life.

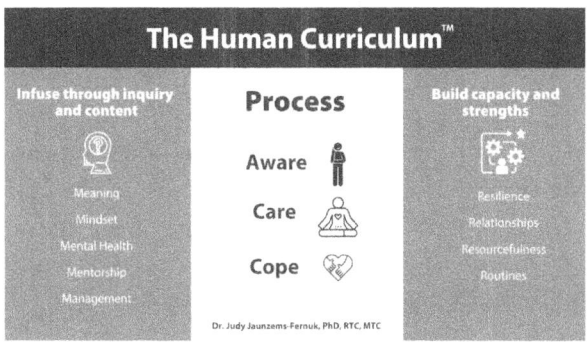

Figure 2: *The human curriculum.*

I designed the Human Curriculum to honour the humans being taught. The curriculum's roots are classroom organisation, lesson development, and teaching and learning strategies that support ACC. Human adversity, risk, resilience, and whole-body health physiology are explored through a process of inquiry in the culminating course project that supports active attention to well-being through self-care (Figures 1 & 2). Active learning is embedded as self-study, requiring students to frame their learning by rooting it in personal experience. The PSTs in this case shared their personal findings with one another through conversation, discussion, and reflective/reflexive activities, which in turn taught others through their experience.

In 2019, the American College Health Association's National College Health Assessment Survey collected responses from more than 43,000 post-secondary students who attended over forty post-secondary institutions across Canada. They noted that *"many students reported experiencing average (31.4%) to above-average stress (46.2%), with nearly 15% reporting tremendous stress levels"* (Linden et al., 2018:i). This increase in mental health needs can also be seen in K-12 environments as well (Canadian Mental Health Association, 2021), highlighting an imperative need to provide support for mental health, especially for PSTs, so that it may, in turn, increase their capacity to support mental health and stress in the classroom.

Active learning theory and methodology

Heading into the fall of 2021, there was much uncertainty about the new nature of hybrid learning environments. At the University where this active learning approach was completed, students were required to be fully vaccinated, wear masks, and avoid many common classroom mannerisms—such as proximity, movement about the space, and eating and drinking in classrooms—and many were asked to stay home and learn asynchronously whenever illness or exposure to coronavirus was suspected. These various levels of engagement made the 'new normal' a tenuous experience. To help build community and connection in the classroom, the instructor decided an active learning model that involved checking in and focusing on self-care through course assignments would be ideal. It was hypothesised that simple engagement, through means of the daily class check-in, might transcend the physical spaces and allow for encouragement and compassion in the event coursework had to move online. Though the check-in strategy had been applied prior to this term, it was never formally studied for its impact on students or reviewed for its potential impact during a pandemic.

Cognitive (Thinking)	Affective (Feeling)	Psychomotor (Doing)
Assignment 1	Assignment 2	Assignment 3
Health Presentation	Literature Lesson Plans	Health Action Plans
Foundational knowledge supporting PSTs understanding of topics that impact health (social, emotional, mental well-being). Topics include: racism & oppression; mental illness; abuse, neglect, bullying or trauma; nutrition & exercise; disorders and disease (ASD, ADHD, FASD)	Application of practical skills through literature and lesson planning exploring identity, culture, diversity, ability, emotions, and stress management for K - 12 students (i.e., sexual orientation or identity; racism, mental illness, difference, disorders, trauma; other adverse childhood experiences, etc.)	PSTs participate in personal and professional development related to well-being in a broad sense by further unpacking their own needs and the development of health-related habits to support resilience: i.e., a health action plan with a focus on learning and applying skills to manage mental illness; disorders such as ADHD; or support stress, trauma, experiences of oppression, racism, or bullying, etc.)
	Active and On-going Mood and Stress Check-in	

Table 1: Course assignments & progression of active learning experience through domains of learning.

Active learning is situated within a constructivist and experiential learning paradigm (Dewey & Dewey, 1915). In this course, active learning was applied through three main assignments that worked in alignment with the active and ongoing check-in process to build mental health-related knowledge, skills, and attitudes of the PSTs (ACC). This active learning approach endeavoured to provide a simple but immersive experience with respect to attending to one's mental health. Within the model, students recorded their temperature (mood, emotional well-being) and stress in a thoughtful process at the start of each class (Figure 4). They then shared their well-being with peers. The check-in allowed for personal engagement with well-being (knowledge and strategies). The active learning process of regularly attending to mental wellness and self-care or growth was combined with embedded semester-long activities that involved several additional active learning components (Table 1).

As highlighted in Bonwell and Eison (1991), the students first learned by becoming involved in and exerting psychological energy while being devoted to their academic experiences (Astin, 1985). This was followed by ultimately using the data to attend to care strategies by completing an action plan assignment, which reflected growth in a chosen area of mental wellness (Bloom et al., 1956; Ericksen, 1984). Throughout our course, students talked and wrote about what they were learning; they shared their rationales behind specific health initiatives; and when asked to apply new coping or emotion management skills to their daily lives, they formulated their learning as an extension of themselves (Chickering & Gamson, 1987). The impact of the active process (ACC) was presented in a cumulative exercise of sharing at the end of the course. Section 3 describes each of these components in detail.

In education, barriers exist to bridging educational theory with practical applications in classrooms; in teacher education, this is known as the 'theory to practice gap' (Allen, 2009; McDonough, 2012; Stough et al., 2015). This gap can dampen teacher confidence in the classroom and lead to burnout in the first few years of teaching (Kutsyuruba & Walker, 2017). An active learning model, providing a context for self-care and personal growth, helps teachers gain transferable skills that may bridge these gaps, especially in managing and mitigating the mental health needs of students. Gadusova and Predanocyova (2018:104) emphasise three levels of influence teachers can use to optimise their practice. These levels are defined as 'necessary areas of development' in teacher education: *"1) cognitive – abilities, dispositions, knowledge, and intelligence; 2) affective – emotions, feelings, experiences, motivation, social relations, and self-regulation; and 3) psychomotor – movement, sensory perception, skills, habits, manners."*, domains first explored by Bloom et al. (1956:14). Holistic development of all three, in theory, and practice, as was seen in this course, can help PSTs transfer and integrate new skills and ideas. Moreover, Gadusova and Predanocyova (2018) recommended developing all three of these areas by integrating active learning into formerly passive learning environments to build integrated skills in students. Table 1 shows how each was attended to in this case.

A constructivist (Piaget, 1971) and experiential (Dewey & Dewey, 1915) learning framework helped frame the reflexive learning pedagogy. Each promoted active and introspective engagement with topics, which explicitly asked students *"to make connections between new information and their current mental models, [by] extending their understanding"* to develop attitudes that may transfer to their practice (Brame, 2016:1), with regards to mental health, self-care strategies, and general well-being. Active learning models, such as those employed in this active learning approach, allow students to experience real-time and real-life engagements with the content, including their reactions to the learning applied therein. In this case, the active learning model challenged students to continually work in the liminal space (Mezirow, 2000) between knowing and actively applying strategies, known as a learning zone of optimal–proximal development (Vygotsky, 1978). The course application relied heavily on four pedagogical orientations: Humanistic (Bloom et al., 1956; Maslow, 1943), Reflective Inquiry (Dewey & Dewey, 1915), Constructivism and Social Constructivism (Bandura & Walters, 1977; Vygotsky, 1978), Transformational Learning (Mezirow, 2000), Relational Learning (Noddings, 2013), and Reflexive Pedagogy (Coburn & Gormally, 2017).

Section 2: The case of active learning

In the health methods courses, students were challenged to complete inquiry and self-study by tracking and sharing daily mental wellness through check-ins: 1) a temperature scale (emotional well-being or mood), and 2) a stress scale (high-low stress level).

These check-ins were followed by encouraging students to share positive affirmations, gratitude, and strategies with respect to managing or coping with stress. Students also engaged with literature on sensitive topics and created lesson plans that considered the potential for classroom tensions (stress), whereby they imagined how to navigate complicated conversations with students and families through topics related to 2SLGBTQ (Two Spirit, Lesbian, Gay, Bi-sexual, Trans, or Queer) identities and relationships; adoption and attachment; perspectives on diseases or disorders; clarity around bullying, racism, oppression or discrimination; and even discussions of suicide, suicide-ideation, loneliness, grief, trauma, and loss in the classroom. In the latter, students critically considered challenging problems, and they were encouraged *"to be creative"* in considering active and ongoing solutions to supporting their student's needs (Brame, 2016:5).

Students created action plans rooted in one area of well-being upon critically analysing their own perspectives and needs throughout the term. Each of the students chose from a selection of non-fiction resources that looked at health through a variety of subjects and lenses personally or professionally: Indigenous perspectives and environmental health (Kimmerer, 2013); trauma and ADHD (Maté, 2017); stress and trauma (Perry & Szalavitz, 2017); physical and mental health (Ratey, 2013), among others (see Table 2). PSTs applied the learning to their own lives, reflecting on and sharing their experiences to support their peers' understanding of how they applied ACC.

Through the sharing and daily exchange of emotional well-being and stress, students also tracked and reflected upon self-care strategies, recognising their needs and how increasing attention to them supported overall well-being. A beginning-of-week ('Monday Memo') from the instructor and end-of-week ('Engagement'), reflection completed by students, supported a reciprocal active process of reflexion on the part of the PSTs and the instructor. Both instructor and students shared ongoing reflections on the impact of course concepts (tensions, stress, emotion management) and how the daily check-in supported them. Aligned with these processes, and intersections of learning, peer presentations, sharing circles, guest speakers, lectures on the Human Curriculum, and various other assignments supported student learning (Figure 2). As noted previously, topics addressed addiction, suicide, loss, trauma, and other painful emotions or disorders, which can cause discomfort or stress. Tracking mental health and overall wellness while discussing these sensitive health topics helped mitigate the emotions faced by the students and instructor. By facing stress directly (through the check-in and self-study), the instructor had a means by which to gauge students' experiences and wellness throughout. With attention to self-awareness practices throughout the term, the students also learned that they could mitigate their stress and care needs through the ACC model: paying attention to (aware) and actively engaging in (care) strategies that could also be used to teach others emotion and stress management skills (cope). Again, a health methods course enhanced the check-in and self-care strategies through projects related to on-going health. However, they could be integrated into any course quite easily, as section two further explains.

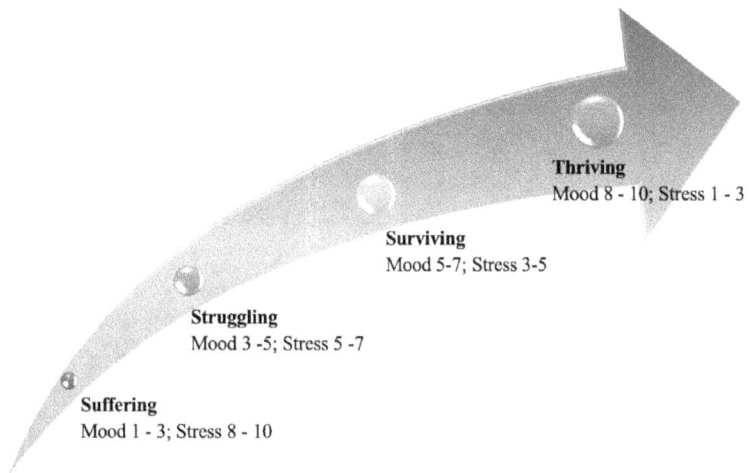

Figure 4: Temperature and stress level continuum.

An introduction to the case of active learning

In a post-secondary course environment, this active learning approach offered undergraduate students an opportunity to take a close look at their personal health in a professional setting while learning about the application of health methods to their personal and professional lives as educators. This active learning approach involved four components to be successful:

Components	Personal health aspects
1. Defining and building a community (and trust) through a common understanding of health and well-being.	Well-being includes an understanding of domains of health: • mental, social, emotional, and spiritual; • development of awareness around the difference between stress and distress; • knowledge of adversity, risk, and resilience; • signs and symptoms of ill health, and coping strategies to increase wellness.
2. Formulation of a clear personal definition of the continuum or spectrum of well-being (Figure 4); actively tracking and sharing mental well-being and stress level at the beginning of each class.	• Students define suffering, struggling, surviving, and thriving for self so that these definitions can be personalised and fluid. • Each student completes a self-assessment daily and tracks their well-being through an active and constructive process that involves reflection, sharing, perspective, and growth; building understanding about the importance of focusing on wellness to impact overall health and support communication of needs, and adequate direction for supports.
3. Assignments that allow for and support personal and professional growth through inquiry (self-study) to support the process of checking in and maintaining well-being.	Growth-oriented active learning processes were strengthened through health action plans. Students recognised personal and professional health needs throughout the term and devised action plans to support them. Non-fiction resources offer choices for the basis of inquiry projects covering an array of topics: • environmental health (Kimmerer, 2013); • management of disorders such as ADHD (Maté, 2017); • trauma-informed (Perry & Szalavitz, 2017), community-based perspectives of thriving with respect to well-being (Borba, 2021; Manilall & Armstrong, 2018); • and other brain, mind, and body-related readings on stress and its impact (Ratey, 2013; Siegel & Bryson, 2012; Siegel, 2015; Tummers, 2011).
4. End of term sharing circle and anonymous student survey.	Opportunities to unpack the meaning of the process and growth for individual students. Students shared experience with the active attention to wellness: from both course assignments and tracking. • Discussions about carrying this practice through to future endeavours support the continuation of therapeutic engagement and self-care and may support teacher burnout.

Table 2: Components to successfully implementing active learning in a health methods course.

An overview of how students work with active learning

Teacher and student mental wellness is just as much a priority for schools in the twenty-first century as academic learning (Jaunzems-Fernuk et al., 2021). For well-being to be a priority, it must be actively attended to through daily teaching, attention, and awareness to students' and teachers' needs. Assessing and reflecting daily complete a process of reflexive action in this course. The active learning focus attended to throughout the term was simple, presented early in the course, as shown in Figure 4, and offered ongoing support. Each time the group gathered, they shared their numbers, reflected, and discussed how they were coping or managing their stress; something that can be done in any classroom. Sometimes, students would also share a quote or mantra that was getting them through a particularly difficult time, or they might share a health-enhancing strategy they were using.

I have been an educator since 2000 and an instructor of higher learning since 2017. Since the beginning of the global COVID-19 pandemic, I noticed a great deal of worry, trepidation, and concern from students who had transitioned quickly from a constant routine of in-person learning and connecting on campus (in some cases, some were struggling already with respect to their mental health), to an immediate stop of everyday social routines and structure. For some students, classes moved synchronously online, and for others, synchronous learning ceased altogether as people scrambled to complete or pick up courses amid lockdown periods. Many students were stuck at home yet had to find ways to access readings, texts, and course support through email, phone, or a new-to-most video conferencing platform. In this emergent state, many watched the world shift in a variety of ways technologically, physically, socially, mentally, and medically, and few returned to in-person work and school for quite some time. This global experience has caused many people's mental and emotional decline (Daniel, 2020).

Following this shift, the University of Saskatchewan settled into a practice that involved one complete year of online learning, as vaccines were rolled out and considerations for a return to campus process (that involved adequate distancing and masking protocol) were considered and then implemented. In the fall of 2021, many in-person learning environments resumed. It was with this return to the classroom that, as a mental health practitioner and educator, I sensed there would be continued trepidation, fear, and the potential for on-going anxiety and stress, as institutions, teachers, and students looked *"for flexible ways to repair the damage caused by COVID-19's interruptions to learning trajectories"* (Daniel, 2020:91). I knew that framing my courses around on-going check-in processes, with attention to the ACC model, could be imperative, and therefore, I planned my courses with the intent of highlighting and then studying the impact of this active learning approach; a practice I used in my own K – 12 classrooms for two decades. Many PSTs entered my course with an awareness of the mental health needs in K-12 environments, as many either had some previous experience in student teaching practicums or as educational assistants (EAs) or leaders in daycares and kid's clubs. A focus on understanding mental health capacity, the needs of twenty-first-century students, and how to attend effectively and impactfully to our health was covered up-front through the Human Curriculum: a relational, humanistic, and developmental learning course design that recognised both a student and instructor experience of mental health and well-being (and need) through learning and application of skills to support self.

This active learning approach could be achieved in a variety of contexts, whether or not mental health was a focus for the course, as the conversation would initially centre on the challenges of any student or profession and any professional tensions therein. The content of various courses may differ. However, the active learning approach could continue to move from the challenges in the discipline to the need for ACC mental health strategies in any context. That is, we all face adversity and stress and require the skills of emotion management and coping at home, school, or work. Some facets of mental health literacy, vocabulary, or mental health first-aid may need to be taught or agreed upon, and some level of relational skill-building and discussions around personal, social, or emotional well-being should be had. These discussions can be done in as little as one class or over the course of several. To have these types of discussions effectively, students would need to feel safe and secure in the classroom space, and this would have to be fostered by the instructor through relational teaching methods (Bandura & Walters, 1977; Bandura, 1999; Noddings, 2013). Trust would also need to be developed, and students would need to feel respected and cared for by their instructor and peers.

The instructor can foster this environment by being vulnerable (Brown, 2012) and remaining open to students communicating their needs. This vulnerability and openness can be achieved by sharing connections or personal stories. Unpacking our perceptions of mental health -personally or professionally- is best done from personal experience and can be an essential feature of learning and relationship building in a course such as this.

As a 'vulnerable' instructor myself, I have found that the more open I am, the more open and willing to share my students are, and thus, the deeper the learning and application of skills become. Suppose students can rely on and connect their well-being in a course to that of their peers or instructor. In that case, they can face challenges together, becoming more open to recognising difficulties and choosing strategies to cope and manage. Sometimes these difficult or tenuous conversations, whereby peers can show one another true compassion and empathy, can be had simply from hearing or seeing the numbers (temperature and stress level) shared by others. This process opens space for conversations between them, especially if the instructor can address one or two students who have particular needs that could be discussed in the context of the class. In my K-12 environments, I found that these short conversations helped mitigate larger problems or stress that could build up over time. Students felt comfortable asking for support and being directed to those in the school or campus who could provide therapeutic interventions. As an essential feature of this active learning approach, students need to feel wholeheartedly connected to the work and invested personally to take action in support of their well-being. They need to understand that the sharing or connecting of the experience of well-being is heard by the instructor and their peers, which can be achieved simply through the practice of checking in.

How I have prepared and organised the active learning

The design of this active learning model starts with teaching about health through a holistic lens: 1) social, emotional, mental, physical, environmental; and moves to teaching 2) with special attention to human development and the impact of trauma, abuse, stress, or neglect; the process is followed by 3) an overview of the impact of systemic issues in schools and communities, such as poverty, racism, discrimination, and oppression. These aforementioned topics can be thoroughly unpacked and can include a combination of lecture, guest speakers, and student engagement in topics (through formal or informal assignments: presentations, research or inquiry projects, sharing circles, class discussions, etc.). Students are taught about the everyday impact of managing emotions when alone with self, at home, in social situations, or in schools and classrooms.

Mental health can be taught as part of, or in addition to, curriculum. Students can be given opportunities to think about how their feelings and managing and coping with stress impact them and others. Research shows that active engagement with these topics supports students' well-being (Kutcher et al., 2016). For university students, particularly PSTs, talking about valuing well-being and offering health services to students is an important factor in academic achievement. Sharing temperature and stress works as a simple tool for addressing important mental health concerns through passively attending to feelings, emotions, and stress. From my experience as a general educator and post-secondary instructor, many students deny experiences of ill health until they are overwhelmed. In the design of this active learning approach, attention to mental wellness was built into the course itself, breaking the stigma and allowing students to learn about mental health as part of the curricula.

The World Health Organization (WHO) emphasises that to be human is to have mental health. In all courses, I also emphasise that experiences that impact mental illness or wellness can come and go throughout our lifetime. Normalising that mental health is human and that we are all susceptible to feeling mentally ill or well can decrease stigma with respect to the topic. Discussions about mental illness and wellness are normalised through attention to self-care strategies that can greatly impact everyone's overall health. These strategies may include breathing exercises, meditations, or exercise. When combined with lectures about the brain, mind, and body (including stress physiology and regulation), students may better understand the physical, mental, and emotional impact of them. Breathing, for example, can be used as a tool that can be practised when calm and called upon in moments of stress, anxiety, or even panic. The experience of critical and active engagement with wellness and health is an experience the PSTs can bring to their future positions as leaders in schools and communities, influencing students and even colleagues to do the same.

My hope throughout the course is that reflexive engagement (action and reflection) can help guide the PSTs choices over their lifetime, the results of which can be used to teach others. In this manner, I feel the PSTs are primed for their roles as therapeutic educators who have learned to apply self-care strategies as health-enhancing behaviours that can be shared and taught to others: 'self-care and then care-give' through ACC (Figure 1). The materials required to complete a cycle of active learning through attention and engagement with health-enhancing behaviours are seen in the following list; however, they can be modified and adapted to any context:

Lecture material

- The Human Curriculum: consisting of mental health awareness & literacy; the brain, mind, body connection (through cognitive behavioural approaches: i.e., think, feel, do); stress physiology & stress management; and behaviour, motivation, and learning theory (consisting of various models: Bloom et al., 1956; Vygotsky,1978; Maslow, 1943; Perry & Szalavitz, 2017).
- Guest presenters, consisting of local government and non-government advocacy groups (LGBTQ, Indigenous Knowledge Keepers, Sexual Health and Sexual Violence Advocacy, BIPOC community leaders).
- Student-led presentations on topics in Table 1 (holistic & health-enhancing behaviours).

Temperature and stress level check-in daily or weekly

Three to five minutes was allotted for daily sharing of temperature and stress at the start of each class. This was done verbally, on paper and passed around, or on Zoom through the use of the chat feature.

Chapter 12

Design of an ongoing self-study through inquiry

The final assignment, which was ongoing throughout the term, allowed for lectures, guest workshops, and readings to be reflected upon, synthesised, and acted upon. Tracking of well-being culminated, and the learning experience (personal or professional growth) was written about in a formal essay style reflection and presented to peers at the end of the course.

Survey

A follow-up survey collected data on the student experience of tracking well-being while implementing health action plans to be used for future course development; and to complete a cycle of active learning for the instructor as well. In this case, a Behavioural Ethics Application for collecting and using student feedback was completed. SurveyMonkey was used for this after course completion.

Section 3: The outcome

This project brought mental health awareness to students through an ongoing check-in process (n=approximately 100 students over three terms). The check-in happened at the start of each class throughout their term in a health methods course. With an active focus on health – well-being and stress levels – to learning about and executing health action plans, the students felt that they had gained valuable and relevant skills that could be applied and shared with future students. Students welcomed the focus on their mental health from a personal and a professional perspective, as was seen in their weekly engagements and action plan summaries (essay and presentation to peers). Students felt heard and supported, and though at times their health took a back seat to the stress of exams and assignments, they felt they could adequately bring the skills, practiced and applied, to other areas of their own lives. All felt active learning centred on well-being was essential for their future classrooms.

Students were offered an anonymous volunteer online survey via SurveyMonkey upon course completion. The survey data was collected with a Behavioural Ethics exemption from the University, and the results are collated below. The students were asked the following questions as part of this survey which was also used for course improvement:

1) Did the tracking, reflection, and/or sharing of personal well-being (temperature and stress level) support your relationships and connections with self, the instructor, or fellow teacher candidates during your course/term?

2) Please explain how the use of a check-in process, such as temperature and stress level, supported your relationships and connections with self, the instructor, or fellow teacher candidates during your course/term.

3) How can attention to the well-being of self (as teacher or student) transition to attention to the well-being of other (peers or other students) in a classroom environment?

4) What is the likelihood of this practice being used in your future classrooms to support K – 12 student learning and/or health?

5) How have your views on 'attention to well-being' changed throughout your post-secondary education Health course?

6) How do these views compare and contrast with your self-identified previous views on health, as well as the practices you have currently or previously observed in school environments?

7) Is checking in on student mental health and/or tracking of our own health in K-12 or post-secondary school environments important? Explain if you can.

The survey given to students at the end of each course served a secondary purpose and gathered valuable student input. It was also part of my own attention to instructional development. As an instructor of health methods and mental health initiatives for PSTs, I am on a lifelong learning journey to support the development of my own practice and that of other educators, with the hope of furthering the use of a therapeutic lens in the profession of teaching.

Chapter 12

Student perspective

One hundred percent of students surveyed felt that the attention to, tracking of, and reflection on student well-being was impactful, positive, and something they would use in their future classrooms:

- *"Before this class, I never used temperature checks, nor did I ever think about implementing them into a classroom. However, with the positive experience I had, I will definitely be using them in my own classroom."*
- *"By doing regular temperature checks, I was more inclined to check in with my emotions regularity throughout the day and have noticed a significant difference in my emotional health. Noticing how this has helped me has encouraged me to include this in a classroom."*
- *"As a whole, this project and process have left me with one insight for all educators: it is imperative to understand and connect with each and every student under your care, without exception."*

In addition, students commented that:

- *"Though most schools 'try' to be aware of mental health, they don't actually do anything to support it."*

They noted that through active attention to well-being, over the term, they were:

- *"Becoming more present by checking in with emotions and stress level."*
- *"It made me more conscious of how this might affect my learning or teaching experience (i.e., teaching when I am mad or learning when I am happy)."*

Several students highlighted the main takeaway from the in-class check-ins:

- *"You can see when someone strays from their normal, and that can be good or bad and can allow you to check-in with them."*

The active attention to well-being through the daily check-in and self-study inquiry projects was so powerful that each student's survey response could have been included in this reflection on the student perspective, as each was a meaningful and authentic response to the power of actively attending to well-being in classroom spaces. The following selections were chosen as reflective of the overall student experience of this active learning approach:

- *"At the beginning of the course, I rarely considered my temperature checks. I know to be courteous and professional, but I did not consider the teacher burnout affects [sic] from unchecked personal well-being."*

- *"I did not realise that certain amounts of stress are beneficial and actually important . . . Attention to well-being does not need to be a special program that you pay for or one that requires a 'life coach'. It can be small things that you do throughout the day to be mindful of your well-being."*

- *"Something I really enjoyed about this class was writing down my temperature and stress level. I think it helps a teacher get a feel for the room and know whether or not to go super heavy on coursework that day or to slow things down, as we all know that when we are stressed, t can be really difficult to retain any extra information as our minds are so fixated on other things."*

- *"I have struggled with my mental health, primarily my anxiety throughout the years. With the help of our class resources and daily check-ins throughout the semester, I am finally starting to understand myself in a way I haven't ever before."*

Student reflections indicated that the check-ins and inquiry projects enabled them to think proactively about their well-being in terms of choosing 'two to three manageable goals... a day'. As a process of active learning, students described they *"felt less alone just seeing how fellow TC's were doing."* Students also felt the instructor could serve as a source of support, as they were directing the self-monitoring of well-being:

- *"I have learned through the novel, our other classroom resources, daily check-ins with myself, with the help of [the instructor], and great classroom discussions more about what I need to do to better myself and my mental health – more in this semester than ever before. I have learned the importance of open communication and the importance of asking for help when needed because there is no shame in that . . . most importantly, I have learned that I am not alone."*

The aspects of this active learning approach as it could be transferred to other courses are reflected in these student reflections:

- *"Personally, I was able to work much better in group projects. I feel that I had more empathy and understanding when other people made mistakes or struggled."*
- *"I learned a great deal about how mental health affects academic performance. I have come to believe that students cannot learn successfully if their mental wellness is not being addressed/taken care of."*

Instructor perspective – my reflections

Mental health, and more specifically, student and teacher well-being, has been a lifelong interest. In my K-12 experiences as a student, and at a time where I could have used it the most, mental health was rarely, if ever, addressed. Many in the health methods courses noted this lack of attention to well-being. After spending close to twenty years (pre-COVID-19) as a K-12 classroom teacher, I saw first-hand the ongoing and imperative need to address mental health as a classroom management strategy and a basic element of care strategy for both students and the instructor. I also have a mental health education background as a trained counselling therapist. However, that is not necessary to bring mental health education to students; only a basic knowledge of mental health and a willingness to be open and vulnerable is necessary. It is imperative that PSTs develop a core awareness of mental health and understand that not only does it apply to us all but that we are all equally susceptible to illness and capable of supporting or receiving support for our wellness.

This course is part of an ongoing focus on mental health for educators at the University of Saskatchewan as a tool to support mitigation of burnout for professionals who work in schools and a method by which quality, therapeutic teaching can be offered to K-12 students. The pedagogy of active attention to well-being throughout the course is something that can be adopted in any classroom, and the resulting skills and practices support us all.

Section 4: Moving forward

This study provides qualitative evidence of the importance of checking in and attending to student well-being. The experience of checking-in with post-secondary students and supporting them to monitor their own health needs in support of self and others was a great asset to the development of this course, and it could serve as an essential aspect of any course. By drawing attention to mental well-being as a core need for all humans and attending to a quick numerical check-in at the start of class, students learn a simple yet valuable tool for defining and tracking their own well-being. The tool helps develop the awareness needed should they wish to seek help, share their needs with instructors or peers, or otherwise engage in care strategies to support well-being. In this case, some students shared that, at times, I was the only one encouraging them to check in on their health, and it was this emphasis that compelled them to not only check-in on themselves but to reach out to others in times of need. The potential of a simple check-in such as this could have far-reaching consequences for those who struggle and for those in a position to help others. The remainder of this course, with a focus on health, allowed for the health check-ins to become part of an actionable plan that was both personal and professional in nature. When these plans were shared with peers at the end of the course, the result proved to be very impactful for students' overall learning.

This work could serve as a call to action for all instructors to begin the process of checking in and attending to well-being in their classes. By also sharing our own connections to mental health, we have the potential to normalise challenges and struggles and, more importantly, strategies for self-care. If an instructor does not have a foundational understanding of mental health, they can use these types of opportunities to refer students to campus initiatives that support mental well-being and demystify and possibly de-stigmatise attending to one's well-being overall. Mental health applies to all of us and, as such, can and indeed should be attended to through classroom connections and interactions.

Conclusion

The execution of this project solidified a core understanding of mental health initiatives for the instructor and the higher-education students. The active learning process of attention to personal well-being proved to be an essential element in the journey of supporting therapeutic processes as imperative for teacher development. These tools have become an increasingly necessary aspect of teaching for the twenty-first-century educator. Through this project's scope, both the instructor and students gained valuable skills, knowledge, and attitudes around health initiatives as they are used in post-secondary environments. As both a concept and a curriculum, health became part of a living experience with personal wellness, and it was an advantage to both the PSTs and their instructor.

This active learning approach could easily be replicated in other disciplines and classrooms. Regardless of whether temperature and stress check-ins were shared aloud or tracked on paper, students would have a collective means through which to be seen and heard emotionally. This research has shown that the simple act of being heard in a classroom can significantly impact coping and management in relation to emotion regulation and stress. Overwhelmingly, students felt that this active process of attending to well-being and stress, even as an awareness piece, was a positive and proactive method of considering personal and professional development pertaining to overall personal health and the development of a therapeutic practice in support of their future students.

About the Author

Judy Jaunzems-Fernuk is a Lecturer, Department of Curriculum Studies, College of Education, University of Saskatchewan, Canada. She can be contacted at this email: judy.fernuk@usask.ca

Bibliography

Allen, J. M. (2009). Valuing practice over theory: How beginning teachers re-orient their practice in the transition from the university to the workplace. *Teaching and Teacher Education*, 25(5), 647–654.

Astin, A. W. (1985). *Achieving educational excellence*. Jossey-Bass.

Bandura, A. (1999). Social cognitive theory of personality. *Handbook of Personality, 2*, 154-96.

Bandura, A., & Walters, R. H. (1977). *Social learning theory* (Vol. 1). Prentice-Hall.

Bloom, B. S., Engelhart, M. D., Furst, E. J., Hill, W. H., & Krathwohl, D. R. (Eds.) (1956). *Taxonomy of educational objectives: The classification of educational goals. Handbook 1: Cognitive domain*. David McKay Company, Inc.

Bonwell, C. C., & Eison, J. A. (1991). *Active learning: Creating excitement in the classroom* (Ser. ASHE-ERIC higher education report, 1991, no. 1). George Washington University, ERIC Clearinghouse on Higher Education, The George Washington University, One Dupont Circle, Suite 630, Washington, DC 20036-1183.

Borba, M. (2021). *Thrivers: The surprising reasons why some kids struggle and others shine*. Penguin Publishing Group.

Brame, C. J. (2016). *Active learning*. Vanderbilt University Center for Teaching. Retrieved from https://cft.vanderbilt.edu/active-learning/

Brown, B. (2012). *Power of Vulnerability: Teachings on authenticity, connection, and courage*. Sounds True, Incorporated.

Canadian Mental Health Association (2021). *Fast facts about mental health and mental illness*. CMHA National. Retrieved from https://cmha.ca/brochure/fast-facts-about-mental-illness/

Chickering, A. W., & Gamson, Z. F. (1987). Seven principles for good practice in undergraduate education. *AAHE Bulletin, 3*, 7.

Coburn, A., & Gormally, S. (2017). Critical reflexivity. *Counterpoints, 483*, 111-126.

Daniel, S. J. (2020). Education and the COVID-19 pandemic. *Prospects, 49*(1), 91-96.

Dewey, J., & Dewey, E. (1915). *Schools of tomorrow*. EP Dutton.

Engelhardt, M. (2016). Examining mental health in schools and the role it plays in supporting students. *SELU Research Review Journal, 1*(2), 17-28.

Enomoto, K., & Warner, R. (2022). Partnering with student leaders: active learning through integration of Peer Assisted Study Sessions into an undergraduate language course. In K. Enomoto, R. Warner & C. Nygaard (Eds.), *Active learning in higher education* (pp. 107-134). Oxfordshire, U.K.: Libri Publishing Ltd.

Ericksen, S. C. (1984). *The essence of good teaching*. San Francisco: Jossey-Bass.

Gadusova, Z., & Predanocyova, L. (2018). Developing teacher competences in a student teacher population. *Education Research and Perspectives, 45*, 93-121.

Gilbert, P. (2014). The origins and nature of compassion focused therapy. *British Journal of Clinical Psychology, 53*(1), 6-41.

Hargreaves, A. (Ed.). (2007). *Extending educational change: International handbook of educational change* (Vol. 2). Springer Science & Business Media.

Jaunzems-Fernuk, J. L., & Kalyn, B. (2018). *Calm classrooms: Teacher behaviours that promote healthy, calm learning environments.* Hawaii International Conference on Education, Oahu, Hawaii, 2018.

Jaunzems-Fernuk, J. L., Martin, S., & Kalyn, B. (2021). Transformative inquiry through the human curriculum. In K. Enomoto, R. Warner & C. Nygaard (Eds.), *Teaching and learning innovations in higher education* (pp. 425–430). Oxfordshire, U.K.: Libri Publishing Ltd.

Ipsos. (2021, February 20). COVID continues to take heavy toll on Canadians' mental health. *Ipsos News Centre.* https://www.ipsos.com/en-ca

Kimmerer, R. W. (2013). *Braiding sweetgrass: Indigenous wisdom, scientific knowledge and the teachings of plants.* Milkweed Editions.

Kutcher, S., Wei, Y., & Morgan, C. (2016). Mental health literacy in post-secondary students. *Health Education Journal, 75*(6), 689-697

Kutsyuruba, B., & Walker, K. D. (Eds.) (2017). *The bliss and blisters of early career teaching: A pan-Canadian perspective.* Word & Deed Publishing Incorporated.

Lawrence-Brown, D., & Sapon-Shevin, M. (2015). *Condition critical—Key principles for equitable and inclusive education.* Teachers College Press.

Linden, B., Gray, S., & Stuart, H. (2018). *National standard for the psychological health and safety of post-secondary students–Phase I: Scoping literature review.* Ottawa, ON: Mental Health Commission of Canada.

Manilall, S., & Armstrong, C. (2018). *Focus on self-regulation.* Edmonton Catholic Schools.

Maslow, A. H. (1943). A theory of human motivation. *Psychological Review, 50*(4), 370.

Maté, G. (2017). *Scattered minds: The origins and healing of attention deficit disorder.* Random House.

McDonough, G. P. (2012). Teaching practitioners about theory and practice: A proposal to recover Aristotle in teacher education. *Journal of Thought, 47*(4), 7-22.

Mezirow, J. (2000). *Learning as transformation: Critical perspectives on a theory in progress.* Jossey-Bass.

Noddings, N. (2013). *Caring: A relational approach to ethics and moral education.* University of California Press.

Olson, H. (2022). Reflection towards excellence – empowering learners to become reflective practitioners. In K. Enomoto, R. Warner & C. Nygaard (Eds.), *Active learning in higher education* (pp. 63-82). Oxfordshire, U.K.: Libri Publishing Ltd.

Perry, B. D., & Szalavitz, M. (2017). *The boy who was raised as a dog: And other stories from a child psychiatrist's notebook - What traumatised children can teach us about loss, love, and healing.* Hachette UK.

Piaget, J. (1971). The theory of stages in cognitive development. In D. R. Green, M. P. Ford & G. B. Flamer (Eds.), *Measurement and Piaget*. McGraw-Hill.

Ratey, J. J. (2013). *Spark: The revolutionary new science of exercise and the brain.* Little Brown and Company.

Schraw, G. (1998). Promoting general metacognitive awareness. *Instructional Science*, 26(1), 113-125.

Siegel, D. J. (2015). *Brainstorm: The power and purpose of the teenage brain.* Penguin.

Siegel, D. J., & Bryson, T. P. (2012). *The whole-brain child: 12 revolutionary strategies to nurture your child's developing Mind.* Bantam Books Trade Paperbacks.

Skovholt, T. M., & Trotter-Mathison, M. (2014). *The resilient practitioner: Burnout prevention and self-care strategies for counsellors, therapists, teachers, and health professionals.* Routledge.

Stough, L. M., Montague, M. L., Landmark, L. J., & Williams-Diehm, K. (2015). Persistent classroom management training needs of experienced teachers. *Journal of the Scholarship of Teaching and Learning*, 15(5), 36-48.

Thompson, N., & Pascal, J. (2012). Developing critically reflective practice. *Reflective practice*, 13(2), 311-325

Tummers, N. (2011). *Teaching stress management: Activities for children and young adults.* Human Kinetics.

Vygotsky, L. S. (1978). Interaction between learning and development. In M. Cole, V. John-Steiner, S. Scribner & E. Souberman (Eds.), *Mind in society: The development of higher psychological processes* (pp. 79–91). Harvard University Press.

Wei, M., Liao, K. Y. H., Ku, T. Y., & Shaffer, P. A. (2011). Attachment, self-compassion, empathy, and subjective wellbeing among college students and community adults. *Journal of Personality*, 79(1), 191-221.

Chapter 13

Teaching from the Native American Circle: A Future Campus-wide Sustainability Project as a Catalyst for Active Learning

Diana Schooling

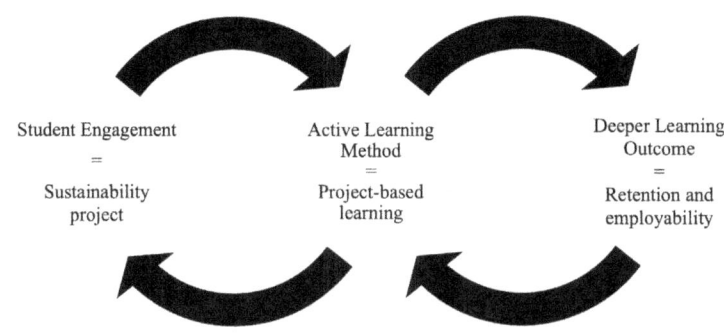

Introduction

This chapter contributes to this book, *Active Learning in Higher Education*, by showing how to engage students in a future campus-wide sustainability project using project-based learning to improve their retention and enhance their employability. Drawing on 'Teaching from the Native American Circle' (Schooling, 2021), the sustainability project has been designed both to improve students' retention and to enhance their employability at the Nisqually Nation Campus of the Northwest Indian College (NWIC) - the only accredited Tribal College serving the educational needs of Tribal communities throughout the Pacific Northwest in the states of Washington, Oregon and Idaho in the United States.

So far, sustainability projects have been partially implemented at several Native American schools around the Puget Sound area of Washington State and are under consideration for post-COVID implementation at the Nisqually Nation Campus of the Northwest Indian College (NWIC). Its inspiration originated from the Sustainable Forestry students at the Seattle campus of the University of Washington. As part of a 'Seed-to-Salad' campaign on their Seattle campus, they devised a student-organised and maintained vegetable garden that feeds their cafeteria (University of Washington, 2009).

This inspired me to envision how and why it needed to be expanded to a full campus-wide sustainability project at any Native American school or college because it is inherently the embodiment of our collective Indigenous deep cultural knowledge. I have been invited to describe the sustainability project in this book on active learning because the project is specifically based on and versed within historical Indigenous knowledge and teaching approaches. I hope that reading about my particular approach to project-based active learning – referred to as 'Teaching from the Native American Circle' (Schooling, 2021) – will be an inspiration that compensates for the fact that the project is not as yet completed. However, it has been partially implemented at other Native American schools in the Pacific Northwest.

NWIC offers five Bachelor's degrees to Native American students. NWIC works cooperatively with Indian Tribal Nez Perce, Muckleshoot, Nisqually, Port Gamble, Swinomish and Tulalip Tribal communities in delivering these degrees. Such communities sponsor classes and programs particularly relevant to Native American students. Indeed, the vision statement of NWIC reads: *"We are committed to our students, the Tribes we serve, and advancing Tribal sovereignty for the protection and enhancement of our homelands and future generations"* (Northwest Indian College, 2022:NP). At NWIC, we work to fulfil our vision using various delivery methods such as onsite teaching, interactive telecourses, video conferencing, online courses, and independent learning (guided by learning contracts). There is a strong focus throughout our offerings on the cultural traditions and Indigenous knowledge of the aforementioned Tribal communities.

In this chapter, I exemplify active learning within a project-based approach to teaching and learning that engages and immerses students in the multilateral facets of sustainability, such as environmental, nutritional, climatic, emotional, and cultural facets. The sustainability project helps establish and maintain an academic campus as a self-sustaining campus, achieved through its students' involvement and continuous engagement in sustainability dialogues and activities, which ultimately improves student retention and enhances employability. The project-based approach paves the way for a student journey through the curriculum using workshop-style mini-projects. Such mini-projects are in line with current recommendations for addressing climate change, which, at the same time, are founded in traditional Indigenous knowledge and teachings.

Reading this chapter, you will gain the following three insights:
1. how sustainability projects can be informed by traditional Indigenous knowledge and teachings to cultivate 21st-century employability skills in students;
2. how to create a zero-landfill campus that can both feed the electrical grid and provide food for students; and
3. how the project-based active learning method enables diverse and inclusive teaching with ease of delivery.

Overview of Main Sections

The chapter has three main sections. Section 1 outlines my background and way into working with project-based learning, and it defines project-based learning as an active learning method. Section 2 describes how a campus-wide sustainability project has been designed to improve student retention and enhance employability. This is followed by Section 3, which presents anticipated outcomes from the sustainability project before demonstrating practical ways to implement the campus-wide sustainability project.

Section 1: The background

Informally, I was introduced to project-based learning by chance when, as a child, I started 'teaching English' the summer after I finished third grade. I corralled all the children in my neighbourhood and convinced most of them to have a 'school' in my living room, as a game for the summer holidays, with me as the 'teacher'. We held the class in my living room on a regular schedule at specific hours of each day, where we collectively wrote, edited, and performed a series of three plays. As each became ready, and we agreed they were the best they could be, I went around to the other children who had turned me down and convinced them to pay five cents each to sit on my patio and watch as the rest of us performed the plays. Several of them saw the fun we were having and asked if they could join the project, but it was nearly the end of summer by then, and there was no time to do the fourth play. Looking back, at age 9, I had created an English curriculum via writing and producing plays and convinced most of my neighbourhood children to join in as a game. I just thought it was fun. And it was just fun for a child who was a natural stickler for proper spelling, punctuation, and grammar. One of the other girls' teachers was so impressed with her grasp of those subjects, compared to her grades at the end of the previous year, she came to me after school started in the Autumn and asked me how I did it. I simply pointed out what I felt: *"Learning is supposed to be as fun as a game."*

Many years later, I enrolled at a university recommended to me by my mentor, retired U.S.-Tribal Federal Judge Wilma Smith-Lees of the Warm Springs Reservation in Oregon State, and co-author of the Indian Child Welfare Act. Wilma said that this university would fit my learning style better than the other ones I had under consideration at the time, as my learning style combines visual and kinaesthetic, which is very common in Native American populations (Peacock & Cleary, 1997). As with most Native Americans, the Western tradition of lecture-based instruction was a struggle for me (Carruthers, 1990). Yet, my university's reflective writing practice with virtual logbooks was a vital feature and was my first formal exposure to project-based learning. My childhood experiences with teaching English as a theatre project enabled me to recognise the validity of the project-based graduate courses as I had already done it without knowing so. In a way, project-based learning had been a natural part of my way of learning. Hence, it is natural that I draw on my own experiences when I engage students in the sustainability project, using project-based learning as the active learning methodology, which I further elaborate on below.

Project-based learning as an active learning methodology

The sustainability project engages students in project-based learning as an active learning methodology (See Enomoto et al., 2022, Chapter 1 in this book – for an in-depth presentation of the concept of active learning and its foundation in Social Learning theory). In a comprehensive definition, Hedge (1993:276) describes project-based learning activities as follows: *"A project is an extended task which usually integrates language skills through a number of activities. These activities combine in working towards an agreed goal and may include planning, gathering information through reading, listening, interviewing, etc., discussion of the information, problem-solving, oral or written reporting, and display"*. In addition, according to Laverick (2018:6), project-based learning must also:

1. *"require students to create an original or authentic product;*
2. *encourage students to think critically;*
3. *be made public and shared with peers, family, community members, and so on;*
4. *encourage collaboration through completion of the project;*
5. *encourage students to reflect during and after completion of the project."*

Bearing in mind the above requirements for project-based learning (to be detailed in Section 2), the campus-wide sustainability project has been carefully designed, drawing on the 'Teaching from the Native American Circle' method (Schooling, 2021), originally informed by the 'Medicine Wheel for Learning and Healing' (Marsh et al., 2016). Figure 1 shows how the 'Teaching from the Native American Circle' method requires (non-linear) circle instruction grounded in critical thinking and considers that all things are connected. The method is based on circle-based instruction consisting of a large coloured circle with an X in its centre. The top of the circle, sectioned off by the X, is white (North). The next section, working down around to the right, is yellow (East). The bottom section is red (South). The left section is black (West). Each of the four elements is represented by different colours: *"yellow (sun, illumination, the Morning Star), red (wisdom, good health, growth), black (rain, purity of water), white (warmth, happiness, generosity, nourishment), as well*

Chapter 13

as the vocabulary of empathy, gratitude, love, and compassion" (Schooling, 2021:345). In addition, the Cherokee Nation culture believes that there are 7 Sacred Directions, not just four as the Lakota have in their culture, and those are: North, East, South, West, Down, Centre, and Up. As shown in Figure 1, Down and Up bring forgiveness, peace, healing, and truth into alignment and are conjoined with Lakota cultural Directions. Together with knowledge at the centre, these comprise what I call the '7 Sacred Directions Pedagogy' (Schooling, 2021).

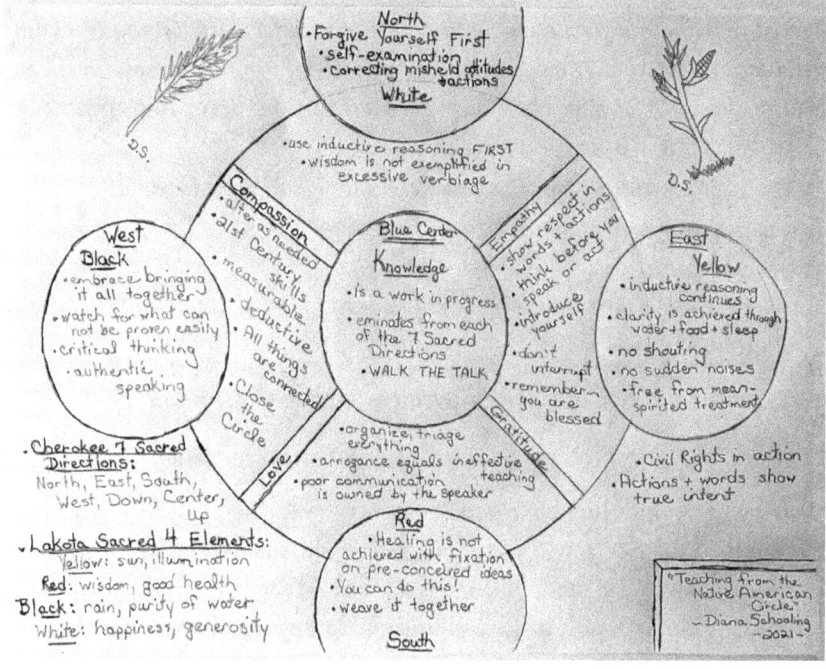

Figure 1: Teaching from the Native American Circle (Schooling, 2021).

As mentioned above, the 'Teaching from the Native American Circle' method (Schooling, 2021) is informed originally by the Medicine Wheel by Marsh et al. (2016). In the same way, the design of the sustainability project is informed by the Research Medicine Wheel (Figure 2) that directly mirrors 'Teaching from the Native American Circle' (Figure 1). As Figure 2 depicts, the Research Medicine Wheel also consists of four elements and their meanings, with triangular points that direct to which colours and components of research align with each direction on the

Wheel. Figure 2 also shows how the four elements of 1) science, 2) math, 3) culture and 4) language are woven together, integrating and braiding them into a cohesive, whole project-based curriculum.

In Section 2, I will detail these practices and how the sustainability project will be run by 'Teaching from the Native American Circle'.

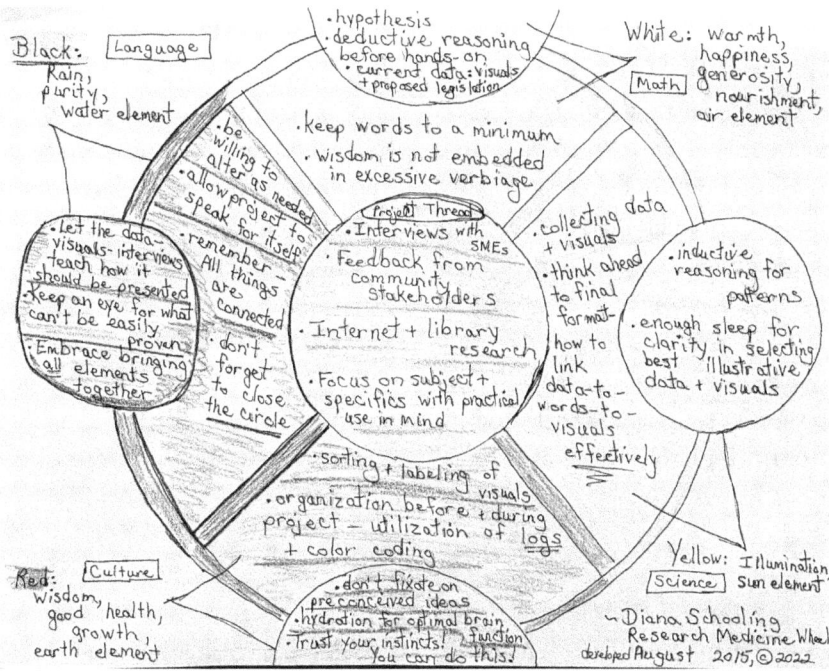

Figure 2: Research Medicine Wheel (drawn by Schooling, 2022).

Section 2: The sustainability project

Ideally, we are all looking to strive for the common good and move our communities and institutions forward. No such community or institution desires to be left behind but rather aspires to remain relevant to the future. Relevant project-based practices are not just beneficial for the future but also work towards ensuring that our higher education institutions continue to provide their original mission statement of service for decades to come. At NWIC, we help do this by providing project-based learning for our students, equipping them with leadership skills and dual-language competencies that will become essential tools for life, regardless of their degree specialisations.

Project-based learning using 'Teaching from the Native American Circle'

Informed by 'Teaching from the Native American Circle' (Schooling, 2021), the sustainability project is designed to improve students' retention and enhance their employability at NWIC. Our sustainability project is informed by the belief that: *"Virtually every discipline, every class, can be proven by a final project, rather than a written exam, and this shows mastery of content in a way no written exam ever could. Writing is already the foundational component of any project for every discipline. In some disciplines, a glossary quiz may be necessary, and in languages, we always have our oral conversational assessments"* (Schooling, 2021:352). When conducting our project-based teaching through the sustainability project, the 'Teaching from the Native American Circle' method provides the concrete directions below.

North

Referring to Figure 1, we start at North and take the first two important steps: 1) self-examination and 2) correcting misheld attitudes and actions. We do so because it is imperative that students are open to the sustainability project and not jump to conclusions. North is also driven by empathy: i) inductive reasoning first, and ii) wisdom is not exemplified in excessive verbiage. Project-based teaching builds on inductive reasoning, and students must realise that wisdom is not exemplified in excessive verbiage. Knowledge has to be created by students during the sustainability project – it is not something already there to be presented by the teachers.

East

We continue at East and take five important steps: 1) inductive reasoning continues, 2) clarity is achieved through water, food, and sleep, 3) no shouting, 4) no sudden noises, and 5) freedom from mean-spirited treatment. We do so because the students while continuing their inductive reasoning concerning the sustainability project, have to be appreciative and respectful to the project, each other and the knowledge created. For instance, they have to learn that they cannot thrive in a project environment if they shout or use power games or are mean-spirited. East is driven by gratitude: i) show respect in words and actions, ii) think before you speak or act, iii) introduce yourself, iv) do not interrupt, and v) remember you are blessed.

South

We continue further at South, which corresponds to wisdom and good health. Here the students go through three important steps: 1) healing is not achieved with a fixation on pre-conceived ideas, 2) you can do this! and 3) begin to weave it all together. This phase is important in the project-based pedagogy because it shows students that it is possible, although the sustainability project may be difficult. At this point, they can start to weave ideas together. South is driven by love. Love to an open process and even a surprising outcome: i) organise, triage everything, ii) arrogance equals ineffective teaching, and iii) poor communication is owned by the speaker. Love is also about nurturing a love of learning and cooperation, which must be done with an open mind.

West

We complete the circular-based process at West, where students begin to 'close the circle'. That is done when they: 1) embrace bringing it all together, 2) watch for what cannot be proven easily, and engage in 3) critical thinking, and 4) authentic speaking. This phase is important because it allows the students to conclude how to implement the sustainability project while still being critical and authentic. This does not mean reaching the 'right' conclusion. Rather, it is concerned with making qualified and critically reflected decisions that can be explained authentically. West is driven by compassion; the Keywords are: i) alter as needed, ii) 21st-century skills, iii) measurable, iv) deductive, v) all things are connected, and vi) Close the Circle.

Blue Centre
The centre of the model is called the 'Blue Center'. This is where students close the circle. They do so by bringing their vision and focus of the sustainability project to the centre. The ideas produced by the students are labelled 'Knowledge', and when speaking of knowledge, we need to remember that: 1) it is work in progress, 2) it emanates from each of the 7 Sacred Directions, and 3) WALK THE TALK.

Designing the sustainability project using project-based learning

Guided by 'Teaching from the Native American Circle' (Schooling, 2021) to facilitate project-based learning successfully, we return to Laverick's requirements (2018:6) for project-based learning and design the sustainability projects that:

1. *"require students to create an original or authentic product;*
2. *encourage students to think critically;*
3. *be made public and shared with peers, family, community members, and so on;*
4. *encourage collaboration through completion of the project;*
5. *encourage students to reflect during and after completion of the project."*

1. Require students to create an original or authentic product
Each product that students create as part of this project-based dual-language instruction will be original/unique to the campus on which it is implemented. Some academic institutions may wish to focus mainly on growing produce within their own culture, while others may want students to grow produce beyond traditional norms. Not every culture grows the same vegetables or fruit trees (for example), and deep cultural knowledge is tied to the land. This means that what is grown is also dictated by how it is grown. Industrial row style farming methods are not expected here, but the methods actually used rather are indicative of the methods of the local culture in which the academic campus resides.

Greenhouses, circular plant beds, and other physical structures will also reflect the local wisdom and culture.

Furthermore, the weather of the particular area must be taken into account, with disaster preparedness and contingency plans, i.e., what to implement if there is a drought, wind storm, and so forth. This requires research into historical weather data and predictions because, depending upon that knowledge, it determines whether plants should be seeded outdoors or inside and whether they should be delayed due to the predictions. Deep historical knowledge must also be considered when considering composting, recycling, and other features involved with moving a campus towards being completely self-sustaining. Cultures have specific methods for disposal and other facets that naturally prevent community diseases from breaking out. No campus can be self-sustaining if community health is not paramount.

2. Encourage students to think critically

Through their planning, coordinating, and reflective logs, students will have to think critically on several different levels. Each stage of the project sets up the success of the next step and the long-term success as a whole, braiding it all together. By combing deep cultural knowledge with modern building, science and health techniques while documenting it all via notes, video, audio logs, photographs, sketches, and schematics, students learn that critical thinking is a multi-layered process and begin to see everything three-dimensionally.

This is of particular value in helping keep English as a second language (L2) learners from getting lost at various times in the project. They can step back and look at the Research Medicine Wheel (Figure 1) and naturally see where they are currently can be 'plugged in,' while their charts, graphs, audio logs, and so forth help them keep on track as they get deep into the 'braid' they are creating, weaving all the elements together into the project. Moreover, students should theorise and anticipate how segments of the project can be improved over the short and long term and what may need to be discontinued and replaced with something else because it might stop working. The students should also consider that some parts of the project are purely for implementation and are not intended to be a part of it for the long term. Here is where the foundation of the story of each facet of the project begins to take shape.

3. Be made public and shared with peers, family, community members, and so on

Video and photographs can be shared via the Digital Media degree students, as they can prove to be valuable for their own projects. Events can be scheduled with local journalists and community leaders to view what is being done, as the University of Washington (2009) did with their kitchen garden project that inspired this inception. As with that project's first sharing on their local television channel, it can be done virtually, in person, or as a hybrid event. It needs to be borne in mind that care must be taken for personal information security. Still, contact methods for anyone who wants to learn more or ask for guidance on how to replicate any stage of this project should be included in every type of sharing of information.

As a possible side benefit of the sustainability project, students' families can be inspired to make their own homes as self-sustaining as possible. Even apartment dwellers can make better choices about the products they use and how they dispose of them, and even contract a plot at a community garden to implement a few of these ideas on a very small scale. The reflective logs can be turned into ongoing reports submitted to various journals, newspapers, or blogs for publication to the wider regional community or beyond. This gives students practice in writing in their heritage language for publication, as well as in English. These are the rough drafts of the story that each piece of the project will tell via media such as journals, podcasts and interviews.

4. Encourage collaboration through completion of the project

Students in other departments, who assist at different project stages, should be encouraged to revisit and see the project's progress and write an updated report on their observances, keeping everyone involved. Further collaboration could be students from the first iteration returning in subsequent years. If they worked on the project during their last year at the specific institution, bring their employers with them to see how the project is going in additional years. Questions such as: 'What has been added?' 'What is not working long-term and has been replaced with something else, and why?' exemplify important critical thinking questions that teachers will need to repeat at each stage of the project to help maintain collaboration through to completion.

5. Encourage students to reflect during and after completion of the project

Written reflective logs should be kept in both the students' L1 and in English. Concepts are embedded in the language of each culture and may not translate well across to English. Nevertheless, this needs to be written first in their L1 so that the elders of their community can help them if they need assistance, and also to comply with the Esther Martinez Native Languages Preservation Act of 2006, which affects any educational institution in the United States that has Native American students enrolled, regardless of age or educational level of the Native American students.

Audio logs should be kept by some students instead. For example, a dyslexic student could face difficulties writing reflective logs but could use audio reflective logs as an alternative. Students with diminished sight could help out with some facets of the program and keep an audio log. And audio logs help with the spoken requirements of the Esther Martinez Native American Languages Preservation Act of 2006, and not just the literacy requirement. All reflective logs, whether written or audio, should be edited and compiled into mid-term and final reports, the latter with an eye towards publication or if they are interviewed for a podcast or news show. We Native Americans believe that all things are connected, so keeping the pieces of the story, i.e., reflective written/audio logs, are a natural process.

A brief overview of how students work with active learning

Native American colleges fall under the jurisdiction and guidance of the Bureau of Indian Education, a division of the U.S. Department of the Interior, the same as our K-12 schools. Under the Indian Self-Determination and Education Assistance Act of 1975, all Native American education from age 21 years and down is 'lumped together' for oversight. This issue is touched upon again in the conclusion of this chapter.

Whether being implemented by high school/gymnasium or higher education students, they will need some instructor oversight as they learn the supply logistics and scheduling skills built into the course and partially serve as the periodic assessment components of the dual-language curriculum. Students will, of course, need to work in several groups, rotating through various foci, spending time as a leader in at least one of the groups. It should also be noted here that this particular piece of the project-based learning design aligns with multiple nations' guidelines and those outlined in 'Youth Leadership in Action' (Burrington, 1995). It is primarily written for higher education institutions that offer dual-language instructions. However, some of the simpler portions of this project-based curriculum have been adopted at Native American high school campuses in the Pacific Northwest of the United States, at their Tribal Nations' discretion.

In the first class in all modules, the instructor will go over the vocabulary terms for the items that will be achieved within the project during its completion. It must be stressed to students that they are not expected to know all relevant vocabulary before the projects start but that they will be learning and reinforcing their vocabulary experientially. Then, at the beginning of each class session, the instructor will go over the vocabulary that immediately pertains to the day's project goals. Students will be responsible for identifying these key vocabulary terms in their first language (L1). Successful vocabulary acquisition will be proven in the content of their final reporting. Flexibility in delivery is important. Anecdotally, I have taught one of my NWIC students via text message when the internet dropped out at her on-Reservation housing during class instruction time and was able to keep her up-to-speed with the in-class activity for their upcoming research essay assignment. This assignment is one of the assessed written tasks in the sustainability projects curriculum.

The campus-wide sustainability projects will run over one academic year and are designed to achieve the following five campus-community goals:

1) feed the student body;

2) learn leadership and other marketable skills;

3) zero-landfill campus;

4) feed the electrical grid, not draw from it; and

5) implement and maintain a self-sustaining campus.

As part of their degree programmes, each student must engage directly in at least three discipline-based sustainability projects and know the vocabulary in their L1 required to engage in the projects. For example:

- build greenhouses and raised beds with netting cover against animals eating the budding produce;
- build watering and hydroponic systems for small fruits and vegetables that grow better via that method, such as strawberries and tomatoes,
- provide composting bins for the cafeteria and culinary department- which also use the above produce;
- establish orchard with symbiotic trees and shrubs; and
- build and install solar panels and generators for supplying the campus, feeding any excess electricity back into the grid.

There will be collaboration options. Students from the Digital Media degree program can work with the math department to illustrate those elements and the culinary and science departments. The culinary department should confer with the math and science department on what is needed exactly and how much. In contrast, the culture and science department need to work together on what traditional foods are and in what season they can be grown, including traditional pest control, such as rabbits, deer, and gophers (a North American burrowing rodent). However, owing to the impacts of the COVID-19 pandemic, specifically, access restrictions, detailing the exact status of the project implementation beyond what is already noted here has been impossible. Most of these schools are in the U.S. Federal Bureau of Indian Education system and must comply with federal pandemic guidelines, not state guidelines. The various Tribal Nation's health department restrictions also apply. Everything is on a critical needs only basis.

By the end of their sustainability projects, students will be able to show their mastery of the above campus-community goals. For their final assessment, they may do a PowerPoint, a video edit of footage taken periodically during the process, or submit a written report in academic English. Notably, the first two options must also include a written short-form report that should be a minimum of three pages, double-spaced, not including the title page. Any books or websites used to aid in the projects must be listed on a reference page; however, if they used oral knowledge or entirely from being shown in person, that must be mentioned in the body of the report, along with who gave them the verbal information and showed them which skill(s). What is more important will be what speaks to the student the most from the material presented and discovered. This process would be the same if a second/advanced level of the program were implemented. It is expected that the first year of students to undertake this project will establish the workshop-style mini-projects with some actual output achieved by the end of the school year. It is not intended to be fully achieved in one school year. Subsequent years will plan how much expansion will be done during their coursework.

In their third or fourth year of undergraduate study, they could align it more to their degree's focus; For example, if they prefer the math design stage, the culinary design stage, the science design stage, actual construction or maintenance, or whether their gifts lie in Digital Media, Language or Creative Arts areas. If any year-end reports were submitted for publication, Indigenous schools would need to receive permission via a conference with that nation's government Council. For non-Indigenous students, their professors should guide them on the plethora of online professional journals that now exist. This should also be done in professional journals and other publications that exist in the students' L1, not just in English. As a dual-language TESOL (Teaching English to Speakers of Other Languages) curriculum, the goal here is that students will be able to function with ease at this written academic level in both their L1 and English.

Section 3: Anticipated outcome

Student perspective

As a result of engaging in the sustainability project, it is anticipated that students will be able to:

- demonstrate how even the smallest campus affects the environment in its community and beyond;
- develop practical application knowledge of math, sciences, health,

nutrition, some basic engineering and water systems; and

- read and write the level of research reports needed for the global community to share in their findings.

These deeper learning outcomes will help improve students' retention and enhance their employability. The anticipated student outcomes learnt through this project-based instruction will help students see how every career, business, and family dinner meal are connected by the choices each community makes. These outcomes include, but are not limited to:

1. math in building projects;
2. biology/chemistry in growing organic and composting, water conservation, symbiotic plants and trees;
3. culinary—how to cook fresh food, when are fruits and vegetables ripe, how to harvest/storage of seasonal foods, drying, canning, freezing;
4. writing: written reports and logs, research skills best practices, government policy writing, grant writing for expansion funding, equipment replacement and/or upgrades;
5. digital media: photographs all throughout, periodic videos, presentation skills and public speaking; and
6. health and medical sciences: seasonal growing and eating, nutrition.

Coupled with the zero-landfill feature, the solar and electrical grid training and the self-sustainability knowledge can help make the students of this proposed sustainability project uniquely prepared for 21st-century careers. Moreover, the training embedded in this project is also therapeutic when viewed from the perspective of trauma-informed practice in higher education. The various aspects of gardening have long been recommended for those who have been trauma-impacted (Millican et al., 2019). Gardening is also non-discriminatory because no single person is doing the vital work. It is all-important work, where each gardening task is integral to the others in the group, being braided together into one whole- mirroring 'Teaching from the Native American Circle' (Schooling, 2021). The group rotational structure and the desired project-based learning align with 'Youth Leadership in Action' developed by Project Adventure, Inc. (Burrington, 1995).

Hollenbeck and Kountouzi (2019:79) state that instructors must make coursework interesting to keep students engaged. They state that this is key to English language acquisition, especially for future career applications in STEM-related careers. This is also critical to students being able to retain those positions. *"We observed that student learning [of] a second language must be purposeful and have a real relevancy to them"*. Mallinson and Charity Hudley (2014:11) noted that research partnerships with STEM teachers are necessary to further cultural diversity and address inequality in STEM, particularly in the United States, stating that *"Establish[ing] a well-defined rationale for collaboration across linguistics and STEM, yield…basic and applied research benefits"*. If the project is to be part of a dual-language instruction model, then care must be given to ensure the students are fully aware of why they are being instructed in these things as a dual-language program. This importance of this dual-language issue is highlighted by Valdez et al. (2016:601), who detail the loss of sight of that in Utah's dual language initiative, nine years after its implementation, arguing that the gentrification, i.e., primarily students of sociocultural privilege, enabled *"a broad pattern of inequitably distributed enrichment education"*.

Moreover, Gonglewski and Helm (2014:3) point out that even business language courses must include *"sustainability pedagogies"* for transformative and experiential learning. This should not be a moot point, given that businesses should have a sustainability statement and plan so that their statement is more than mere words. Bowden (2010:16) warns that without this, previously, businesses have become disconnected from their surroundings via the resulting *"commodification of food, labour, and the environment"*, arguing that interconnectedness through sustainability is a critical *"process whereby these interlinked systems maintain themselves and each other"*. Students need to see, touch, and experience how math, science, and even academic writing are interconnected to be able to demonstrate beginning-intermediate-advanced competencies in these areas. Not just by watching documentaries or listening to lectures. Without these safeguards of hands-on learning, the objectives will never achieve the stated outcomes; it will only be busy work with no real-world applications able to be attained.

Teacher perspective

Cates (1990:41) believes that, through sustainability education from language teachers, *"poverty, prejudice, and pollution"* are addressed through *"effectively acquir[ing]"* English as a 'lingua franca' that empowers students *"with the knowledge, skills, and commitment required by world citizens to solve [these] global problems"*. This *"is a pedagogical approach"*, she stresses, *"not just a new teaching technique"*. Founded in a four-point Medicine Wheel concept, she further notes that: *"...peace, human rights, development, and the environment..."* through language education are *"the four content areas of global education"*.

Our students will go out into a world where companies expect them to have some hands-on experience already. This project-based learning enables graduates to articulate that they have a multiplicity of interests and have knowledge and experience from differing industries that they can apply for any employer. If they have other project-based learning experiences, it further enhances their employability. Via building their portfolio during their rotating involvement in the project, students will acquire marketable skills, such as, but not limited to:

- writing for social change;
- project management at all levels throughout the implementation and maintenance of the project's needs;
- learning how to interview and coordinate with Subject Matter Experts in each facet that is braided throughout the project;
- networking with community stakeholders via facilitating community listening sessions;
- proving they can successfully manage workshop-style research, ordering and tracking a variety of supplies; and
- connecting knowledge-skills-identity to prove understanding of multiple industries.

Overt deliverables provided include preparation for flexibility in various roles, such as moving back and forth between project leadership, practical project support, and project development and supply-side logistical assistance. United States Congressional Representative Derek Kilmer has stated employers are already asking him for guidance on finding such trained employees (Kilmer, 2022). Employers are also asking him to spearhead requiring the regular updating of innovation methodology, such as this, via Congressional Act, so there is constant availability of flexible, interdisciplinary persons to hire (Kilmer, 2022).

Section 4: Moving forward

Until the sustainability projects are enacted and reflected upon at NWIC, it is difficult to determine how to move forward. The moving forward will emerge from detailed analyses of the project-based learning model's effectiveness and its constituent parts, from feedback from the staff and students involved in the different sustainability projects. This could take the form of a combination of qualitative surveys, questionnaires, and interviews of available students and staff. An onsite tour of the current stages of each facet of the project is the optimal method for gaining this critical knowledge. Information gleaned could take the form of a report for each module, which could inform future iterations of such project-based learning at NWIC. Accessing any available data from those educational institutions and districts that have implemented similar project-based learning activities will also be useful in developing our sustainability projects at NWIC.

In terms of adding to the actual number of sustainability projects (see Section 2), one possible suggestion for future expansion is campus-based chickens with nesting coops for eggs. A plan for care/maintenance outside of school is in session—including securing against wild animals such as coyotes and foxes at night. Implementing such a project would likely rest on both how successful the other sustainability projects proved to be and the logistics of putting such a new project in place. Similar considerations would be needed to expand into other husbandry mini-projects, such as shellfish farming, like some Tribal Nations in the Pacific Northwest of the U.S. already do on a small scale. Another project could be sheep and llama, with the wool production involved in each being included, as is typical of the Tribal Nations of the U.S. Southwest. The possibilities for future expansion will vary greatly, at both NWIC and elsewhere, depending on the unique needs of each campus. The beauty of this project-based instruction is that it is also very customisable while teaching career and academic English (or whatever L1/L2 is used) through the various essential aspects that need to be implemented regardless of location. This means that students gain the local career skills needed, not just an overview of the pieces that will 'plug-and-play' anywhere.

When considering sustainability projects on a broader scale, for example, a university in Thailand will not have the nuanced community needs to meet as will a university in Norway. So, for any academic institution considering implementing such a sustainability project, it is not recommended to attempt to implement all facets of this project-based instruction all at once. Instead, each academic institution should determine which cultural foundations require which pieces to be commenced first. Some may emulate the University of Washington (see the Introduction) and implement a kitchen garden as a single first step. In contrast, others may want to start with compost for the existing food disposal and then integrate the kitchen garden later. The time of year the project is started will be a huge factor unless the campus physically lies somewhere where there is nearly a year-round growing season.

Conclusion

Today, we train tomorrow's leaders, Elders and Council/Parliament. It is imperative that we provide immersive, culturally appropriate, comprehensive training, such as project-based learning based on sustainability with climate change foundationally in mind. We thereby work towards restoring our educational standards via truly traditional project-based instruction, incorporating Indigenous theoretical knowledge. Even the very business of national governance is all project-based. And given the state of climate change, public health concerns, and other events that have already occurred -necessitating such a richly complex curriculum as this- we must take the additional steps to ensure that we have these leaders in our communities who can build and maintain sustainable community support systems for the future of our collective nations. Similar to the way the European Union is set up, in the United States, there exists a 'Nations within a Nation' status. Tribal Nations are sovereign governments in their own right, yet they physically reside within the borders of the U.S.; some laws apply everywhere regardless, but others do not. While this is a complicated relationship that cannot be detailed here due to space, it needs to be mentioned to provide further context, which helps in understanding this sustainability-focused chapter.

About the Author

Diana Schooling is an Adjunct English Faculty member and Student Advisor at Northwest Indian College, Nisqually Nation Campus, in Washington State, U.S.A. She can be contacted at this email: dschooling@nwic.edu.

Bibliography

25 U.S. Code, Chapter 14, Subchapter 11, §5301 (1975). *Indian Self-Determination and Education Assistance Act.* United States Congress.

120 Stat. 2707 Public Law 109-394 (2006). *Esther Martinez Native American Languages Preservation Act.* United States Congress.

Bowden, R. (2010). Teaching English for sustainability. *Journal of NELTA,* 15(1-2), 16-21.

Burrington, B. (1995). *Youth leadership in action: a guide to cooperative games and group activities.* Dubuque, IA: Kendall/Hunt Publishing Company.

Carruthers, S. (1990). Learning styles and Native American students: A study of learning preferences of students at Bay Mills Community College. *Tribal College: Journal of American Indian Higher Education,* 1(3), 21.

Cates, K. A. (1990). *Teaching for a Better World: Global Issues and Language Education. The Language Teacher,* 14(5), 3-5.

Enomoto, K., Warner, R., & Nygaard, C. (2022). Passive learning and active learning in higher education: their underpinning learning theories and consequences for teaching and assessment. In K. Enomoto, R. Warner & C. Nygaard (Eds.), *Active learning in higher education* (pp. 1-34). Oxfordshire, U.K.: Libri Publishing Ltd.

Gonglewski, M., & Helm, A. (2014). Sustainability pedagogies for the business language classroom. *Global Business Language,*19(1) 2.

Hedge, T. (1993). Key Concepts in ELT. *ELT Journal,* 47(3), 275-277.

Hollenbeck, J., & Kountouzi, B. (2019). Using motivation in the instruction of English language learning for STEM and economic secondary education for Bulgarian learners. *Bulgarian Journal of Science and Education Policy,* 13(1) 71-79.

Kilmer, D. (2022). *New Investments in America's Infrastructure*, January 2022 Constituent Newsletter for the 6th Congressional District, accessed via email subscription.

Laverick, E. K. (2018). *Project-based learning*. ELT Development Series. Virginia: TESOL Press.

Mallinson, C., & Charity Hudley, A. H. (2014). Partnering through science: Developing linguistic insight to address educational inequality for culturally and linguistically diverse students in US STEM education. *Language and Linguistics Compass*, 8(1), 11-23.

Marsh, T. N., Cote-Meek, S., Young, N. L., Najavits, L. M., & Toulouse, P. (2016). Indigenous healing and seeking safety: A blended implementation project for intergenerational trauma and substance use disorders. *International Indigenous Policy Journal*, 7(2), 1-37.

Millican, J., Perkins, C., & Adam-Bradford, A. (2019). Gardening in displacement: the benefits of cultivating in crisis. *Journal of Refugee Studies*, 32(3), 351-371.

Northwest Indian College (2022). *Vision statement*. Retrieved from https://www.nwic.edu/about-nwic/#our-history

Nygaard, C., & Dobozy, E. (2021). A learning centred, five tier model of innovation in higher education. In K. Enomoto, R. Warner & C. Nygaard (Eds.), *Teaching and learning innovations in higher education* (pp. 19-46). Oxfordshire, U.K.: Libri Publishing Ltd.

Peacock, T. D., & Cleary, L. M. (1997). Ways of learning: Teachers' perspectives on American Indian learning styles. *Tribal College*, 8(3), 36.

Schooling, D. (2021). Teaching from the Native American Circle: An innovative teaching framework. In K. Enomoto, R. Warner & C. Nygaard (Eds.), *Teaching and learning innovations in higher education* (pp. 339-356). Oxfordshire, U.K.: Libri Publishing Ltd.

University of Washington (2009). *Sustainability: From Seed to Salad*. Retrieved from: https://green.uw.edu/news/seed-salad

Valdez, V. E., Freire, J. A., & Delavan, M. G. (2016). The gentrification of dual language education. *The Urban Review*, 48(4), 601-627.

www.ingramcontent.com/pod-product-compliance
Lightning Source LLC
Chambersburg PA
CBHW071556080526
44588CB00010B/927